Police Liability

Police Liability

Lawsuits Against the Police

Dennis M. Payne
Michigan State University

CAROLINA ACADEMIC PRESS
Durham, North Carolina

ISBN: 0-89089-144-3
LCCN: 2001097413

Carolina Academic Press
700 Kent Street
Durham, North Carolina 27701
Telephone (919) 489-7486
Fax (919) 493-5668
E-mail: cap@cap-press.com
www.cap-press.com

Printed in the United States of America.

Contents

Preface

This book examines fifty-two actual cases litigated against police officers and their departments or jurisdictions. Written for working police officers, their supervisors and managers, students of police administration, and the citizens who pay the bills, it is designed to alert them to several pitfalls that can occur in police operations, and which can lead to law suits against the police. Another purpose of the work is to provide the readers with insights that will assist them in the development of stronger and more meaningful policies, improved training, closer supervision, and more accountable discipline. When such initiatives are taken, the result could be fewer law suits against the police.

Not all of the fifty-two cases discussed in this book are favorable to the police. To be sure, police officers make mistakes. Some of these mistakes were honest errors resulting from a lack of appropriate training or supervision, and thus they drew the attention of attorneys adept in negligence law. A few suits resulted from actions teaken by police officers that were neither logical nor ethical. Though rare, these cases could have resulted in criminal prosecutions. However, the majority of the cases reviewed in this book represent examples of sound police work, but were litigated due to the loss of life sustained by innocent victims associated with police actions.

The total cost of negligence suits against America's police departments is unknown. Damages against the police agencies discussed in this book ran into the millions, but that was only a portion of the total costs incurred. Even when the outcomes were successful, the agencies paid costs for attorney fees, insurance premiums, expert witness fees, and countless hours of officers' time off the job—with concurrent loss of productivity. The public trust placed in the police of America requires, among other things, that the police managers strive to reach goals of operating as effectively and efficiently as possible, as circumscribed by the Constitution and the law. The author hopes that this book will assist them in achieving those goals.

Introduction

The topic of police liability is of paramount concern to police administrators, individual police officers, insurance underwriters, attorneys, plaintiffs' attorneys, police trainers, and policy makers as well as the governmental entities that provide the tax-supported operating capital for the police agencies. Police liability should be of the utmost concern to the general public. They are the ones who ultimately bear the brunt of liability suits in the form of increased taxes or reductions in services resulting from the monetary losses incurred from liability actions.

Indirect effects from the plethora of police liability cases include increased potential of general community mistrust of police officers, a demand for public involvement in police policy development, and a stronger demand for public police accountability. The latter may be in the form of variants of police review bodies. Public involvement in police policy development and strong demands for public accountability can have positive outcomes, however, such public initiatives are frequently viewed by some police agencies as counterproductive. Other positive outcomes include the identification of poor practices and enhanced training.

Of course, there are potentially negative outcomes attached to police liability suits as well. Though perhaps isolated, an individual officer's response to such conditions may be to recoil from the apparent threat to one's autonomy and discretionary decision-making. Such a reaction may manifest itself by lying, stress, failing to completely report the facts, shading the facts, mistrust of supervision, and alienation with the public. Such a polarizing effect can erode contemporary efforts to embrace the community in the process of developing community, or problem-oriented policing. It may in the long run retard the full development of an effective operational reality for community policing.

There is no simple solution to this problem in the operations of contemporary American policing. To be sure, the onslaught of police liability cases has increased drastically since the enactment of the 1964 Civil Rights Act and particularly with regard to Title 42 United States Code Section 1983, but it did not start there. Section 1983 is viewed by some as the nation's grievance procedure, though public grievances with the police did not start in 1964. The act only provided a method for the public to formally process those grievances and obtain redress, often in the form of monetary awards.

This work is intended to highlight issues, based on actual cases, that have a bearing on such conditions, and hopefully provide some understanding of the mind-set of the police and citizens when they confront each other in the forum of a law suit brought against the police to redress a real or perceived wrong by the citizen-plaintiff.

Police Environment in U.S. Cities

From the mid 1840's to the late 1920's, policing in America, particularly in the large urban areas of the northeast, could be described in general terms as the political era. In the major cities of the United States the police had close ties to the political hierarchy. Frequently, obtaining a police job was dependent on one's political connections. Favors to ward bosses were frequent and preferential treatment existed in a quid pro quo style. Operationally, the police were close to the community in which they worked. Officers walked beats, knew the people on their beats, and interacted with community members on a regular basis. The police at that time dealt with crime as it arose, and in many cases the police performed many social service duties, such as taking care of the poor, dealing with derelicts, running soup kitchens, and handling medical and social emergencies (Cole and Smith 1999). In these cities it was common for police to provide sleeping places and food for the homeless. Such services and an order maintenance police philosophy engendered support from the citizens. Most rural communities depended primarily on the county sheriffs for law enforcement. In the more rural south, policing was quite different due to its association with slavery, and in the west policing was very limited, depended on local marshals, and vigilantism was not uncommon.

The professional era, from 1920 to 1970, can be viewed as the time in which the police changed from an emphasis on order maintenance to one of professional law enforcement with an emphasis on crime fighting. Though no one condition ushered in the professional era the Wickersham Commission report in 1931 to President Hoover was pivotal. Other conditions attributed to the movement away from order maintenance include the great depression and prohibition. The Progressive Movement with its demands for clean government and police reform called for de-politicizing the police. Several educated police leaders also had a major impact in changing the police to a more professional stance. Cole and Smith (1999, 77) outline six elements of the professional era:

1. Police force should stay out of politics,

2. Members should be well-trained, well-disciplined, and tightly organized,

3. Laws should be enforced equally,

4. Police force should use new technology,

5. Personnel procedures should be based on merit,

6. Main task of the police should be fighting crime.

The community policing era began in the early 1970's and continues today. Interestingly, this period is marked with a call for greater emphasis on keeping order and providing community services. It appears the police may have come full circle in terms of their external emphasis. This period was preceded by the civil rights movements of the late 1950's and 1960's, the urban riots of the late 1960's, and the campus disorders of the early 1970's. It is not surprising that the Civil Rights Act of 1964 was enacted during a period of public cries for help, charges of police brutality, and the development of citizen police review boards to monitor police actions.

The professional era was marked by a disengagement of the police from the people. The use of radio and patrol cars, in lieu of walking the beat, distanced the police from the people. The emphasis on crime fighting and tallying of numbers of arrests was felt by the people and they responded. Clearly, the external environment of policing was sending serious messages for reform once again. In describing the causal texture of the environment, Emery and Trist (1971) described the most complex texture as a turbulent field. They noted the ground could be conceived as being in motion. Others referred to those years as the assault on the establishment. The police, one of the more visible functions of the establishment, received the brunt of the public dissatisfaction with the status quo.

Several values were tested and formed during this period. Some segments of the public were pro-police response, others were anti-police response and others, probably the majority, were somewhere in the middle or just unconcerned. Likewise, many police values were formed along similar lines. The transition from the professional era to the community policing era is an example of the police adapting to external forces and demands.

Case Studies

From 1986 through 2001 the author has consulted and provided expert opinion on over two hundred police liability cases involving local, state, and federal governmental agencies. This work is an examination and analysis of fifty-two of those cases. Of course, caution should be exercised in accepting the term expert in regards to the author. A preferred definition was provided by a U.S. District Judge in Detroit when the author was testifying on one of the cases analyzed in this work. In Handcock (1995) after an examination to establish the author's expertise, counsel for the defense moved that the author be accepted as an expert in police administration, policy, and operations. The Judge said, "No, I will not accept him as an expert, but I will allow him to testify due to his experience, background and education. If the jury listens to him, he is an expert. If they do not, then he is not."

Method

The book is organized into six chapters. Chapter 1 provides an overview of police liability and outlines common pleadings of impropriety. Chapter 2 through Chapter 5 provide a review of literature on each topic and fifty-two case analyses. Chapter 6 summarizes the author's findings and conclusions with several recommendations.

Chapter 2 focuses on the police use of force on fifteen use of force cases. Chapter 3 deals with police pursuits and examines eighteen police pursuit cases. Chapter 4 provides the analyses of thirteen police procedure cases. Chapter 5 examines police procedures and actions taken in six homicide cases investigated by the police.

Each case analyzed in this book is factual. The author chose to use fictitious names and dates to provide anonymity to the parties involved. However, the intervals between the dates and the times used in the description of the cases are accurate.

General Observations on Police Law Suits

In many police liability cases, no matter how well the police perform in the originating incident, the possibility exists that they may be sued. Moreover, the best of work by the police may be nullified by the decisions of a jury. Personal observations over the past fifteen years and two hundred such cases reveal an emerging social philosophy in such matters, which the author calls "the Somebody Has to Pay Syndrome." Furthermore, financial considerations, regardless of the merit of a particular case, frequently have an effect on the outcome of lawsuits. Whether a community is self-insured or retains an insurance underwriter for it's liability claims, someone at the policy level has to make a decision whether to go forward with a defense or settle the claim against the police department.

For example, it is not uncommon for a police community to be sued for fifteen million dollars in actual and punitive damages for a wrongful death claim resulting from a police pursuit. The police may have followed the law and their pursuit policy to the letter, and the agency may appear to have a solid basis for defense. However, an administrator, empowered to make such decisions, must consider the financial risks associated with going forward.

Such administrative decisions must consider opinions of mediators deciding a twenty percent likelihood of fault, the potential fickle nature of a jury, the total cost of defense, and not knowing what will come from an officer's testimony on cross-examination. Settling a case may be an attractive alternative for the administrator, the jurisdiction, or the insurance carrier.

An unintended outcome of these decisions is the frequent frustration and animosity felt by the officers involved. Officers who honestly believe they did everything right frequently feel they should have their day in court. In a sense, a jury that finds for a plaintiff and decides for three million dollars in punitive damages is taxing its own community. Perhaps, as Emery and Trist (1971) noted, the ground is in motion again. That is, the external environment of the police, the public, is sending signals to the police that they are not satisfied with the state of police-community relations, and, in many cases, the way the police conduct their business.

It is not the purpose of the author to reach conclusions as to why there are so many law suits against the police in contemporary society. Such a formulation has too many complex variables. However, it is a contention of the author that the manner in which the police conduct their work, implement their procedures, conduct pursuits, apply force, and conduct investigations often have a direct bearing on the instigation of a law suit.

Range of Issue Examined

In the chapters that follow, several operational issues are examined. The chapter on the use of force examines how the force was used, the context of the encounter leading to the use of force, how well the officers' actions were documented, and the appropriateness and legality of the force used. The chapter on pursuits addresses whether a pursuit should be initiated, when a pursuit should be terminated, how equipment should be used, driving conditions, the manner of driving, officer testimony, due care and caution, and the level of documentation of the events. The chapter on police procedures looks at the effects of language barriers, search warrant execution, protection of innocent people, medical treatment, wrongful arrests, following accepted procedures, interrogation and warnings, and agency accountability. The chapter dealing with investigation of homicide focuses on the extent of the investigation, the handling of the crime scene, the nature of the reporting, the need for detail, the supervision of the case, discipline and accountability. All of the cases analyzed here highlight the need for proper training, complete reporting, documentation of detail, supervisory oversight, discipline, and public accountability.

Police Liability

Chapter 1

Commentary on Police Liability

Police Liability

One of the more pressing issues facing law enforcement today is the liability of officers, their departments and the jurisdictions they serve. Regardless of their size, police agencies and their officers are vulnerable to liability suits. Carter and Payne (1989) noted it is a real possibility that court judgments rendered in cases of departmental liability may exceed the agency's insurance coverage and completely drain the resources of a small jurisdiction. Though larger law enforcement agencies may account for the bulk of the law suits, this may be true only because more officers work in those departments. The fact remains that smaller law enforcement agencies also have a high probability of being named in a lawsuit. Moreover, a smaller agency may be less prepared to successfully defend itself because they are less likely to have effective training, supervision and comprehensive policies and procedures (Benson, Payne and Trojanowicz 1990). Liability of a law enforcement agency and its officers may be based on either state or federal law, and may be either criminal or civil in nature.

Criminal Liabilities

Criminal liabilities are the least likely to occur against a police officer except in the most egregious circumstances. Under federal law, the most probable criminal liabilities for improper police officer behaviors would be found under Title 18 United States Code,

Section 242, Criminal Liability for Deprivation of Civil Rights, and Title 18 United States Code, Section 245, Violation of Federally Protected Activities.

Under state law, an officer may be charged with a violation of the penal code provisions specifically addressing public officers for offenses such as official oppression or official misconduct. Moreover, an officer could also be charged with standard criminal violations such as assault and battery if an officer used excessive force against a person. Though such criminal charges may be rare, the potential exists. Furthermore, one can assume that if an officer's conduct is so egregious as to warrant criminal charges, the likelihood is good that the officer, the department and the jurisdiction will also be civilly sued for the behavior. The standard of proof in a criminal case is beyond a reasonable doubt, but in a civil case the standard is by a preponderance of evidence. The latter need only show that it is more likely than not that an officer acted improperly.

Civil Liabilities

Unlike criminal cases, the probability that an officer, the department and the jurisdiction may be civilly sued is rather high. Such suits may be based on either state tort law (and in some cases state civil rights law) or federal law under the Civil Rights Act of 1964.

State Tort Law

A tort may be defined as a civil wrong, either intentional or unintentional (as when caused by negligence), wherein the action of one person causes injury to the person or property of another in violation of a legal duty imposed by law (del Carmen and Carter 1985). In the case of tort suits, there must first be a duty on the part of the officer or the department to act with due care to the suing party. If that duty of care was breached and the breach of that duty was the proximate cause of the injury to the party as a result of that breach, then liability may be established. Injury in such cases is not limited to physical injury, but includes the rights of the person at issue. There are a number of torts for which officers may be held liable including, but not limited to, wrongful death, use of excessive force, invasion of privacy, libel or slander, malicious prosecution, negligent vehicle operation, and negligent administration of first aid.

Federal Civil Rights Law

The most widely-used provision of the law used in police liability cases is Title 42 United States Code, Section 1983. Such deprivations of civil rights cases are termed 1983 cases. In order for a plaintiff to establish an officer's or department's liability under Section 1983, four elements must be present:

1. Defendant must be a natural person or a local government
2. Defendant must be acting under color of law
3. Violation must be of a constitutional or federally protected right
4. Violation must reach a constitutional level (see del Carmen and Carter 1985).

Despite the articulation of these elements, experience has shown that plaintiffs have been able to establish the presence of these elements with comparative ease. If liability is established under Section 1983, the plaintiff may request declaratory relief, injunctive relief, and/or monetary relief. In declaratory relief, the court, after a plaintiff has fulfilled the burden of proof of the 1983 elements, declares the officer(s) and/or department acted improperly and bears liability for the actions in question.

Injunctive relief means the court grants a plaintiff's request for some change in operations or behavior. For example, if a department has been found to violate a citizen's rights because officers have been inadequately trained, an injunction may mandate that the department establish a specifically delineated, on-going training program. Similarly, if it is found that a department had an inadequate procedure for review of citizen complaints, the injunction could mandate proper citizen complaint and review procedures. The impact of injunctive relief is such that a court can mandate policy and even managerial activities that the police department must follow. Needless to say such actions can be costly for jurisdictions.

Monetary relief exists when the defendants are required to pay the plaintiff the cost of injuries suffered as a result of the officer(s) actions. Actual damages can also be collected for expenses such as medical bills, property damage and lost wages. Punitive damages refer to pain and suffering experienced by the plaintiff as a result of the injury. In most jurisdictions, there is no limit for monetary relief, which can easily be in the millions of dollars. If the relief assessed exceeds a jurisdiction's ability to pay, that jurisdiction must then account for its responsibility through other sources such as the general fund, sale of property or even issuance of bonds.

In addition to the various forms of relief, a plaintiff may also collect reasonable attorney's fees from the defendant. Clearly, law enforcement agencies are well advised to take an aggressive preventive approach to liability problems rather than suffer the experiences of a lawsuit.

It is not the intention of this author to take a stand for or against liability claims. It is his opinion that the Civil Rights Act of 1964 is good law. People in a democratic society should have a means of redress from improper governmental actions. As a social control agency of government, the police can, through their discretionary decision making, deprive citizens of their liberty, interpret what is legal and illegal, therefore defining who is criminal and who is not, and in some cases take the life of a citizen. However, some cases observed over the years strain one's logic and give rise to doubt as to whether the system is being misused. It is likely that such skewed cases are aberrations rather than the rule. Whether a particular case is an example of use or misuse of the law is a matter of personal interpretation and is always open to argument. Argument is the basis for civil trials.

Skewed Cases

There are some jury decisions that appear so far afield that they could cause many to suspect the ultimate purpose of the Civil Rights Act and the credibility of the system. Caution should be exercised when viewing such cases. Nevertheless, skewed cases are particularly troublesome for individual police officers who are most often the focus of such matters. Two such skewed examples are provided here. A few years back in California a plaintiff attempted to gain entry to a school building by forcing open a skylight on the roof. The skylight broke under his weight and he fell two stories to the floor, seriously injuring himself. He was charged with the felony of breaking and entering. He subsequently sued the school district for his injuries claiming they erred in not having installed bars across the skylight to prevent such injuries. The plaintiff prevailed and was awarded six figures in punitive damages. The second case involved a motorcyclist and his wife, who were struck by a police car responding to an emergency. Neither party was seriously injured and there appeared to be little doubt as to the police department's liability. Under the claim of pain and suffering, one of the two plaintiffs claimed a loss of consortium with the marriage partner as a result of mental trauma. The other plaintiff suffered a broken big toe. The jury awarded the person claiming the loss of consortium $120,000.00 and the plaintiff with the broken toe received $ 80,000.00.

Common Pleadings of Impropriety

Liability may be either direct or vicarious. Simply stated, direct liability means the individual directly caused the resultant injury to a plaintiff. Excessive force against a person, an arrest without probable cause or damage to property during an unlawful search are all examples of direct liability. Similarly, a supervisor may be directly liable for what he/she does personally, such as ordering a subordinate to conduct a strip search or a body cavity search without the appropriate legal grounds and statutory safeguards.

The trend in 1983 suits is vicarious liability. Indirect or vicarious liability is substituted responsibility where the supervisor and others in the chain of command, up to and including administrative officials and the elected officials, are held liable for the actions of their subordinates. The basis for vicarious liability is accountability, but a common reference to vicarious liability is the "deep pocket." The deep pocket refers to a practice reportedly begun during the industrial revolution period. Plaintiffs began to name corporations in their injury suits on the basis that the corporation might be vicariously liable for an injury sustained. The posture was that the corporation could be responsible due to its established practices, policies, or supervisory actions. The corporation had far more assets than an individual supervisor, thus the term, deep pockets. Similarly, contemporary plaintiffs name the officer, the chief or sheriff, and the jurisdiction in hopes of finding the deep pocket. Persons in supervisory, administrative and policy making positions have the responsibility of ensuring that subordinates perform their tasks in a fair and lawful manner. When this type of performance does not occur it may indicate that the superior officers and officials have failed to take reasonable and proper care to ensure a subordinate's compliance with the law.

To establish vicarious liability, a plaintiff must show that the police department acted negligently or with deliberate indifference in permitting the alleged improper police behavior to occur. It is also generally required for the plaintiff to show that the improper behavior was part of a pattern of behaviors. One case of excessive force will not automatically bring vicarious liability. However, in circumstances where an obvious and gross violation occurred, the pattern may not be necessary (Carter, Payne and Embert 1997).

Benson, Payne and Trojanowicz, (1990), Carter and Payne, (1989), and Payne and Carter, (1997), note eight general areas where vicarious liability may arise. (For expanded detail see del Carmen 1985).

Negligent Hiring

Liability may result if it is shown that an individual was unfit for appointment as an officer, that such unfitness was known to the agency or that the agency should have known about it by conducting a thorough background investigation, and that the unfitness for duty was foreseeable. Such liability highlights the importance of thorough background investigations.

Negligent Assignment

This may occur with the assignment of an employee to a task or job without determining whether or not the officer is prepared to perform the responsibilities incumbent for that job. Such liability may also occur if an officer is kept in an assignment after he/she was found to be unfit. Placing an officer in undercover work without proper preparation is just one example. Keeping an officer assigned to a jail who has a history of being abusive to prisoners is another.

Negligent Failure to Train

This allegation assumes a subordinate has not been given sufficient training to provide the skills, abilities and knowledge required to properly perform the job. Examples may include deadly force cases in which the plaintiff claims inadequate firearms training, discrimination cases in which the plaintiff claims lack of human relations training or constitutional rights cases in which it is asserted that officers lack adequate training in criminal law, criminal procedure or civil rights.

Negligent Entrustment

Negligent entrustment exists when there is a failure of a superior officer to properly supervise an officer's use of equipment or facilities entrusted to him/her on the job. Entrusting an officer to carry or use a firearm, or a baton, or drive a police vehicle without adequate preparation and direction in their use could constitute negligent entrustment. del Carmen (1986, 318) observed that "the test of liability is deliberate indifference." Negligent entrustment highlights the need for police administrators to insure proper training, to properly test the trainees, and good record keeping of the training.

Failure to Supervise

The failure to supervise includes circumstances in which a supervisor, at any position in the chain of command, was negligent in handling the responsibility to insure that subordinates were handling their jobs in accordance with the law. Liability could also arise in cases in which a supervisor failed to regularly enforce organizational policy. Failing to take action when subordinates regularly violate policy or law and tolerating a pattern of discrimination are examples of failure to supervise. It is important to note that in order to prevail under this concept a plaintiff must show (a) a pattern of such behavior, (b) the supervisor must have known of the behavior and (c) the supervisor failed to act to remedy the improper behavior.

Failure to Direct

A police agency has the responsibility of telling employees of the specific procedures, conditions and limits associated with the performance of duties. Officers must be informed of the proper circumstances and conditions when they may use firearms and must be told what conduct is permissible and what is not. In addition to the procedures and potential consequences associated with improper conduct officers must also have the processes for arrest, interrogation and holding of criminal suspects clearly articulated to them. The best defense to "failure to direct" is a comprehensive policy and procedure manual. Moreover, such a manual may also support defenses against the allegations of the failure to train and the failure to supervise. However, the existence of such a manual is not enough. Officers must be trained it its meaning and understand its contents and implications. This practice should be fortified with regular testing and all of the work should be well documented.

Negligent Retention

Negligent retention occurs when a police department fails to take appropriate disciplinary action and, perhaps, fails to appropriately re-train an officer who has demonstrated unsuitability for the job to a degree of dangerousness to the public. The test is: was the employee unfit for training and did the supervisor know or should he/she have known of the unfitness? (del Carmen 1986, 318). When such conditions exist and the department retains the individual officer then the department's actions may be considered negligent and the charge of liability could arise. When a department does take definitive action and fires an officer for such behaviors, but a civil service board or the collective bargaining agreement calls for reinstatement of a fired officer, the department is left with a dilemma. To put such an officer in the same position again will only bring further liability. To place such an officer in a less exposed position will bring ill feelings from other officers and complaints of favoritism. Either way a department loses.

Failure to Protect

Failure to protect asserts that the police have failed to take some affirmative or preventive action which would have protected another from harm. Though the failure to protect allegation focuses on the individual behavior of the officer, vicarious liability attaches when there were foreseeable actions the police administration should have taken to prevent the officer's indifferent or negligent behavior. In virtually every type of call or action a police agency performs, the potential for liability exists. It is of paramount importance for administrators and elected officials to recognize this fact and take a preventive posture on matters of liability by proactively addressing the areas wherein the susceptibility to liability is high.

Chapter 2

A Review of Literature Concerning the Use of Force and Case Analyses

The Use of Force

Fazo (1985), writing of the finality of the use of deadly force, notes that the consequences of the use of deadly force are not reversible. She also pointed out that the decision not to use deadly force can also mean finality. "a hesitation or conscious decision on the part of the officer could very well result in the death of the officer or another person the officer is sworn to safeguard" (54).

In encounters with persons arrested, except in those cases where voluntary submission is present, the police often resort to the use of some degree of force to complete the arrest process. The standard for the use of force is to use only that force necessary to overcome the resistance offered by the arrestee. The least amount of force is the preferred norm. Where there is no resistance, the slightest amount of force may be excessive.

The majority of American police departments rely on reference to a force continuum provided in their training curricula. That guideline ranges from the lowest level of persuasion or firm orders up to and including the use of deadly force. Officer's actions are predicated on the level of resistance given by the person being arrested. For example, it may be passive resistance, active resistance such as pulling away, or armed attack. With each level of resistance a corresponding police response is recommended. A major premise of the continuum is escalation and de-escalation. That is, as the level of resistance is reduced, the level of force must be correspondingly reduced. Likewise, as the level of resistance is increased, the level of force is increased. At best, the continuum is a guideline. There is a good deal of overlap between the steps to be taken and much is left to the interpretation and training of the officer. Most arrest situations take place in a matter of seconds or a minute or two at most. In a force situation the conditions can change rapidly and degrade quickly. This area of police response is open to a number of 1983 suits against the police with charges of excessive force.

Not only is an officer vulnerable, but the municipality may also be vulnerable since the decision in *Monell v. Department of Social Services* (1978). In that case, it was made clear that a municipality could be sued if it maintained an unconstitutional custom, practice or policy that was deemed the cause of the constitutional deprivation. O'Linn (1992) holds that gaps in typical use of force polices or use of force training could unwittingly bring the jurisdiction into liability. She lists seven failures on the part of a municipality that could lead to liability under *Monell.*: (1) Failure to Incorporate Use of Force Continuums, (2) Failure to Incorporate the Continuum in the Training, (3) Failure to Train Administrative and Supervisory Personnel, (4) Failure to Use Consistent Standards of Evaluation, (5) Failure to Provide Continuous Review of Use of Force Incidents, (6) Failure to Provide Specific Guidance, and (7) Failure to Publicly Acknowledge the Department's Position.

Donnely (1978) emphasized the need to properly and thoroughly investigate an officer's actions in a case of deadly force and likened such investigations to those of homicide investigations. The author of this book recommends investigation of any complaint of the use of force, deadly or otherwise. As part of his Abuse of Authority Typology, Carter (1984, 226) defines physical abuse/excessive force as "(a) any officer behavior involving the use of more force than is necessary to effect an arrest or search, and/or (b) the wanton use of any degree of physical force against another by a police officer under the color of the officer's office."

Police experts, as well as police trainers and administrators, must ask themselves several questions when addressing claims of excessive use of force by police:

Was the use of force necessary under the conditions confronting the officer?

Was the level of force employed legal?

Was the level of force more than was required?

Did the plaintiff suffer injury from the use of force?

Was the injury consistent with the level of force used?

Was the use of force the proximate cause of the injury?

Was the plaintiff's action a proximate cause of the injury ?

Was the injury an unintended injury caused by plaintiff's resistance?

Was the officer's action in keeping with departmental policy?

When the resistance ceased did the force cease?

Was the level of force proportionate to the level of resistance?

Was the departmental policy reasonable and in accord with case law?

Was the officer properly trained in the proper use of force?

These and other questions arise in almost all law suits against the police for the use of force.

Constitutional Standards

The guiding case for the use of deadly force in the United States is *Tennessee v. Garner* (1985). In *Graham v. Connor* (1989) the court extended the 4th Amendment to all use of force cases in investigative stops, arrests and other seizures. The *Garner* court ruled that deadly force is a seizure within the meaning of the reasonableness standard of the 4th Amendment. The court held that it was constitutionally unreasonable to use such force unless it was necessary to prevent the escape and the officer had probable cause to believe that the suspect posed a significant threat of death or serious injury to the officers or others. *Garner* does not apply to excessive force without seizures.

Elements of *Tennessee v. Garner*

The reasonableness requirement makes it clear that if an officer has probable cause to believe that a suspect poses a threat of serious physical harm, either to the officer or others, it is not unreasonable to prevent his/her escape using deadly force. The person must be viewed as dangerous and not just as a felon. The decision also requires some warning should be given where feasible. The elements can be viewed as: (1) a suspect threatens an officer with a weapon, or (2) an officer has probable cause to believe the suspect has committed a crime involving the infliction of or threat of infliction of serious harm, and (3) the officer has given some kind of warning where feasible. It should be noted that the first two elements are disjunctive and the third is conjunctive.

Deadly force is defined by the Model Penal Code as that force the actor uses with the purpose of causing, or that he knows to create a substantial risk of causing death, or serious bodily harm, 3.11(2). An application of the Model Penal Code definition can be seen in *Pruitt v. the City of Montgomery* (1985). In that case if the police used force that was intended to or likely to cause death or serious injury, the lower courts have construed it to mean deadly force. An eighteen year old was shot by an officer who said that he did not intend to kill him. The person did not die, but did sustain permanent injuries. The city said it was not deadly force because they only shot at his legs to stop him. The court applied the Model Penal Code definition and said it was deadly force. However, all attempts to apprehend a person which results in death are not necessarily seizures. In *Cameron v. Pontiac* (1987) two suspects ran from a burglary of a residence. One of the two burglary suspects gave up, but the other, Cameron, escaped. During his escape Cameron jumped a fence adjacent to an expressway, ran onto the paved portion of the expressway and was killed by a passing vehicle. Cameron's claim of illegal seizure did not hold up. The *Cameron* court noted that the plaintiff was not seized within the meaning of the 4th Amendment because the officers' firing at him did not stop him or in any way restrain him.

Other Applications of Deadly Force

Crawford v. Edmonson (1985) involved two robbery suspects. One of the two turned toward the police with a gun in hand. Officer Edmonson fired a shot gun and pellets from the shell he fired hit both suspects. The facts showed that at least one of the two suspects was armed, they were working together, and the officers yelled "Halt" several times before firing the weapon. The court held that the unarmed person was not an innocent bystander. Edmonson, it was determined, did what any reasonable person would do in firing the gun.

In a similar vein in *Amato v. U.S.* (1982) one bank robbery suspect sued for wounds inflicted by the FBI in a shoot-out which was triggered by a second suspect firing the first shot. In the next thirty-three seconds, eleven agents fired their weapons thirty-nine times, unleashing two hundred and eighty-one bullets and shot gun pellets that killed one suspect and wounded Amato sixty-five times. The shots fired by the FBI agents put 141 holes in the robbers' car as well. Mr. Amato alleged he did not fire his weapon and was trying to surrender. The court said a person like Mr. Amato acting in concert, under such circumstances, may have forfeited his right to surrender if his co-conspirator fired and used deadly force against the police and the police feared he would continue to do so. Though it appears that the number of shots fired at Amato was excessive, it should be noted that multiple shots are not intrinsically wrong.

The theory that there are different degrees of deadly force and that any actions to increase the probability of success are excessive is not well founded. Based on the examination of details of past shootings, law enforcement experience has revealed that the human body is capable of absorbing the shock and damage of several shots, and a person with such wounds may still be capable of returning fire for an extended period of time. Only those wounds which disrupt brain functions or the upper spinal cord can immediately incapacitate. Some shots, though fatal later, may not stop immediate hostile action. It has been determined that an officer cannot pause after each shot to see if the criminal has ceased his action that prompted the first shot. Courts have indicated that the Constitution does not require an officer to use a minimum of violence when attempting to stop a suspect from using deadly force against the police or others. However, as noted in *Bauer v. Norris* (1983) where a plaintiff did not physically resist an arrest or physically threaten a officer, the court held that any force used would be excessive. The 8th Amendment prohibition against unnecessary infliction of pain may also apply.

Tennessee v. Garner (1985) literally declared the fleeing felon statute as unconstitutional and placed limits on when an officer is constitutionally allowed to use deadly force. A primary issue in that opinion was that such cases should be viewed in light of the 4th Amendment proscription against illegal seizures. It noted that when a person is shot dead they are in fact seized. That court , however, did not address other uses of force which were less than deadly force.

In 1989 in *Graham v. Connor*, the court applied the 4th Amendment objective reasonableness test to all cases of force, deadly and nondeadly, and did away with the substantive due process test used earlier in *Johnson v. Glick* (1974). *Glick* required consideration of whether the individual officers acted in good faith or maliciously and sadistically for the very purpose of causing harm. Essentially, the four part test of *Johnson v. Glick* included: (1) the need for the use of force, (2) the relationship between that need and the amount of force that was used, (3) the extent of injury inflicted, and (4) whether the force was applied in a good faith effort to maintain and restore discipline or maliciously and sadistically for the very purpose of causing harm. The *Connor* court felt that test was incompatible with a proper 4th Amendment analysis. For a determination of whether the force used to effect a seizure is reasonable under the 4th Amendment requires, said the court, a careful balancing of the nature and quality of the intrusion on the individual's 4th Amendment interests against the countervailing governmental interest that is at stake.

The Objective Reasonableness Test

Proper application of the objective reasonableness test requires attention to the facts and circumstances of each particular case, including the severity of the crime at issue, whether a suspect poses an immediate threat to the safety of the officers or others, and whether he is actively resisting arrest or attempting to evade arrest by flight. Moreover, the court said that the reasonableness of a particular use of force must be judged from the perspective of a reasonable officer on the scene, rather than with the twenty-twenty vision of hindsight. The court further clarified the test and said the calculus of reasonableness must embody allowance for the fact that police officers are often forced to make split-second judgments about the necessary amount of force in circumstances that are tense, uncertain and rapidly evolving.

To be sure, the grave decision by an officer to employ deadly force is frequently made in a very short period of time. Matulia (1984) feels that the authority to use deadly force is the most critical responsibility placed on police officers. Officers must balance several conflicting points of view and do so instantaneously. Matulia's points include the right of an officer to protect his/her life, the duty to protect the public lives, the duty to suppress violence, the authority to use reasonable force that is both reasonable and necessary, the right of the jurisdiction the officer represents to be protected, and the right of the individual to be presumed innocent until proven guilty. Matulia (1984) describes some obligations police administrators have in this regard. They are responsible for controlling police officers' authority to use deadly or other forms of force. They are required to develop polices, rules, and regulations but with enough latitude for self-protection built into the policy. They should develop training programs to prepare officers, physically and mentally, to carry out their duties under the policy. They should support officers when they are acting properly and discipline them appropriately when they act outside the policy. A citizen's constitutional rights are protected under proper policy, training and discipline.

Most research has shown that when police confront suspects, force is used infrequently and the type of force used is at the lower end of a continuum toward less severe (Cole and Smith 1999). Garner et al. (1995), in their research in Phoenix, found the largest predictor of use of force by the police was the use of force by a suspect. In that study, police used some form of physical force or the threatened or actual use of a weapon in twenty-two percent of the surveyed arrests (Gaines, Kaune, and Miller 2001).

Determining when the amount of force used is excessive requires a close examination of the facts on a case by case basis. Even then, those using force tend to feel the amount used was proper and sufficient to overcome the resistance, whereas those receiving the force tend to feel it was excessive. Quoting the Christopher Commission, Gaines et al. (2001) note the Commission's attempt to qualify excessive force: "an officer may resort to force only where he or she faces a credible threat, and then may only use the minimum amount necessary to control the subject" (ix).

It is this author's opinion that though much has changed in policing in the past forty-five years, providing a precise calculus for determining what is excessive and what is not is at best difficult. In contested cases, the final decision on what is excessive and what is not will be made by a judge or jury in a civil proceeding in a state or federal court or in a criminal trial in either a state or federal court.

Many variables confound determination of the truth in such matters. Among those most often observed are: (a) biases of plaintiffs or defendants, (b) racial issues, (c) experience of all parties involved, (d) desire for financial gain, (e) desire to prevent financial gain, (f) efficacy of policies, (g) enforcement or lack of enforcement of policies, (h) lying, (i) media coverage, (j) political climate, (k) community polarization and (l) the absence or presence of sound supervision and training. Other factors that may have an impact on the outcome of excessive force suits include the credibility of the officers and their departments, the skills and abilities of the litigating attorneys, the expertise of experts when used and the world views held by members of the jury.

Use of Force Cases

The following fifteen cases concern allegations against the police of an excessive use of force. The author was retained in each of these cases as a consultant and provided expert testimony at depositions and trials as they arose. Some of the cases were settled prior to giving testimony. Others were settled after providing deposition testimony, and some cases went to trial. These cases are presented and analyzed to provide some insight into the nature of such cases and their dispositions and, where appropriate, suggestions are made for policy and operational improvements so that civil suits can be or might be avoided in the future.

The names of officers, plaintiffs, and agencies are omitted. In many cases the term "case settled" refers to agreements between plaintiff's attorney and defendant's attorney. Such decisions often include consideration of the underwriter's or jurisdiction's concern for costs associated with going forward measured against the risk of loss and potential jury awards. Moreover, recommendations of the mediation panels are always considered. A settled case should never lead to an automatic inference of negligence or liability on the part of the defendants, although that may be one of the critical considerations in reaching such decisions.

An expert has an obligation to his/her client to be objective and honest at all times, to examine all the facts available and to apply his/her experience and education to the facts as observed. In some cases that means advising counsel that the case does not have merit or that his/her clients were in fact negligent based on the consultant's background, experience and education. Objectivity requires an expert to inform counsel of the strengths and weaknesses of a case.

Case 1: Exigent Circumstances

Facts

The incident occurred in a suburban area of a large metropolitan county served by several police agencies on an early summer evening. The police agency received a call from a psychologist, after he had received a call from the plaintiff's wife, and he reported the plaintiff was hiding in a barn on his property, fired one shot from his shot gun, and may commit suicide. A dispatcher, who reached the plaintiff by phone, was told by him if the police came near his house he would kill the officers. Two departments responded. Four officers of the primary agency and two from a back-up department met prior to exposing themselves to possible gunfire and made a plan. One officer was assigned to guard the exit from the property. One officer would approach the barn past the house, and two officers would serve as his backup. Two others would go behind the plaintiff's house and work their way toward the barn.

As one officer was passing the front porch of the house the plaintiff appeared on the porch and ordered him off the property. He was emotional, profane and hollering. The two officers from the back-up department looked through a doorwall as they passed the back of the house. They could see the plaintiff standing on the front porch; he was talking to an officer, and behind him against a wall and within his reach was a shot gun. They entered the house and came out on the porch. Plaintiff turned and assaulted one of the back-up officers. All of the officers present attempted to handcuff him. He was strong and resisted being cuffed, swinging wildly. In an attempt to get his attention and his arms down, an open hand slap was given to him in the face, then the testicles. He was finally handcuffed and arrested for assault on a police officer and resisting arrest after an active fight. Plaintiff claimed he was pistol wipped. He did not complain of injury at the time, but did have some scratches and bruises. Plaintiff later pled guilty to both charges.

Six months after his arrest the plaintiff was involved in a motor vehicle accident in which his vehicle went into a ditch. He did not report that accident or seek treatment. Days later he experienced headaches, saw a physician, was diagnosed with a subdural hematoma and had surgery. As an apparent result of the surgery, he was in a constant vegetative state for life. His estate sued the physician and collected, and then brought suit against both police agencies claiming the slap, six months earlier, caused the subdural hematoma.

Issues and Factors Considered

A first consideration was the force used by the officers in attempting to gain control of plaintiff's arms to see if it was excessive. An important issues was whether the two officers' entry into the plaintiff's home was a violation of plaintiff's 4th Amendment rights. Departmental procedures had to be examined to determine whether the officers followed policy and to find out if their actions were consistent with accepted police standards and practices. A final consideration was whether the officers had a right to be on and stay on the plaintiff's property.

Commentary

Officers were proper in responding to the report of a potentially suicidal person, who reportedly had fired a weapon, threatened homicide and was hiding in a barn. Until the barn was searched the officers did not know whether the plaintiff was the person reported to be in the barn. In this situation, because they saw a gun within the plaintiff's reach, the officers' entry into the house was a response to an exigent circumstance. A warrant for entry was not needed. Under the circumstances it is deemed reasonable to assume that fellow officers were in fact in a dangerous position had they not entered to disarm the plaintiff. After the plaintiff assaulted an officer, they had a duty to arrest him and they used a minimum amount of force to overcome his resistance to being handcuffed.

Both agencies had a comprehensive use of force policy and all officers had documented excellent training records. Long guns were left in the patrol cars and the officers did not have batons or flashlights with them at the time. They met and formulated a plan prior to being committed and that plan included isolating the possible gunman and then when confronted, de-escalate the situation. The author had no criticisms of the officers' actions and no suggestions for improving their response in this matter. The author's conclusion was it was a text-book case of proper police response. The author testified in a jury trial in the U.S. District Court in Wayne County, Michigan. The jury deliberated for less than an hour and determined a no cause of action in favor of defendants.

Case 2: Forced Entry to Patrol Car

Facts

This case took place in mid-winter in a medium sized industrial city at 1:00 a.m. Two officers entered a tavern, well known for its problems, to conduct a liquor inspection. Once inside, one officer observed a man falling backwards out of the men's room and landing on his back. Another man, the plaintiff, came out of the men's room, fell upon him, struck him in the face with a fist and then reentered the men's room. One officer entered the men's room and found plaintiff at the urinal with his pants undone. He grabbed his arms, arrested him for assault and handcuffed him behind his back. The plaintiff asked to have his pants pulled up as they were open and slipping down. The second officer obtained the identification of the assaulted person and released him. Plaintiff was then taken out of the tavern in front of several patrons with his pants falling down. He was taken to a patrol car and ordered to get in. He refused and asked to have his pants pulled up and buttoned before he got in. The officer did not comply, but used his knee to the back of plaintiff's knee to facilitate his entry into the car. The first attempt at bending plaintiff's knee failed. He was then kicked by the officer in the knee area. He collapsed and was put in the car. During this time his partner stood by the tavern door several feet away and had no memory of what transpired at the car. The plaintiff's knee was fractured. He was lodged in jail and there was no mention in the reports of his being treated for his injuries. A later check of the assault victim's record revealed he was wanted by that department on a felony warrant for rape.

After interviewing witnesses and reviewing deposition transcripts of the officers and witnesses, the following sequence of events emerged. Plaintiff bumped into the second man when entering the men's room. That person left and returned with a beer bottle and threw it at the plaintiff, nearly hitting him in the head. Plaintiff then pushed him out of the door, to the floor, jumped on top of him, hit him in the face and returned to the urinal. The police arrived and, after witnessing the plaintiff hit the man, arrested the plaintiff. Four witnesses, including a waitress, stated plaintiff did in fact have his pants falling down as he was being escorted out of the bar. His wife-to-be and uncle followed them out of the bar and asked the officer to pull his pants up, but they left when threatened with an arrest for interfering. The second officer did advise the plaintiff that he had a right to sign a complaint for felonious assault against the man who threw the beer bottle at him, but nothing else was done. Details of the use of force in the police report were vague and incomplete.

Issues and Factors Considered

The officer had a right to arrest plaintiff for a misdemeanor committed in his presence. He also had a right to handcuff him and place him in the patrol car. While it is not a right to have one's pants pulled up, it was certainly reasonable to have done so. Doing so might have reduced the need to use force to get the plaintiff in the patrol car. That aside, when a person, who is under a legal arrest, resists being placed in the car, a degree of force can be used. The issue here is whether the kick to the knee, which caused the plaintiff's injury, was excessive. Physicians who were deposed testified that the only way the injury could have occurred is from a lateral kick. If in fact, the kick was lateral it was excessive. That type of kick does not bend one's knee, but is only designed to injure. The failure of the officer to use good judgment and lift the man's pants was a proximate cause of the need to use force. Walking a person through a crowded tavern with his pants falling down is demeaning and unnecessary, but not negligent. The officer's stated purpose for not stopping to help plaintiff close his pants was to avoid inflaming the crowd, but in fact by acting the way he did the officer had a greater chance of inflaming the patrons.

On deposition the officer was asked why he did not comply with plaintiff's request and he said that he did not have to. Interestingly, his partner, who stood outside by the front door to the tavern most of the time, claimed he saw very little and none of the force used. The author seriously doubted that officer's honesty and from experience knew he should have been assisting his partner. He did not offer an explanation of why he stood by the tavern door and could not see what two other witnesses clearly observed. It was concluded that he did not wish to testify against his partner's behavior, nor did he wish to support it.

The department requires a use of force report to be filed after such incidents, but none was filed. The officer did not know he was required to do so. If, as the other officer said, plaintiff could sign a complaint for felonious assault, one could wonder why the other man was not arrested based on probable cause. Very little investigation was done at the scene and it was days before it was learned the assaulted person was wanted for rape.

Commentary

There were alternative methods for getting the plaintiff in the car. Several witnesses, albeit favorable to plaintiff, told the police the "other guy" started it, but that fact is not in the police report. The primary issue in this case is whether the second blow to the knee was a missed attempt to buckle the knee from behind or a punitive kick to the side of the knee causing the fracture. In any case, it was the opinion of the writer that the officer over-reacted, did not avail himself of alternatives, including help from his partner, and did not comply with his agency's policy. He also did not fully investigate the matter in keeping with accepted police practices. The determination of the type of kick was left to medical experts. Depositions were taken and the matter went to a mediation panel. The case was settled before trial and plaintiff was given a settlement. A review of the agency's policy leaves an objective reader with the idea that the policy is "we vs. them." Prior to this case the department did not investigate verbal or telephone complaints on excessive force. A Complaint Policy Review Board was formed five years prior to this incident. That board was designed to meet quarterly. In the five year period leading up to this complaint there were no minutes of any meetings and the city admitted it had not met in over a year.

The paternalistic manner in which complaints against officers are investigated, the implicit disinterest by supervisors by failing to hold officers accountable, and a lack of after-action behaviors by supervisors sends a clear message to officers. That message is that it is all right to use excessive force and little or nothing will happen to you when it occurs. The department should revise its use of force policy, train all officers as to its contents and hold officers accountable when they are found to disregard it. If a review board on force is to be maintained it should meet as required and keep minutes for review. A review of the use of force should be conducted by supervisors at the time of such occurrences and supervisors should require reports by officers involved in the use of force. No action was taken against the officer for failing to file a use of force report. The administrative atmosphere of the police department was in need of serious improvement.

Case 3: A Shoot-Out Inside a Dwelling

Facts

This incident started in late morning of mid-summer in a metropolitan suburb. A woman called the police reporting that her son and husband were fighting over a shot gun in her home and she felt her son was going to shoot her husband. Two officers arrived, heard yelling from within the home and through a front window saw a man waving a long gun in the front room of the house. When the officers reached the porch, the plaintiff's mother let the officers in and then ran out screaming her son had a gun and was going to shoot his father. Upon entering the home the officers saw the son holding a shot gun and struggling with his father. The son broke loose from his father's grip and ran to a back bedroom. The officers immediately got the father out of the house. They took up positions in rooms adjacent to a long hallway in the back of the house where they could have a view of the door to the bedroom.

Several attempts were made to talk the man out of his weapon. The son came out of hiding and pointed the shot gun at the junior officer who was exposed in his position. The senior officer fired two shots at the son, who then retreated to the bedroom. The senior officer crawled down the hall to check on the son's condition. On entering the room he found the son pointing the gun at him and again the officer fired two quick shots and retreated to cover. The son came out of the room for the second time with the gun in hand and the junior officer fired two shots. Finally, the senior officer entered the bedroom, found the son on his knees pointing the shot gun at him and fired two more shots. He then wrestled the gun away from the suspect who was wildly kicking and yelling. The son did not die from his wounds, but suffered serious wounds including the loss of his testicles. The prosecutor declined to issue a warrant for the son because in his opinion, the son's mental state prevented him from forming the intent required for culpability.

Issues and Factors Considered

The first question addressed was whether the officers had a right to be in the house. The second issue was once in the house, did the officers who were partially exposed to gun fire have a right to shoot at the suspect? Another issue is whether the officers gave any warning to the son or attempted to use less than deadly force to handle the situation. Plaintiff's attorney took the position that the officers should have set up a command post outside, as recommended by his expert, rather than enter the home and then wait for backup. Other issues considered included whether the officers were acting under a reasonable policy, whether they had the right to use deadly force and whether they were in an exigent circumstances situation.

Commentary

The officers in this case took decisive action based on information they had to intercede and protect the life of a person in immediate danger. They were confronted with three things: (1) they had information from the mother of the son's possible intentions, a view of someone in the front room with a long gun, and the scuffle between the father and his armed son upon their entry; (2) these three observations provide a reasonable person a basis to conclude that an exigent circumstance exists; (3) to leave the premises under such circumstances would have been a neglect of duty and an unnecessary endangerment to the father and others.

Setting up a command post in lieu of entry would not be proper as this was not a case of a barricaded gunman. The exigent circumstances required immediate action to prevent death or serious injury to another. The officers shot at the son because they thought they were in danger of death. Under such conditions police officers have a right to defend themselves and they are not required to retreat. Moreover, under these circumstances it was prudent to maintain control of the person in the bedroom, who had pointed a shot gun at least twice at the police in order to prevent his escape and the possible broadening of danger to others.

The agency policy provides proper guidance. Among other things, it states deadly force is restricted to the apprehension of persons, who in the course of crime threaten deadly force...or if the officer believes the person sought poses a substantial risk, or will cause death or serious bodily harm if his/her apprehension is delayed. Officers are allowed to use deadly force to protect themselves or other persons from death or serious injury. In this matter the defense prevailed. The manner in which the officers acted was within the deadly force guidelines. Their tactical action was appropriate.

Case 4: A Claim of Injury During Booking

Facts

A middle-aged woman was arrested for driving under the influence of alcohol. The Preliminary Breath Test (PBT) indicated a blood alcohol level of .152 which was over the level allowed and considered under the influence. She was handcuffed after her arrest and brought to the police station. At the booking room, she was being transferred to another part of the jail. One officer led her down a hall and had hold of her collar. At a ninety degree turn at the end of the hall she went one way and the officer tried to lead her another way. She fell and claimed she then fainted. Plaintiff claimed she pleaded with officers not to handcuff her hands behind her back due to illnesses. The officers note when she was told she was going to be handcuffed she put her hands behind her back. She did mention a blood disease but did not complain and walked into the police department under her own control. After her fall she was taken to the hospital by the police, was administered four stitches to her forehead and then released. Subsequently, she saw a doctor who told her she never should have been cuffed and that she had a possible closed head injury. She also saw a dentist for a chipped tooth. Her primary claim was that the handcuffs hurt her so much they caused her to be unsteady on her feet.

Issues and Factors Considered

One issue is whether the officers were correct in handcuffing the plaintiff. A second issue was to see if the department handcuffing policy allowed for variances in handcuffing procedures. A detailed review is required to determine whether the officer had a hold on her collar as stated. Other factors include whether the officers had a duty to protect her once she was in custody and whether the officers' actions were the proximate cause of her injuries. Finally, it should be determined whether her injuries were in fact connected to the fall.

Commentary

Interestingly, the officer denied having any hold on the plaintiff when walking her down the hall, but on deposition he testified that he lost his grasp of her collar. Such discrepancies open the door to criticism and provide plaintiffs and potential jurors with a basis for thinking the police are lying. The policy of the department does allow variance in where the hands are placed during handcuffing, and leaves these decisions to the officers' discretion based on the circumstances. The police report was written in a rather matter of fact way and there was no mention of pain from the plaintiff. Plaintiff had a long history of surgeries and other maladies. One fact in the police report is salient: when the officer attempted to turn plaintiff to the right, her left foot just stopped and she tripped and fell. However, that detail was not in the police report. The degree of intoxication could well have been the precipitating factor in the plaintiff's fall. Police reports should contain every detail of which the officers are aware since it is too late to amend such reports after the fact.

The failure of the police to provide detailed reports in every case may be an oversight, or officers may not consider such detail important on less than spectacular cases. Nevertheless, later, when sued, such reports provide plaintiffs with a basis for suspicion of a cover-up. A nexus between the fall of plaintiff and the police action could not be made. There was no evidence of use of force. Though police do have an affirmative duty for the protection of a person arrested, there did not appear to be any breech of that duty here. Plaintiff's attorney chose not to go forward.

Case 5: Misuse of Chemical Agents

Facts

At 10:30 p.m. on a humid August night in an industrial city of 45,000, a group of hospital staff and friends were gathered in a rented clubhouse of a condo complex to honor a surgeon who was being transferred to another hospital. The room and the surrounding area were on private property. Due to the high temperature and humidity, the clubhouse windows were open and the music was loud enough to cause the complex superintendent's wife to call the police and report a loud party. Prior to calling the police, a maintenance worker was sent to the room to tell the participants to keep the noise down. The music was turned off and those in attendance began cleaning up.

The first officer to arrive noted in his report that he was sent to "disperse a loud party." The first officer called for assistance, and within minutes six additional officers responded to the scene with their emergency lights activated. The first officer approached the clubroom doorway and encountered a young Hispanic male holding a cup of beer. He ordered the man to either go back inside the room or throw the beer out. He threw the contents out and some of the beer spilled on the officers shoe or trousers. The officer grabbed him, spun him around, and arrested him for what he believed to be an assault. At the patrol car, the Hispanic party-goer refused to put his arms behind his back for handcuffing and asked why he was being arrested. Immediately, he was maced in the face, handcuffed and placed in the patrol car. A sergeant, standing nearby, observed everything that took place and took no action to supervise or stop the officer.

One party member asked the guest of honor, the plaintiff, to inquire as to the arrest of one of his friends. He met the officer at his patrol car and said, "I think there has been a mistake here, officer. I would like to speak to you." The officer told the plaintiff to get back. After asking to speak to the officer the second time, the plaintiff was grabbed, spun around, pushed against the patrol car and arrested. The plaintiff asked why he was being arrested, and he refused to put his hands behind his back until he was given a reason. He also was spun around and maced in the face. He was then handcuffed and placed in another patrol car. The plaintiff denied that he was told to back away by the officer.

A nurse friend of the plaintiff, standing nearby, said "Jesus Christ, what is this the Gestapo?" The officer told her not to use those dirty words. On her second utterance she also was arrested for interfering with an officer. She was handcuffed and placed in the patrol car, but she refused to put her legs in the car until she was told why she was being arrested. At that point she too was maced in the face. Other officers, in their depositions, testified the party was not out of control, but was peaceful and breaking up. The first officer said the young man threw a cup of beer in his face, but the sergeant refuted his statement and said some beer may have hit part of his uniform. A post-incident investigation was instituted by the department only after a law suit was filed by the plaintiff. The internal investigator concluded that excessive force was not used during the incident. An investigation was not conducted into possible violations of departmental policies.

Issues and Facts Considered

The first issue is whether an officer's order to empty a cup of beer onto the ground or go back inside was legal, considering it occurred on private property. Another issue is the whether the police have a right or duty to disperse participants of a party. The latter should be viewed in light of the 1st Amendment. A primary consideration is whether asking an officer a reasonable question rises to the level of interfering with an officer. The policy has to be reviewed to determine if it prohibits macing persons in handcuffs. Moreover, the policy should be examined to see if there are other alternatives recommended before macing a non-combative or non-resistant person. One should question whether the utterance of "Jesus Christ" in connection with one's appraisal of a poor arrest is a violation of the law. An examination of the department's policy regarding loud parties should also be made.

Commentary

The police response of seven patrols was far beyond that which was required. The first officer labors under an ideal that loud parties and assemblies should be dispersed. When asked why he used mace rather than persuasion or a form of a hold he said, "It is better than pulling their arms out of their sockets." The over-response by the police and their rapid arrests of two persons who were not unruly or loud at the time tended to accelerate the incident.

The original call to the police was placed by the maintenance person who also told the party-goers to turn down the music volume. Several persons described him as intoxicated, abusive, and profane. The policy of the department is to give a warning on such matters, but it is not their policy to disperse. A proper response from a reasonable officer would include stating his purpose, asking those in attendance to quiet down, and then leaving. Removal of such persons from private property is not within the authority of the officer.

Another officer at the scene testified that the party was quiet, orderly, and breaking up upon his arrival. Response to so-called nuisance calls does not require an emergency response. It is doubtful that the officer had the right, on private property, to order a person to dispose of his beer or go to jail. The indiscriminate macing of those arrested only escalated the situation. The department policy forbids macing anyone who is handcuffed. The force continuum, included in the agency policy, requires persuasion or ordering prior to the escalation of using mace. Most of the officers who gave depositions said their policy is to give warnings at such events. The arrest of the plaintiff for two inquiries was patently illegal and without basis. The macing of the plaintiff was not called for as the officer was not being attacked or facing any resistance. It was clear that the plaintiff was arrested for what the officer thought he might do rather than what he did. Thus it was a baseless arrest.

The lack of patience and awareness of the officer led to the arrests. A serious lack of training and discipline was present in the agency. The sergeant, observing these activities, failed to take any administrative control, yet other officers at the scene supported the plaintiff. The force policy of the department views mace as an escalated form of force and should be used only when officers are attacked or are given physical resistance. The case was settled out of court after depositions were taken. The mediation panel's recommendation was heeded and the plaintiff and the female arrested were both given financial settlements. Ironically, the plaintiff, prior to this incident, had been an ardent supporter of the police and a member of the Fraternal Order of Police. The plaintiff did not suffer permanent injury to his eyes. The officer was exonerated and no discipline or retraining was imposed. The department, in failing to discipline the officer and investigate for policy violations, set a pattern for future mishandling of similar incidents. Such a record can only open the agency to future vulnerability in lawsuits. This method of handling citizen complaints sends a definite message to the officers working the streets. That message is the department will not hold officers responsible for the use of force.

Case 6: Shooting of Unarmed Robber Appropriate

Facts

This case occurred during the summer months in an industrial city of 45,000 just prior to midnight. Four undercover officers, working a surveillance detail, received a tip from a confidential informant that a certain black male who was over six foot five inches tall was going to rob a twenty-four hour drive-in beer store. His address was given to the officers. They set up surveillance on his house and the only drive-in beer store in the city. Shortly before midnight a suspect fitting the description left the house, went to the bushes near the porch and retrieved what appeared to be a sawed-off shot gun. He was observed walking to the drive-in beer store and entering with something that looked like a weapon held close to his side. A few moments later, he ran out carrying a paper bag in his left hand and a long dark object cradled across his right arm.

Officers in two cars gave chase. He ran a short distance and entered a long driveway next to a house. One officer followed him down that driveway in his car and the other went to the adjacent house to cut him off behind the homes. The pursuing officer bent over in his car seat as he rounded the rear corner of the house to avoid being shot. He then exited the vehicle and took cover behind the car door. The officer saw the suspect running into a wooded area behind the house. The officer hollered "halt" and the suspect stopped, swung around to face the officer and pointed what the officer believed to be a shot gun in the officer's direction. The officer fired one shot and his bullet struck the suspect in the spine.

When he and the back-up officer got to the suspect he was lying on the ground with money around him that had apparently fallen out of the bag. The officers also found a black coin drawer from a cash register but no shot gun. Other officers checked the beer store and learned from the clerk that the plaintiff had pointed a sawed-off shot gun at him through a cage style structure and demanded money. As the clerk passed him the coin drawer through the cage window, he simultaneously grabbed the shot gun and pulled it into his cubicle. The plaintiff was charged and convicted of armed robbery and sentenced to prison. He was hit in the spine and was permanently disabled. He sued claiming excessive force and that the officers did not have probable cause to make an arrest, thus their firing on him was illegal.

Issues and Factors Considered

The confidential informant had been used in the past and was deemed credible. The suspect's description was accurate. Officers armed with this information followed him and observed him as he entered the drive-in store with what appeared to be a weapon. Those conditions coupled with his rapid exit and attempted escape gave officers probable cause to arrest him. Turning and facing the officer with what appeared to be a weapon provided that officer with reasonable grounds to believe he was about to be shot. Robbery armed is a serious life-threatening felony and thus within the scope of *Tennessee v. Garner* .

Commentary

The reports of each of the surveillance officers were well documented and complete. The department convened a shooting review board and exonerated the officer. In as much as it was dark and the actions of the suspect indicated a robbery, the officer had a right to defend himself from what he thought was an attempt to shoot him. At a distance of fifty feet in the dark, under these circumstances, it is not unreasonable to think that a fourteen inch dark object being pointed at him was a weapon. All four officers had extensive experience and good training records. A civil trial was held and the defendants prevailed. Officers have to make split second decisions in such matters and, when viewed from a reasonable officer at the scene, one is hard pressed to second guess the officer's action. The plaintiff filed a subsequent law suit against the city while incarcerated and that suit was later dismissed.

Case 7: A Fatal Shooting under Questionable Conditions

Facts

In a large midwestern city at 9:30 p.m. in the summer months, two officers on patrol observed a suspicious circumstance. A lone male was bending over a vehicle parked at the curb with its hood up doing something to the engine. The officers decided to investigate a possible stolen car situation. They pulled behind the vehicle, got out and asked the person what he was doing. He said that he was trying to get the car started. He also said the vehicle belonged to his girlfriend and he gave the police her name. One officer ran the license on the computer while the other officer patted the person down and found he was not armed. The registration check revealed the vehicle was registered to the name the suspect provided, but it also showed she was wanted on an outstanding traffic warrant for a civil infraction. The officer in the patrol car yelled to his partner, "there is an outstanding warrant." At this point the young male fled on foot.

One officer chased him on foot and the other chased him with the patrol car. The fleeing suspect ran across a busy six-lane street, entered an alley and jumped a wooden fence, entering the back yard of a residence. The officer on foot took up a position behind the house in the alley, and the second officer watched the front of the house. Both officers could hear the person moving around in the yard. A third off-duty officer saw this person running past a restaurant as he was leaving it. He followed them, identified himself to the officer in the alley asking: "What do you have?" The response was "We have to catch that fucker." Again he asked what they had and was given the same response. The third officer took up a position in front of the house facing the wooden fence near a gate.

The third officer gave the following scenario in his report. He said he saw the suspect raise his head over the fence and ordered him to "freeze" which he did. He said the young man put both arms over the fence gate. He then approached the gate and, while changing his weapon from his right to left hand to get his handcuffs, the suspect grabbed the barrel of his weapon and they tugged back and forth to gain control of the officer's weapon. He reported the gun went off and the suspect dropped. The gun was then dropped on the street side of the fence.

Twenty minutes after the incident the senior officer of the three reported the incident to headquarters. Detectives and a senior command officer came to the scene accompanied by a crime scene specialist. The detectives picked up the officers weapon, handled it, passed it around and then put it in a plastic bag to protect it for fingerprints. The officer's account was provided to the command officer at the scene and he was relieved of duty. The suspect was found dead inside the fence with a shot to his forehead. Later, no identifiable prints were found on the weapon. A hearing board was convened within one week and the officer was exonerated and returned to duty.

Issues and Factors Considered

The facts surrounding the investigative stop were examined. The reasons the officers pursued the running male were also addressed. The question of probable cause was also looked at in detail. An investigation was made into the actions of the third officer. Reports on the methods used by the detectives and the crime scene specialist were reviewed as was the conduct of their investigation as to the reasonableness of their actions. Other issues relevant in this suit included the appropriateness of the use of deadly force and the agency's response.

Commentary

A criminal record check was run on the twenty-one year old black male who was killed. He had no criminal record and was not wanted for any crime. The officers did have reasonable grounds to investigate a suspicious circumstance and thus conduct an investigative stop. Their pat down during such an investigate stop was within the Terry v. Ohio (1968) guidelines. They also could have chased him, but it is doubtful they had probable cause to make an arrest for any crime. In some cases the Supreme Court has said that one who is being investigated who runs may provide a shift from reasonable suspicion to probable cause. However, the officers already knew the traffic warrant was not for the suspect and they knew the car was not stolen.

The handling of the crime scene investigation was seriously lacking. The officer's weapon was handled by at least two detectives before placing it in a bag. That action compromised any evidentiary value. The crime scene specialist took measurements of the gate and photos of the body. That specialist, in his deposition, said that he estimated the distances measured by stepping them off as opposed to using a tape measure. Those actions were less than professional. The officer who claimed his weapon accidentally discharged was five foot nine inches tall. The victim was over six foot tall. The gate was five foot high, but the bullet entered the victim's head at a downward 45 degree angle. Blood spatterings were found on the inside of the gate half way down its height. Physical evidence indicates the victim was likely shot while crouching behind the gate and not as indicated by the police. If this conclusion is correct then deadly force was used against a person who had not committed a crime of any kind. The agency's administrative post-shooting review of this matter was very rapid and the conclusion was, in this writer's opinion, inconsistent with the facts. An affidavit with the expert's opinions and conclusions was submitted to plaintiff's attorney. The police agency settled the matter quickly before a trial by paying the family of the deceased man a quarter of a million dollars. It was the author's opinion that the officers fabricated the facts of the shooting and the department relinquished its responsibility to run a proper post-shooting investigation. There was no evidence in the materials reviewed that the prosecuting attorney was contacted to determine criminality.

Case 8: A Fabricated Shooting

Facts

The plaintiff, a young man in his twenties, was driving a motorcycle on a county road just outside of a small village. He knew the license plate on the cycle had not been properly transferred and he was serving weekends in the county jail for driving on a suspended license. A reserve village police officer recognized him and attempted to stop him. Fearing he would have to return to jail for the license violation, the cyclist fled for a distance of four tenths of a mile and ran into a ditch. As he was getting off his cycle, the officer arrived and grabbed his arm. He pulled loose from the officer's grasp and ran through the yards of a series of homes in the village. At one point he turned around and saw the officer trying to get over a fence he had just jumped over in his flight. He heard the officer yell, "Stop or I'll shoot." He then heard a shot fired. He continued to run and entered the village post office where he was employed. After he entered the post office he hid behind some boxes.

The officer's report is similar to the plaintiff's account up to the point of the shooting. His police report indicated that he shot at the person after he saw the young man turn and face him and saw two flashes from a gun held in the man's hand. The chief of police and the pursuing officer entered the post office and arrested the plaintiff. En route to the jail the chief asked him where the gun and the stolen motorcyle were.

At the preliminary hearing the officer testified that he saw two flashes from the man's right hand and heard two loud bangs. He then called for back-up with several police units responding. No gun was ever found and the motorcycle was not stolen, but improperly registered. The prosecutor requested a polygraph examination and a credible polygraph operator found no deception in the young man's responses. A second polygraph test was run with similar results. The prosecutor's polygraph operator noted it was the strongest case he has seen of non-deception and wished he could give a polygraph test to the officer. The prosecutor dropped the charges of assault with a weapon against the plaintiff and the plaintiff was freed. A credible witness at a car wash saw the young man run by and moments later the officer asked him to call for back-up, then the officer fired one shot. A passing motorist saw the officer at the scene of the motorcycle accident and said the officer had his weapon out as he approached the cyclist.

Issues and Factors Considered

One issue is whether the officer had a right to use his weapon if in fact he was not fired upon. Another issue is the pointing of a firearm at a misdemeanant. One should examine the evidence, reports, and witness statements to determine if the evidence confirmed or disconfirmed the officer's version of the facts. Was the officer lying? The department would have to be checked to see if it had a shooting review process in place and, if so, was it initiated. Another task was to determine whether the chief conducted a detailed investigation prior to charging the plaintiff with such a serious felony. Another issue is to determine whether a search was conducted for the alleged weapon the plaintiff reportedly had in his possession. One should also ask if it would be proper to discipline an officer if it was learned he had fired a warning shot or filed a false report. Lastly, it should be determined if the chief had interviewed witnesses that could shed light on these and other questions.

Commentary

A metal detector search of the field, in which the alleged firing took place, was conducted twice by a private investigator and no gun was found. Two witnesses were located by the investigator whose testimony disconfirmed the officer's account. The officer drew his weapon on a misdemeanant after the plaintiff's accident. It appears the officer fired a warning shot and lied to cover his actions. The department had a shooting review process, but did not use it. No search was made for the alleged gun and the officer's weapon was not checked by the chief. The use of a weapon in a traffic case is improper. No objective investigation was conducted by the officer's superior officer, but such investigations are required by their own policy. Discipline was not considered or implemented. After the polygraph results were received, and the prosecutor dismissed the charges, no further action was taken by the department. Warning shots are specifically prohibited by the department. A small out-of-court settlement was given to the plaintiff. This case points out the need for proper administration and accountability. The duty of a superior officer to follow his/her own policies is critical. Failure to act on several important factors in this case violated the public trust. In this particular matter, the failure to properly conduct the business of policing also resulted in the incarceration of the plaintiff and the added expense of unnecessary attorney fees.

Case 9: A Failure to Document the Use of Force

Facts

This case involved two suspects in a robbery armed of a pizza store. Two suspects entered the store and said, "This is a stick-up, give me all the money." One clerk did not believe the suspect and said one gunman pulled up his shirt and she saw what appeared to be the handle of a gun. The second clerk did not see the gun, but did hear "this is a stick-up." Both clerks gave clear descriptions of both suspects and reported they both left the scene on bicycles. A short while after receiving the report the police found two suspects riding bicycles nearby and gave chase. Both suspects fit the descriptions given by the clerks. One cyclist claimed he knew nothing of the robbery and did not know his partner was going to rob the place. The second suspect was caught nearby and ordered at gun point to get off of the bicycle. The police had their firearms pointed at him. The suspect reported that he was pushed against the patrol car and then hit on the back of the head with a gun or flashlight. He then shoved the officer away and ran off. The police report does not mention the use of force, but only that there was a short scuffle. The second suspect was later captured hiding in some bushes of a nearby house. Again, the police report only noted an arrest after a scuffle. The injured suspect had a laceration on the front of his forehead. His complaints of injuries were numerous. The suspect that was injured had a large roll of money on his person at the time of his arrest. He was treated for two one-inch lacerations to his forehead.

Issues and Factors Considered

The first issue is whether the police had probable cause to stop and arrest the suspect and the right to use force under the circumstances. One should check to see if the policy of the department addresses the use of flashlights as an appropriate weapon. If force was in fact used by the police it should have been reported in the police reports.

Commentary

The police department policy forbids the use of a flashlight as a weapon except in cases where deadly force is allowed. None of the police reports indicated any specificity on the use of force, but only refer to two scuffles. A use of force report was not submitted by the officers. The police did have probable cause to arrest the suspect based on him fitting the description, being on a bicycle in the vicinity and having a roll of money on him. There was no documented evidence to support a reason to strike the suspect on the first encounter, and no reason to justify striking him on the second encounter in the bushes. Oddly, the injury reported by the plaintiff to the back of his neck does not match the injury of two lacerations to his forehead. Moreover, the plaintiff alleges a series of injuries not indicated in the reports.

The case was settled out of court to avoid a trial. Failure on the part of the police to properly document their actions and using force without documented justification appear to be the reasons the settlement came about. A lack of follow-up and internal investigation into the officers' actions reduced the credibility of the police department. Failure on the part of the police to accurately document their actions, particularly when some level of force is used, invites law suits. Police administrators that do not fully investigate all claims of the use of force send mixed messages to officers and provide plaintiffs with justifications for law suits, whether there is merit or not on their side. Officers who feel that their agency will not properly investigate claims of the use of excessive force by felons have little reason to control themselves.

Case 10: A Caged Cougar Leads to a Claim of Excessive Force

Facts

At the scene of a previous raid by the Treasury Department's Alcohol, Tobacco and Firearms unit, and other cooperative force units searching for explosives at a residence, the police assisting those in the raid were assaulted by a woman attempting to protect her daughter. At the home of those suspected of keeping explosives the police found a caged cougar in the yard. An animal control officer summoned to the scene arrived and was attempting to take the animal into custody until its legal status could be checked. The daughter of the home owner was bodily protecting the cougar by draping her body over the cage. When two police officers attempted to dislodge her, her mother came out of the house and verbally assailed the officers. One officer attempted to hold her back and he was kicked in the groin and upper leg area. She was ordered back into the house so the animal control officer could do his job. She was warned on four occasions to desist or be arrested, but she continued her tirade and assaults. She was then arrested and taken to the patrol car. One officer held her arm and she reportedly complied by putting her arm behind her back for handcuffing. Once in the patrol car, she became violent and kicked out the windows of the police car. Later, in court, she pled no contest to the charges, but showed up wearing a cast on one arm. After filing a law suit for excessive force in her arrest she was examined by two physicians. One said she had a fracture and the other said she did not.

Issues and Factors Considered

A first issue to check is to determine if the police department had an adequate use of force policy. A second issue is the training of the officers in the policy. The next issue was to examine the materials and depositions to determine if the force that was used was consistent with proper police procedures. Once these issues were reviewed, a determination had to be made to see if the force was excessive and whether the agency investigated the plaintiff's claims.

Commentary

The department had an excellent use of force policy and both officers involved had extensive and documented training records. The force used by the officer in this matter was minimal. He only used enough force to hold the woman back who had already kicked him. There is some question as to the injury she claims. She did not complain of any pain when being handcuffed and did in fact help by placing her hands behind her back. The incident was investigated by the department and no fault was found. The matter was settled without a trial for minimal costs. The police reports gave sufficient detail and corroboration to inform any reasonable reader that very little force was used. The department's sound policy, documented training and appropriate follow-up for accountability was instrumental in keeping the costs of the suit down. Without such factors the department could surely have suffered a considerable loss.

Case 11: Shooting a Tire to Stop a Person from Harming an Officer

Facts

Two officers responded to a family disturbance. While responding, a second call to the police reported a shot was fired and the suspect was near a white semi-truck and trailer in the driveway. On arrival one officer blocked the truck's exit with his patrol car. The suspect was in the driveway, and the second officer, who had exited his patrol car, warned him not to get into the truck. He got into the truck anyway and quickly backed up toward the blocking patrol car. He then abruptly stopped and pulled ahead just twenty feet from the patrol car.

The second officer activated his overhead lights, went to the cab of the semi, pointed his weapon at the driver and then ordered him out of the semi. The suspect then backed up again. Feeling he would ram the patrol car parked behind the truck with the officer standing near it, he fired his weapon into a tire of the vehicle. The suspect stopped after first hitting the patrol car. He was forcefully taken from the cab, subdued and arrested. Witnesses from inside the house said the person was swinging wildly at the officers. Plaintiff claimed the officers lacked probable cause and denied swinging at them. He also claimed they illegally searched him and he did not know it was the police. He maintains he got out of truck compliantly and that the officers kicked him in the testicles.

Issues and Factors Considered

The first issue is whether the officers had probable cause to arrest the plaintiff. A second issue is whether the amount of force used was excessive. A primary issue is whether the officer had a right to fire his weapon into the plaintiff's tire. A final issue is whether backing up a vehicle like the plaintiff did, could be perceived as an assault with a motor vehicle.

Commentary

The officers had a right to order the plaintiff not to enter his vehicle since it was, at that time, an investigatory stop. The description of the suspect's vehicle was accurate. When the plaintiff refused to exit the vehicle when so ordered and backed into the patrol car, the officer felt his partner would be injured and fired to stop him from being injured. Once this was done, the arrest of the plaintiff for assault was reasonable. The judge felt probable cause existed. Plaintiff was ordered to the ground, but only sat down. He was then forcibly put on the ground. The fact that officers searched him for a gun supports their belief that he was armed per the call that a shot was fired. The plaintiff's claim of injury was false as none were found. Though a preliminary police report was made, the officer did not have any field notes he claimed he made and used to construct their report.

Three witnesses in the house support the officers' accounts of what transpired. Not keeping their investigative notes does however open the door to suspicion. When field notes are made and retained they not only support the writing of a police report, but become strong evidence in a law suit. When they are mentioned, but not retained, it gives rise to reasonable suspicion and often supports a plaintiff's claim. The criminal charge against the plaintiff was reduced and he pled guilty. When charges are dismissed or reduced by prosecutors, plaintiffs often use this as a basis for law suits. Cases that are particularly well-documented and include all the elements of the crimes charged are seldom reduced. Plaintiff received a small settlement perceived to be nuisance value by the agency.

Case 12: Shooting a Mentally Disturbed Person

Facts

In the early afternoon of a summer month, an officer was summoned because a neighbor reported a man was sitting out in front of his house on the curb with a shot gun across his lap. A reserve officer was sent as a back-up. On arrival the first officer took up a protected position behind the side of a church across the street from the plaintiff. He then racked a shell into his shot gun. Not known to him at the time, two other officers, who were driving down the street toward the suspect, report when they got parallel to the plaintiff he rose and pointed the shot gun at them. Those two officers stopped their car and laid down on their seats. A few moments later they pulled ahead again and the plaintiff again pointed the weapon in their direction.

The complainant in this case was a police buff who used his radio to reach the police. Though the plaintiff had fired a single shot into the church it was not clear from reviewing the reports whether it was prior to the officers' arrival or after their arrival. The complainant reported that multiple shots were fired.

It was learned that the police had been called on the plaintiff's odd behavior in the past. Once he had decorated saw horses and placed them in the street as if to hold a phantom horse race. He also had painted his cat. He was frequently reported to the police for acting strangely in his yard. The responding officers in the car were not aware of the first officer's location by the church. The first officer reports he yelled to the plaintiff on three occasions to drop his weapon. Neighbors reported hearing a total of two shots fired. The first officer reported that after the plaintiff had fired into the church, he rose, took a position behind a utility pole, and aimed toward the officer. At that point, the officer fired at him striking him with multiple shot gun pellets. Throughout the incident, which took just over one minute, the officers were taking their cues from the citizen who had a police radio. Communications between the officers was non-existent.

Issues and Factors Considered

It was significant that the entire action took just over one minute from the time the first officer arrived until the plaintiff was shot. Assigning a reserve officer with a questionable training background to a serious incident may be ill-advised. Officers driving in front of a man with a shot gun on two occasions was neither safe nor a good police procedure. There was no evidence that the officers attempted to isolate the plaintiff or try to clear the area of possible civilian victims. Officers' awareness of the plaintiff's mental background would be an issue to consider. If it is a practice to allow a citizen with a police radio to participate actively on such a scene, such a practice should be reevaluated. One should examine if there is a nexus between the officers closely approaching the plaintiff in their patrol car and his firing a shot at the church.

Commentary

The plaintiff, according to his family, had severe mental problems, and as of late his condition had been deteriorating. The police were aware of his past behaviors. The officers in the patrol car used very poor approach procedures by driving directly in front of the plaintiff. Their action could have easily excited the plaintiff. Several neighbors were unnecessarily exposed to gun fire from the plaintiff, but nothing was done to contain the situation. One neighbor said that plaintiff was pointing the gun in several directions, but the officer that fired his weapon said that it was pointed at him. The police response to this unfortunate incident may well have precipitated the plaintiff firing his weapon into the church. Follow-up investigation reports by the police agency administrator were not available. All the police involved said that the procedure they used was their standard procedure. It appears that there are training deficits in the police department, however, the attorney for the plaintiff withdrew the law suit based on the assumption that the police fired on the plaintiff to protect their own lives. Had the suit gone forward it is reasonable to think that the actions of the police in this one minute response coupled with poor reporting and less than a sound response could have easily led to an assumption of proximate cause in the injury of the plaintiff. Very little assessment of the situation was done by the police. The plaintiff became a paraplegic as a result of his injuries. Training on the special handling of persons with known mental disorders is considered customary training for police. Those departments that do not provide such training are vulnerable to suit when such persons are the objects of the force police use.

Case 13: Unintended Injury while Resisting Arrest

Facts

Two officers were called to a spousal abuse complaint and given entry to the house by the plaintiff's wife. The police were summoned after a nine-year-old daughter ran to the neighbors to report the assault on her mother. The wife told the police she was choked and thrown to the floor. The daughter said that her father dragged her mother by the hair after throwing her to the floor. The officers observed red marks on the wife's neck and due to current spousal abuse laws did not need a complaint signed by the victim, although at the time she said she wished to sign a complaint.

When officers attempted to interview the plaintiff, he refused to speak with them, acted belligerently and smelled of alcohol. He later said that he had between twelve and fourteen beers. The officers decided to arrest him for spousal abuse as the plaintiff worked his way to a counter top that had knives on it within his reach. To avoid further problems the officers forced the plaintiff to the floor, though he resisted violently, and placed him in handcuffs. He did go down hard to the floor. One officer said the plaintiff bumped his eye as he hit the counter top on the way to the floor. Plaintiff sued the police claiming excessive force and denial of medical treatment.

Issues and Factors Considered

The police agency has an excellent use of force policy and the officers were trained in that policy. The officers responded appropriately to the circumstances presented to them. Their arrest of the plaintiff was both legal and proper. The amount of force used was in keeping with the resistance given, but officers cannot control unintended injuries that could arise from a forceful arrest. The fact that knives were within reach of the plaintiff supports the mode of arrest. The officers were given admittance to the home by the victim. The department has a good regulation on medical treatment and it was documented that the plaintiff was taken to a hospital shortly after being processed for his arrest. A supervisor was present at the scene of the arrest.

Commentary

Spousal assault victims often change their story from what was said at the time of their complaint. Despite the reports of plaintiff's wife at the time, at her deposition she said that she was never hurt, she was not choked, and she did not wish to pursue the matter. The fact that the plaintiff suffered a broken collar bone and two broken bones near his eye surely had some impact on the mediators' decision to recommend a ninety thousand dollar settlement for the plaintiff. The ability of plaintiff's wife to share in that settlement may or may not have been a factor. There was no doubt the police did not deprive the plaintiff of medical treatment. The plaintiff was arrested at 7:06 p.m., jailed at 7:25 p.m. and taken to the hospital for treatment of his complaints at 8:00 p.m. The defense accepted the ninety thousand dollar mediation recommendation and the case settled. Under the circumstances presented to them it appeared that the officers' actions in making the arrest were appropriate and that excessive force was not used. Plaintiffs are often injured during the act of resisting and the police are not always in control of what unintended injuries a person could suffer when forced to the floor for handcuffing. The highly volatile conditions of the plaintiff, within reach of knives, and fighting with the police at the time made it reasonable to make a forceful arrest. Nevertheless, the police are always vulnerable when the injuries incurred seem more severe than the force reportedly used. They become more vulnerable when a victim changes the facts originally provided.

Case 14: Wrong Person Killed by the Police

This case involves a police officer of a medium-sized department in a city with a population of less than twenty thousand who shot and killed the wrong person. The officer was summarily fired for failing to adhere to the agency's use of force policy. Subsequently, there was a protracted collective bargaining issue over improper firing. After being cleared in the shooting by a prosecuting attorney's investigation, the officer was later charged with second degree murder in the courts by the state attorney general. The family of the shooting victim sued the officer and his department.

Facts

Having just completed a previous run from a report of a gun complaint, the officer was advised that there were two young males walking in a neighborhood and one of them was reportedly wanted by his department on a warrant for homicide. This was not a recent murder warrant as the wanted person had been at large for some time. Descriptions of the clothing and general description of the men were given to the responding officer. Upon arrival at the scene the officer saw two men and one of them generally fit the description given by radio. It was later learned that the wanted person was described as having hair fashioned in cornrows, and he was wearing a coat with a fur collar. The officer turned his patrol car around to check out the two suspects, but they had entered a two-story dwelling. He checked out of service without explanation and entered the dwelling. On entry to the residence he found two youngsters in a hallway. The told him two men had just entered the upstairs apartment. The officer knocked on the upstairs apartment door. A woman answered the door and said there were no men in the apartment. The officer saw one male in the kitchen and entered uninvited. The man observed in the kitchen did not fit the description of the murder suspect, and he said that he was there alone. The officer then noticed a second person hiding behind a wall who did generally fit the description, including the type of jacket and pants reported. He approached him and asked the man for identification. The man told him he did not have any identification. At that point the officer started to frisk the person for offensive weapons, whereupon the man ran down the hall. He yelled for him to halt, but the person jumped out of a second story window, on to a porch roof, and then on to the ground.

The officer pursued him through the apartment. As he reached the window, with his weapon drawn, he yelled at the running suspect to halt. The suspect, now in the back yard, turned and reached into his back pocket. The officer felt he was reaching for a gun and fired three shots killing the man. It was learned he was not armed but was reaching for a set of keys that were mounted on a large key holder. The victim did not have cornrow styled hair and there was no fur on his jacket. Subsequently, it was learned that this officer had previously arrested the real wanted person and there was some question as to whether he made that distinction at the time.

The county prosecutor conducted an investigation into the shooting, determined it was self-defense, and declined to authorize a warrant charging the officer. The officer stated that he drew his weapon and fired three times as he thought the suspect was going for a gun. He drew as the suspect started to turn. He said that he had no doubt it was the wanted person. The officer previously said his weapon was already out when he arrived at the upstairs window.

Issues and Factors Considered

There are issues that could support a good faith defense and negative aspects to this case that do not support the officer. In favor of the officer, he saw two males who generally fit the description and were of the correct race. The two observed suspects were near where they were reported to be. Though the descriptions were not exact, they were reasonably close. The officer was not close enough on the street to see the distinctive hair style. His suspicions were raised when he saw they went into a house and went into an apartment. The officer was lied to at the door by the woman and then saw one male in the apartment. His suspicions would be further enhanced when the victim had no identification, fled down the hall after the attempted search and jumped out of the window. Leaping out of a second story window under these circumstances indicates a great deal of fear. Running across the yard, turning rapidly and facing the officer while reaching for something from a back pocket, coupled with his previous flight, could lead to a reasonable suspicion that the person was armed and about to fire.

Boding against the officer's action is the fact that he knew the person who was wanted on the murder warrant and had previously interrogated him. The suspect had been at large for some time. The officer was not in any immediate danger when the victim was in the yard as he had cover behind the window and wall. He did not wait to see what he was reaching for, moreover, he stated he saw nothing in his hand. The issue of probable cause is a critical issue in this matter and determining probable cause depends on the articulation of what an officer thought at the time, and the basis of his thoughts.

Commentary

The description being close, albeit not exact, the location of the suspects, their furtive actions, being lied to, and the method of the victim's escape, all could provide reasonable grounds to believe that the person focused upon was the one the officer sought. This conclusion would lead to probable cause to search, seize, and arrest. As to whether it provides sufficient conviction to shoot is an open question depending on other factors. If in fact the officer felt that he was about to be shot, his actions could be warranted. If, on the other hand, he recognized the victim as not being the one he had previously arrested, or if he had not been told of the cornrow hair style by the dispatcher, then his actions would be negligent. At worst, he made a mistake in judgment and an identification based on good faith, albeit factually wrong.

The officer's tactical decisions were examples of poor police procedure. He should have isolated the suspects and called for back-up and further information. Going into the house alone under these circumstances is a dangerous act. Failing to inform the dispatcher that he was going into the house was also a poor procedure. The department was also negligent in sending a lone officer to pick up someone wanted for murder. Reflecting on the *Tennessee v. Garner* standards one should consider where a suspect poses no immediate threat to the officer, and no threat to others, the harm of not apprehending him does not justify the use of deadly force to do so. The *Garner* case requires a serious life-threatening felony, an attempted escape and some warning to be given if feasible. All of those elements were present in this case. However, it also requires that the suspect threaten the officer or another. That element is problematic with these facts. Further confusing a reasonable conclusion from the facts of this case, the *Graham (1989)* court noted that the reasonableness must be judged from the perspective of a reasonable police officer on the scene, not based on hindsight, and should take into account the fact that police officers are often forced to make split-second judgments about the amount of force that is necessary in a particular situation. Obviously, one prosecuting attorney felt that the officer's actions were reasonable. Another prosecutor, assigned by the Attorney General of the state, thought otherwise and initiated prosecution.

The author declined to defend the officer's action unless and until he learned whether the officer was told of the cornrow hair style of the actual wanted person. Furthermore, it appeared likely that he may have or should have been aware of the identity of the real murderer because he had previously arrested and interrogated him at length.

Case 15: Force and Arrest Arises from Improper Parking Violation

Facts

A female police officer was dispatched to a tavern in a small farming and industrial city of less than twenty-five thousand. She was given explicit instructions to advise the tavern operator to move her vehicle from its illegally parked position on the street in front of the establishment. This action was prompted by several calls from other business owners in the area and was subsequent to previous warnings of such parking by the plaintiff. Upon entering the tavern the plaintiff identified herself and the officer asked to speak with her in private. The plaintiff refused to meet with the officer in private so she was told, in the presence of her patrons, of the parking violation and was asked to please move her vehicle. The officer described the plaintiff's demeanor as hostile and upset. She said the plaintiff told her she was not going to move the vehicle. Moreover, the officer testified that the plaintiff followed her verbal refusal to comply with derogatory racist remarks directed at the officer. The plaintiff denied making the racial slurs. The officer returned to her patrol car and saw the plaintiff come out and move her vehicle to a parking area behind the tavern. The officer said, because of her adherence to good community relations, she followed the plaintiff to the parking area in an attempt to explain her enforcement order and to establish rapport with a member of the business community.

When the officer approached the plaintiff and tried to explain her actions and discuss her differences, the plaintiff refused to discuss it with her and threatened to have her job. She further told the officer she was going to meet with the chief of police and continued with other derogatory remarks. At one point behind the tavern the plaintiff ordered the officer to get out of her way and she pushed the officer into her own parked police vehicle. At this point, the officer grabbed the plaintiff's arm and told her she was under arrest. After her arm was grabbed the plaintiff struggled while resisting arrest and the plaintiff and the officer slipped on the icy pavement and fell to the ground. Once on the ground, the plaintiff began to scream and continued to resist. She was told on several occasions to stop resisting and struggling. The officer then tried to assist the plaintiff off the ground, but she refused to cooperate. When the officer started to get up she was kicked by the plaintiff. The officer sprayed the plaintiff with pepper spray Freeze P to stabilize her and control her. A witness watching these actions yelled to the plaintiff, "For heaven's sake, do what the officer tells you to do and stop!" That man then assisted the officer in getting the plaintiff off the ground. She was held against the patrol car, handcuffed and transported to the police station.

En route to the police station the officer asked plaintiff if she was all right. She said her face was burning. When asked if she was hurt in any other way she responded in the negative. When the plaintiff entered the police station the duty clerk also asked her if she was injured. She was told she was not injured. At the police station the plaintiff was given a water rinse to ease the pain of the spray. The plaintiff sued the agency and the officer. She claimed she had a torn rotator cuff and the incident aggravated an aortic aneurysm condition.

Issues and Factors Considered

The issues here are whether the officer had legal grounds for an arrest, and whether in making the arrest she used reasonable or excessive force. A secondary issue is whether it was wise for the officer to confront the plaintiff in the rear of the tavern in an attempt to assuage her feelings.

Commentary

First, the officer's attempt to get the plaintiff to move her vehicle was proper and done in good taste. Her concern for not wanting to embarrass the plaintiff by discussing the situation in public was sound. She was carrying out a lawful order from her superior to prevent further parking violations. Going behind the tavern would generally be considered good police practice to defuse a situation. Such discussions can often prove fruitful in re-establishing good police community relations.

Once the plaintiff pushed the officer, solid grounds existed for an arrest for assaulting a police officer. The plaintiff's kicking and screaming while on the ground required that she be controlled. After the attempt to verbally control her failed, the use of a spray was an appropriate response to gain control. This level of force is minimal considering the resistance and active fighting displayed by the plaintiff. Such efforts are designed to de-escalate active resistance and to reduce the need for additional force. The spray was used only after verbal commands were ignored. One must grab an arm in order to be properly handcuff a person who refuses to cooperate. The officer had legal grounds for an arrest and used minimum force to effectuate an arrest. Testimony from a physician later revealed that there was no documented relationship between this incident and the plaintiff's aortic aneurysm. The injury to the plaintiff's rotator cuff, if it was caused by her fall to the ground, was the result of her self-induced resistance to a lawful arrest or as a result of her slipping on the icy ground and not clearly related to the officer's actions. Unintended injuries incurred by combative arrestees who actively resist arrest are not in the realm of excessive force. The officer had two options. She could have either arrested the plaintiff or she could have walked away. Walking away under these conditions would be unacceptable for a police officer.

Summary

Police administrators that promulgate sound and reasonable polices, train their officers in the meaning and purpose of the polices and supervise officers to assure compliance with the policies have much less to fear from Section 1983 suits. Those agencies that retrain and test their officers periodically, and initiate appropriate discipline when required, are even in a stronger position. Police officers who document all of their actions in force cases in great detail are best prepared should a law suit arise. Moreover, greater detail and documentation in police reports could reduce the number of dismissals of police cases by prosecutors. Dismissals and reductions of charges are often a stimuli to law suits.

All police agencies should have an open and operable citizen complaint procedure that affords all members of the community the opportunity to air their grievances. Police administrators are well advised to have systems in place to monitor officer conduct and track the use of force complaints against individual officers. Such computerized risk management databases are used in the more enlightened police agencies.

Departments that overlook lying, falsification of reports or less than adequate reporting only invite liability suits. Those that choose not to strive for accountability will find their cases seriously weakened if not indefensible. Such is the grist for the mediator's mill. Though many officers fail to fully document each step they took in a particular incident, it is frequently a manifestation of "familiarity breeds contempt" rather than a covert cover-up that is often alleged. However, on the stand under cross examination an officer is hard pressed to appear credible when asked, "If the use of force happened the way you say it did officer, why isn't that in your report?" or "Did you fail to include anything else in your report?" A suit based on the concept of failure to train is enhanced for a plaintiff if an officer, when asked under oath about the contents of the use of force policy replies, "I know we have such a policy somewhere, but I can't tell you what is in it."

It is the author's contention that the proper day to day management of a police agency is critical in avoiding liability suits or worse. It is common for supervisors to sign off on their subordinates' police reports. Unfortunately, many of the reports are not carefully reviewed. A close review of an officer's conduct, based on the report, could shed light on potential anti-constitutional actions or tendencies to do so. Early warnings are often discovered by close case supervision or after-action briefings. At that time, corrections can be made and documented, further investigations can be conducted and, if necessary, appropriate counseling or discipline can be initiated. Three years after the fact it is far too late to make adjustments in the formal record of the agency. When field notes are taken to support the written report it is always a good practice to retain them with the original file.

Managers who overlook poor police work, push aside violations of policy or attempt to justify improper or illegal actions by members of their commands, all to avoid public or internal criticism, are on dangerous ground. Subordinates soon learn what the "brass" will accept and what it will not, regardless of the written policy. At some point in time such conditions may erupt into a full blown public assessment of corruption or incompetence. Individually, members of the public will seek redress in the form of 1983 suits. Where there is little or no confidence in the police or, worse, contempt for the police, such suits will be commonplace. Literally, the ground will be in motion.

Chapter 3

A Review of Literature Concerning Police Pursuits and Case Analyses

Police Pursuits

Police pursuits can be dangerous and deadly. Because police officers tend to under report the pursuits they are involved in we may never know the true level of dangerousness of these tactics. Under reporting skews the final outcomes and it may be much less dangerous overall if the true number of pursuits were known. Regardless, police are continually being sued by third parties resulting from injuries and deaths surrounding pursuits.

Those particularly interested in these police tactics and their outcomes include police administrators, police trainers, insurance underwriters, jurists, legislators, researchers, attorneys, and the media. Police administrators are concerned with the elements of policy, liability, and the appropriate level of restrictiveness to guide the behaviors of their officers. Police trainers seek to develop the safest and most effective means of conducting a pursuit. Underwriters are concerned with the costs associated with the damages and injuries which often result from pursuits, as well as the reduction of the costs associated with litigation. Jurists are concerned with decisions that strike a reasonable balance between the state's need to apprehend violators of the law and the public's interest in being free from unreasonable risks of harm. Moreover, they must decide questions of law applicable to the conduct of a pursuit. Legislators must address political pressures from a broad base of constituents. Legislators also attempt to enact reasonable legislation that balances both public and governmental interests. Researchers seek to discover valid data for analyses upon which informed decisions can be made. Furthermore, they identify several variables and attempt to determine the relevance of such variables to the negative and positive outcomes of pursuits. Attorneys, representing their clients' best interests, have interests in the facts of their particular actions, as well as pursuit data in general. The media's focus on the more spectacular pursuit outcomes reflects their interest in marketable news. However, due to the frequency and nature of police pursuit accidents in which persons are killed or injured, the media maintains a general interest in pursuit research as well.

Determining an accurate rate of pursuit accidents, injuries or fatalities is dependent on knowing the total number of pursuits conducted in the jurisdiction under study. Wide variations between officially reported pursuits and the actual pursuits conducted can skew the rates being examined. The accuracy of the accident or injury rate of a particular police department's pursuit experience may be of little interest or solace to a surviving family member of one killed as the result of a pursuit. As previously indicated, several others do have an interest in examining the relative dangerousness of the pursuit phenomena, as might be indicated by the injury, accident and fatality rates.

Falcone (1994), referencing Falcone, Wells and Charles (1992) reported an alarming disparity between the official record of pursuits and those reported unofficially. Falcone et al. (1992) stated the under estimations may be by a factor of five to fifteen times. Falcone et al. (1994) reported field interviews indicated not all pursuits are reported. They noted a lack of a consistent definition of a pursuit and an avoidance of liability may account for a failure to report. Moreover, they called for determining the accuracy of this possible liability avoidance technique. In their work, officers reported slightly more than one pursuit per officer per year. That figure was six times the number reported in their administrative survey and fifteen times the estimates of Auten's study in Illinois (Auten 1990). Falcone et al. (1994) also suggested a sizable "dark figure" of pursuit: that is, those pursuits not reported by the police for a variety of reasons. Substantial variations were found within and among police departments with regard to the frequency of pursuits reported by officers.

They also suggested officers under-report their pursuits for two basic reasons: (1) they feel restrained by a policy that is in conflict with their ideology and (2) they fear discipline when they act according to their inclinations. The failure to report pursuits is easily concealed because law enforcement is a low visibility activity. Payne and Corley (1994) found fear of discipline, liability issues and the impact of law suits were positively associated with the failure to report a pursuit by Michigan State Police officers. Moreover, zero ordered correlations showed officers' involvement in law suits, knowledge of other officers' involvement in law suits and previous disciplinary experiences were positively associated with the failure to report. The reported correlations were low, but all were significant at the alpha .01 level. Policy restrictiveness and a policy of pursuit discouragement were also associated with an increased failure to report pursuits.

Falcone (1994) stated under-reporting was done in an attempt to avoid scrutiny by supervisors or administrators and to avoid unwelcome paper work. Based on officer interviews, Falcone (1994) learned that officers felt those who flirted with eluding the police were usually stopped within a short distance and issued a ticket for the precipitating offense. As a result, no official record was made and the situation was handled informally by officer discretion.

Crew (1992), conducting a study of the Houston Police Department before and after the implementation of a new policy, reports pursuits dropped forty percent during two seven month study periods. The author concluded that the drop was either a result of a real reduction of pursuits or a change in officer and supervisor reporting behaviors. He concluded two kinds of behaviors may have contributed to the reduction. First, officers may have stopped reporting pursuits to dispatchers. Second, they may have actually reduced their number of pursuits due to the policy or because it wasn't worth the paper work.

Payne (1997) noted police officers who fail to report pursuits, particularly those with positive outcomes, may be working against their own best interests. Plaintiffs' attorneys frequently cite accident and injury rates when describing the dangerousness of pursuits to juries. Failing to report pursuits, as usually required by policy, clearly inflates the accident and injury rates. Higher rates may even encourage some litigators. Ironically, officers who fail to report to avoid liability may in fact be contributing to increased litigation and thus become their own worst enemy.

Interest in police pursuits has permeated every branch of the criminal justice system and legislatures have considered limiting the practice of high speed pursuits. Arguments regarding the usefulness of pursuits are polemic. Some view all high speed pursuits as inherently dangerous and opt for severe restriction or abolishment of pursuits. Others predict the dangers which could result if pursuits were abolished and take a position that the need to apprehend fleeing offenders outweighs the potential negative outcomes.

Proponents maintain that avoidance of pursuits constitutes a failure by law enforcement to perform its duty. Such a policy would create an atmosphere of lawlessness that would allow traffic violators and felons alike to escape capture at will. Proponents also feel that such a position is inconsistent with the basic purposes of law enforcement. Opponents of pursuits perceive the risks as too costly and appear to question the basic utility of pursuits. The issue of police pursuits has been so sensationalized, it presents an inaccurate picture of the problem and leads the public to fear and openly criticize police pursuits (Barth 1981).

Clearly, the safety and security issues surrounding police pursuits are paradoxical. The police are sworn to protect and serve their community and maintain order without unduly endangering the public. Enforcing the law requires the pursuit of offenders which may place the public at some risk. The balancing point rests somewhere on the scale of the need to protect the public from an unreasonable risk of harm when pursuing and the need of the state to apprehend. However, advantages of a high-speed pursuit are somewhat obscured by the inevitable disadvantages. Though accurate numbers are unknown, pursuits can result in property damage, injuries and deaths.

A determination of the dark figure of pursuits by Charles et al. (1992) suggested the police do not report many pursuits. Under-reporting of pursuits by the police frustrates attempts to describe the scope of the problem. If the true number of pursuits without negative outcomes were known, it might strengthen the proponent's position. Nonetheless, threats of lawsuits, adverse media publicity and negative public opinion often surface in the wake of pursuit-related accidents. Moreover, the cost of legal defense for the police is considerable, and jury awards for damages often run in the millions.

A question frequently posed in the wake of litigation against the police concerns whether pursuit of fleeing offenders is worth the risk. When a pursuit terminates in injury or death the litigation that follows reduces police resources. The media, as well as the police, seldom report successful pursuits. The public, exposed to negative and spectacular outcomes, reasonably form an impression that all high speed pursuits end in tragedy. Yet, it is the police officers on patrol who are the primary decision makers in pursuits. Guided by training, policies and their own perceptions, they must continually determine whether to pursue a fleeing car, continue a pursuit or terminate a pursuit. They must not only determine what tactics to employ but must also exercise continual judgment in evaluation of variant environmental conditions when making pursuit decisions.

In response to pursuit litigation responsible law enforcement administrators have been obligated to revise their pursuit policies. These revisions are often more restrictive and may result in complex policy statements that are designed to solicit preferred officer behaviors. However, if the rationale for such policy changes and restrictions are not understood, officers may not view policies as a guide for their decision making, but rather a restriction upon their discretion.

The majority of pursuit research has addressed the existence or nature of policy, environmental conditions, dangers and pursuit outcomes (Alpert 1989; Alpert and Dunham 1990; Kennedy et al. 1992; Charles et al. 1992; Charles and Falcone 1992; and Falcone et al. 1992).

Some favor highly restrictive policy or abolishment (Beckman 1983, Urbanya 1991), while others recognize the dangers but hold that apprehension outweighs the outcomes, provided there is strict enforcement of policy (California Highway Patrol 1983; Hannigan 1992; and Britz and Payne 1992). An examination of officers' perceptions and opinions relating to pursuits provides yet another important dimension for police administrators to consider when constructing or implementing pursuit policy (Falcone et al. 1992; Charles and Falcone 1992).

The discretionary decisions made by patrol officers become the focal point in a litigation. Non-conforming attitudes or beliefs may be attributed to the socialization of police officers, attitudinal responses to current litigation against the police, a desire to perform one's duty, general frustration over the apparent lack of impact of the criminal justice system or lack of training and supervision.

Viewpoints on Pursuit Policy

Views held on the appropriate content and restrictiveness of pursuit policies also vary. Fennessy et al. (1970) reported police agencies that had instituted pursuit policies had adopted one of three models: (1) the officer judgment model, (2) a restrictive model, and (3) a model of discouragement or prohibition. Whetsel and Bennett (1992) call for attitudinal changes in pursuit policies, where compliance should be anchored in the cognitive, emotional, physical and spiritual dynamic of every individual. Territo (1982) found considerable variations among the policies he studied and recommended strong controls on the operation of police vehicles in pursuits and other emergency responses. Morris (1993) notes that many agencies do not have a pursuit policy and of those that do, the policies are frequently ambiguous or misleading. He concluded that pursuit policies must be specific to ensure a common understanding. Charles and Falcone (1992) discovered there was considerable confusion among officers regarding pursuit policy. Kennedy et al. (1992) report seventy-nine percent of the policies they studied fell into the officer judgmental category, and more restrictive policies were more likely to be seen in cities with a higher population density.

A special commission in Canada concluded that despite potential hazards to human well-being, failing to uphold the law by means of vehicle pursuit may pose a much greater threat to the well-being of society in general (Solicitor General Report, 1985). Alpert and Smith (1991) proposed that determining the appropriate policy, which balances deterrence and citizen safety, is the key element in obtaining the desired police reaction to motorists who flee the police. Auten (1990) reported that twenty-one percent of all the police agencies studied did not have any written guidelines governing the activities of police pursuit operations. Falcone et al. (1992) recommended police agencies should have well-developed highly restrictive police pursuit policies and stringent procedures for their departments.

Pursuit Training

Training has also been problematic. Earlier training in pursuit driving could be accurately defined as precision driving with an emphasis on skill and vehicle handling. Though pursuit related training has been in place for years in one form or another, the character of that training has changed. Initially, police pursuit training reflected the "get your man at any cost" attitude, tempered by a concern for officer safety (Kroeker and McCoy 1988). Later, trainers espoused concerns for the officer, the suspect and the public. Training emphasis changed from a purely physical skill orientation (Basham 1978; Clark 1976; Dougherty 1961; International Association of Chiefs of Police (IACP) 1965; IACP 1968; Schultz 1979; Traffic Institute 1981) to an emphasis that added policy issues and restrictions in addition to skill development (Auten 1985; Auten 1991; James 1980; Fyfe 1989; Halloran 1985; and Wisconsin DOJ 1984). This change of operational focus may be attributed to the stimuli of empirical research and the growth of lawsuits arising from the use of Section 1983 suits. Falcone et al. (1992) discovered police agencies generally equate emergency driving training with pursuit training, when in fact the two do not possess the same content.

Accident Outcomes

The California Highway Patrol Study (CHP 1983) conducted from April through September 1982 involved ten police agencies from Southern California and the highway patrol. The 683 reported pursuits reflected an accident rate of twenty-nine percent (N=198), an eleven percent injury rate (N=75) and a one percent fatality rate (N=7). All officers who participated in that study were asked to complete a survey instrument for each pursuit conducted.

Beckman (1986) conducted a study utilizing a modified version of the CHP questionnaire from April 1984, through September 1984. Nine states and two U.S. territories were sampled. Each officer who had participated in a pursuit was asked to complete a survey instrument. That study of 424 pursuits revealed an accident rate of forty-two percent (N=178), an injury rate of fourteen percent (N=59) and a fatality rate of three percent (N=12). It was not clear whether the reports were completed after the fact or at the time of the pursuit involvement. It is not known whether all officers from each department were to report all pursuits or the researcher relied on an officer sample from each agency. Regardless of the criticisms that can be made of this and other studies, Beckman (1986) did provide accident data useful for this analysis. Interestingly, pursuit profiles provided were quite similar to profiles reported elsewhere.

Alpert and Dunham (1990) conducted a detailed two-phase study in Dade County, Florida. Phase I involved an analysis of pursuit policies from numerous agencies in the country. Subsequently, a model policy was developed and adopted by all Dade county police agencies. Phase II, 1985 through 1987, involved an empirical analysis of pursuits involving members of the Metro-Dade and Miami police departments. Metro-Dade's three-year participation resulted in 819 pursuits and Miami (1986) resulted in an additional 133 pursuits for a total of 952 pursuits. The accident rate was thirty-three percent (N=310) , the injury rate was seventeen percent (N=160) and a slightly less than two percent (N=7) fatality rate was reported.

Auten (1991) conducted a study from January through December of 1990 of eighty-six participating police agencies in Illinois in which all officers were to complete a survey instrument after each police pursuit. A total of 286 pursuits were reported. The accident rate was approximately forty-one percent (N=118), including a twelve percent injury rate (N=34) and a 1.4 percent (N=4) fatality rate. The two largest agencies in Illinois, the State Police and the Chicago Police Department , were not included. Auten (1991) warned that any attempt to generalize the data to the entire state must be done with caution.

In their study of fifty-one Illinois police departments, Charles et al. (1992), conducted four separate surveys: an officer survey, an administrative survey, a police field interview form and an administrative telephone survey. In the officer survey segment officers reported 875 pursuits (Falcone et al. 1992). The accident rate of the 875 pursuits was thirty-four percent (N=298), the injury rate was seventeen percent (N=149) and the fatality rate was two percent (N=15). Differences in reporting existed between the administrative and officer surveys. The administrative section reported a pursuit accident rate of twenty-six percent, a nine percent injury rate and no fatalities. Researchers conjectured that some "telescoping" of data may have occurred.

Accident Outcomes From Other Studies

Alpert and Dunham (1990) cited data from the Ontario, Canada, Solicitor General's committee report on 6,757 pursuits between 1981 and 1984. The data represent pursuit information from all police agencies in the Province of Ontario. The agencies involved ranged in size from five to five thousand officers. The results of that report revealed an accident rate of thirty-three percent (N=2246), an injury rate of ten percent (N= 642) and a fatality rate of .4 percent (N=26).

In conjunction with the adoption of a new pursuit policy, the Chicago Police Department collected data in 1984, but the actual time span was not reported. The 741 pursuits reflected an accident rate of twnety-four percent (N=178), an injury rate of five percent (N=37) and a one percent (N=7) fatality rate (Patinkin and Bingham 1986).

Focusing on their rural police agency experiences, the Kentucky State Police collected data from May 1989, through April 1990 using intra-agency teletypes. That study resulted in 235 pursuits with an accident rate of twenty-three percent (N=53), a six percent (N=13) injury rate and a .4 percent rate of fatality (N=1). The lack of specificity on the method of data collection hinders a determination on validity and reliability (Oechsli 1990).

The North Carolina Department of Motor Vehicles conducted a very limited study of pursuits by their officers from November 4, 1968 through November 10, 1968 in response to the claims made by the Physicians for Automotive Safety (PAS). Fennessy et al. (1970) reported major flaws including the number of cases (N=44), questionable questionnaire training and the short duration of the study. Of the forty-four pursuits reported, eleven percent (N=5) resulted in accidents with a five percent rate of injury (N=2) and no fatalities.

The Michigan Emergency Response Study (MERS) Phase II of 197 pursuits revealed an accident rate of thirty-three percent (N=65), a seventeen percent (N=33) injury rate and one fatality resulting in a .5 percent fatality rate. These ten studies reveal a mean accident rate of thirty-two percent, an eleven percent injury rate and a fatality rate of one percent (Payne 1997).

Accident Outcome Rates Often Questionable

An accurate number of pursuits in a particular jurisdiction may never be revealed due to under reporting of pursuits by the police. However, the reports of accidents, injuries and fatalities are less likely to be concealed owing to their outcomes, reporting requirements and public nature. Accident data may represent a constant, but police pursuits are easily concealed by failing to report their initiation. Officers may issue a citation, release a person, lose an eluder or voluntarily terminate a pursuit without reporting the incident. Police officers who fail to report pursuits not only do a disservice to their agencies, but confound assessments of accident, injury and fatality rates. For example, in phase II of MERS respondents reported 197 pursuits and sixty-five accidents resulting in a thirty-

three percent accident rate. However, a verification of traffic citations issued for fleeing and eluding during the study period revealed
400 such citations. Consequently, a more accurate accident rate
would have been sixteen percent. Interestingly, the accident and injury rates among several studies are quite similar.

Mandatory reporting of pursuits within jurisdictions could vastly
improve data collection and analysis. In the meantime, close examination of pursuit outcomes, regardless of rates, provides a useful
area for research. Determining the number and nature of injuries incurred by those involved in pursuit accidents would enhance an objective analysis of pursuits. For example, in the sixty-five MERS accidents there were thirty-three injuries. The police were injured in
eight percent of the accidents (N=5) but all of them were serious injuries. Among the twenty fleeing suspects injured, twenty-six percent (N=17) suffered minor injuries and five percent (N=3) were serious. Third party injuries occurred in twelve percent (N=8) of the
accidents. Eleven percent (N=7) were minor injuries and one (1.5
%) was a fatality. The police were the least likely to be injured.
Third parties were somewhat more likely to be injured than the police, and fleeing suspects were most likely to be injured. These figures are limited to the 197 MERS pursuits and the sixty-five resultant accidents, thus no inferences are possible (Payne 1992).

Liability Issues

Though departments may have sound pursuit policies, the individual officer must still constantly weigh the hazards originally created by the suspect against the future hazards that may be created
by a pursuit (Schultz 1979). The officer must also decide whether
the violator will continue to be a hazard if he or she does not give
chase. Scafe and Round (1979) believe a police pursuit is justified
only when the necessity of immediate apprehension outweighs the
level of danger created. Similarly, the court in *Lee v. City of Omaha*
(1981), ruled that an officer has a duty to balance the need to apprehend violators against due care and the well-being of the general
public.

Some courts have ruled that officers have a duty to the community which they are sworn to protect. Others, such as *Smith v. City
of West Point* (1985), have ruled that the police are under no obligation to let suspects leisurely escape. Nonetheless, the police do
have a duty of care with respect to the manner of the chase. This

manner of chase is set forth in pursuit policies, statutes and court decisions and can be found under reasonable care guidelines (Michigan Complied Laws Annotated 1979). Hence, it is important that police administrators design pursuit policies that clarify issues and guide behavior because neither the police nor their jurisdictions are exempt from liability. Some authors believe total abrogation of governmental immunity is on its way and assert that courts now start from the premise that "...liability is the rule and immunity is the exception " (Koonz and Regan 1981, 65). Consider for instance, the position presented in the Michigan Compiled Laws Annotated 691.1405 (M.C.L.A.):

> Governmental agencies shall be liable for bodily injury and property damage resulting from the negligent operation by any officer, agent, or employee of the governmental agency, of a motor vehicle of which the governmental agency is owner, as defined in Act No. 300 of the Public Acts of 1949, as amended, being sections 257.1 to 257.923 of the Compiled Laws of 1948.

Until recently, courts have held individual officers, their departments and municipal governments liable for their actions and those of the fugitives they pursue. Thus, sound pursuit policy, appropriate training and close supervision are of paramount importance in all emergency response driving. Some of the more common concepts and principles that must be thoroughly understood by officers and reflected in their pursuit driving behaviors include the duty of due care, public safety, liability, the definition of an emergency, reasonableness, balancing the need to apprehend against a risk of harm to the general public and adherence to agency and statutory standards (Payne 1992).

Sound pursuit policies, where they exist, frequently reflect complex concepts outlined in court decisions, statutory obligations and preferred officer behaviors. The initial reporting of a pursuit brings the elements of the policy into play. The failure of an officer to initially report a pursuit, as may be required by a policy, can raise serious doubts later about the efficacy of the police agency and may lead to inferences that officers are not in compliance with other portions of the policy (Payne 1992). This is particularly so when unreported pursuits have negative outcomes.

Those other portions of the agency's policy may address factors of negligence, clarify bounds of pursuit reasonableness, define emergency situations and specify correct use of emergency equipment.

Thus, officers should not only be knowledgeable about their particular pursuit policy, but understand in a broader context issues and factors that give rise to the need for a sound pursuit policy (Wayne County Sheriff 1986; Dearborn Heights Police 1986; Lansing Police 1984; and Oak Park Police 1986). For instance, officers, whose judgment may eventually be tested on the stand, may find it provident to understand how negligence and reasonableness are legally operationalized. Failure to testify intelligently in these matters only invites large judgments against public agencies.

Negligence

Negligence is generally determined by the triers of fact, utilizing a reasonableness standard. That is, the question would be to determine what any reasonable, prudent emergency driver would do under all the circumstances, including that of the emergency (*Rutherford v. State* 1979).

In determining reasonableness, factors such as speed through intersections, views of traffic, road and weather conditions, the need for an emergency response and other drivers' negligence are considered. Once reasonableness is determined, proof of negligence consists of evidence showing a duty to the injured party, a breach of that duty and an injury proximately resulting from that breach. Furthermore, such injury must be so related as to be the proximate cause thereof (*Brooks v. Lundeen* 1981).

In *Kuzmics v. Santiago* (1978) it was noted that vehicle code exemptions have been designed to require a plaintiff seeking recovery for any damage caused by an emergency vehicle to prove recklessness rather than ordinary negligence. Therefore, conduct is considered reckless when the officer intentionally disregards the safety of another by failing to perform an act that the public is entitled to or performing an act which endangers the public. Other courts have held that officers engaged in high-speed pursuit of traffic violators are protected by statute where they observed basic standards of reason and due care (*Marion v. City of Flint* 1976; *Powell v. Allstate Insurance Co.* 1970; and *Hammon v. Pedigo* 1962).

Negligence in Civil Suits

Many cases are brought against the police in both federal and state courts and the theories that are standard for the courts are often mutually exclusive. Generally, state claims against individual police officers can be brought only for gross negligence. Such negligence is defined as " conduct so reckless as to demonstrate a substantial lack of concern for whether an injury results." The officer's jurisdiction can not be found vicariously liable except for negligent operation of the motor vehicle, as set forth in Michigan for example in *Fiser v Ann Arbor* (1983). Allegations of negligent training, negligent entrustment, etc., generally have no place under state statutes. A federal claim must be based on the deprivation of a protected right and more often have to amount to conduct that shocks the conscience of the community and is viewed as outrageous.

Vicarious liability is not applicable to civil rights violations, however since *Canton v. Harris* (1989) civil rights actions against municipalities are allowed for deliberate indifference for inadequate training. Being unsatisfactorily trained will not be enough to impose liability unless the plaintiff shows that the identified deficiency in the municipal training program is closely related to the plaintiff's ultimate injury and that the city policy makers know "to a moral certainty" that their police officers will be required to participate in a particular task for which they need training. Moreover, the failure to train must be so obvious that a failure to do so could properly be characterized as deliberate indifference to a constitutional right. The court went on to say that the need for the training must have been plainly obvious to the policy makers who, nevertheless, are deliberately indifferent to the need.

In *Galas v. McKee* (1986) the court said the minimal intrusion on a traffic offender's 4th Amendment rights occasioned by officers participating in high-speed pursuits does not outweigh a longstanding police practice considered essential to a coherent scheme of police powers. The court went on to decide that the use of high-speed pursuits is not unreasonable and thus does not violate the 4th Amendment (Winslow 1989).

Some Courts Move in an Opposite Direction

For the last several years countless law suits have been filed against the police where the eluding driver crashed into innocent motorists. Most of them have been cases in which an innocent third party was killed. Several such cases involved multiple fatalities. A typical pursuit scenario would involve the police attempting to stop a motorist for a traffic violation or because of a suspected felony. The eluder would refuse to stop, speed up or take other evasive action. During the pursuit the eluder would run a stop sign or traffic signal and crash into an unsuspecting motorist killing the occupant(s). The culprit would often be driving a stolen car and be uninsured. The police in such scenarios were not physically involved in the crash and would be anywhere from one hundred to five hundred feet behind the speeding vehicle to upwards of two miles behind. Plaintiffs, recognizing there were no opportunities to collect from the eluders in most cases, would bring suit against the officers and their jurisdictions because of the deep pocket potential. Several juries have awarded millions of dollars in such cases.

Two cases referenced in this work are such cases in point. In one case, a protracted pursuit, there was no physical contact with the speeder, the officers never got closer than five hundred feet during the pursuit, and the police had in fact canceled the pursuit. At the time of the fatal crash the nearest police officer was over two miles north of the accident scene. Yet, the jury awarded the plaintiff two and one half million dollars. Another case involved several departments. The closest officer was within a few hundred yards of the crash and observed the crash; however, he was not from one of the involved departments. The jury in that matter dismissed all but the originating department, which at the time of the crash was miles away and had discontinued the pursuit. In that case the jury awarded the plaintiff's family one and a half million dollars. Those suits were premised on the idea that an officer could be "a" proximate cause due to the implied dangerousness of their driving.

In a recent case of *Robinson v. City of Detroit* (2000) the Michigan Supreme Court addressed the issue of proximate cause and reversed *Fiser v .Ann Arbor* (1983). This movement by the court is also becoming evident in California and elsewhere, but has yet developed into a national trend. The *Robinson* court has set a reasonable standard in regards to pursuit operations and liability. They concluded that the individual police officers are immune from liability because their actions were not "the" proximate cause of the plaintiff's injuries. In short, they held that plaintiff's injuries did not, as a matter of law, result from the operation of the police vehicles where the police cars did not hit the fleeing car, physically cause another vehicle or object to hit the vehicle that was being chased or physically force the vehicle off the road or into another vehicle or object.

The court also overruled *Roger v. Detroit* (1988) and held that an officer's decision to pursue does not constitute the negligent operation of a vehicle. Though the police do owe a duty to innocent bystanders, in the context of a police pursuit no duty is owed to the fleeing motorist. That court notably stated that the police, out of concern for public safety, must sometimes allow fleeing suspects to get away. They also said, however, it would be absurd to conclude that the police, out of concern for the safety of a fleeing criminal suspect, must cease a pursuit of the fleeing suspect or risk possible civil liability. They made clear there is a duty to innocent persons but not to wrongdoers. A paramount issue in the *Robinson* opinion was only when the officer's driving itself is a direct cause of an injury would the question of negligence be submitted as a fact question to the jury. The determination should not turn on how the officer was conducting the pursuit but, rather, on what effect the manner in which the officer drove his vehicle had on the cause of the accident. The court defined proximate cause as meaning the one most immediate, efficient and direct cause preceding injury. In the author's experience of testifying in over fifty-five police pursuit law suit cases in sixteen years all but two of those cases were predicated on the idea of "a" proximate cause. This case puts to rest those ill-conceived cases in Michigan. Hopefully, other courts in the country will take notice and limit such suits to gross negligence encounters and use the standard of "the" proximate cause.

Emergencies

Policy makers may wish to define emergency situations and pursuits according to the statutes and regulations which are often mirrored in their pursuit policy. Though some courts have ruled in order for statutory exemptions to be in force, police must be involved in emergency situations, no universal definition of an emergency situation has been established. Rather, each situation is judged and evaluated on a case by case basis. For instance, in *Hamilton v. Town of Palo* (1976), the court found that an emergency call does indeed exist when, upon receipt of a message, an officer truly believes an emergency exists and has reasonable grounds to believe the same. Further, in *Simkins v. Barcus* (1951) the court held that even if the situation was not in fact an emergency, the police were not liable if the officer involved honestly believed it to be an emergency.

Several court decisions shed further light on what is and what is not an emergency. The interpretation of the term emergency varies from one jurisdiction to another, but there is a common understanding. The *Sells v. Monroe County* (1987) case dealt with the issue of whether the deputy sheriff responding to an alleged emergency accident reasonably believed he was responding to an emergency at the time he was involved in a vehicular collision. That court ruled that whether the police officer was on an emergency run was a factual question to be determined by a jury, and counsel for the plaintiff in an action for a wrongful death of the driver killed in the collision spent considerable time arguing that the police officer was not responding to an emergency call when the collision occurred. The officer in this case was responding to a head-on collision. The issue arose when it was brought to the attention of the court that a state trooper was already at the scene and attempts to notify the deputy failed. See also *Holser v. City of Midland* (1951) and *Hoffman v. Burkhead* (1958).

Lakoduk v. Cruger (1956) determined that the test for determining whether a publicly owned motor vehicle is, at a given time, responding to an emergency call is not whether an emergency in fact exists at that time, but whether the vehicle is being used in responding to an emergency call. Whether the vehicle is being so used depends upon the nature of the call that is received and the situation as presented to the mind of the driver.

Pursuits by police are generally considered to be runs at high speeds of motorists who are taking some evasive action to avoid capture. However, it is important to note that the above definition is inclusive only of a typical pursuit. There are other runs, "... often at higher than normal speeds or under such adverse conditions, that could be considered in a broad definition of pursuit " (Payne 1992, 8). For example, a police officer attempting to stop a motorist on a snow covered roadway at forty miles per hour may be equally as hazardous as a ninety mile per hour pursuit on a clear, dry, four-lane expressway.

In 1982, in *City of Akron v. Charley*, an Ohio court held that a cruiser loses preferential right-of-way when driven without an audible signal. The court in *Semple v. Hope* (1984) stated that the vehicle with lights and siren engaged keeps its preferential emergency status. Interpretations abound as to the finite meaning of the term emergency. Several years ago in *Rowe v. Kansas City Public Service Co.* (1942) the court ruled that the call to an accident constituted an emergency situation. *In Rankin v. Sander* (1953) the Court ruled that if an officer received a call to investigate "trouble" it could be considered an emergency run. *Spencer v. Heise* (1958) held the investigation of a death could be considered a response to an emergency situation. *Agnew v. Porter* (1969) ruled that a call to help or assist fellow officers at a high school brawl could also be considered an emergency.

Emergency response driving is not limited to the typical police pursuit, but may include responses to alarms, medical emergencies or crimes in progress. In terms of the overall goal of public safety, it would seem proper to include all such classifications when examining risks to the public. Many statutes regulating police driving behavior address emergencies, apprehension of those violating the law, pacing speeders, chasing those suspected of violating the law and silent responses to crimes in progress (MCLA 257.603b, 1979).

Emergency Equipment

Similarly, officers should know and understand why the proper use of emergency equipment is important from both a procedural and liability perspective. Pursuits in which visible and audible emergency equipment were not operating and which have resulted in an accident involving the fugitive and a third party have not been looked upon favorably by the courts. Failure to use a siren during pursuit constituted negligence on the part of the officer (*Alexander v. New York* 1976). *Reed v. Winter Park* (1971) held in the event that a siren was not activated, negligence could be based on a failure to warn. Emergency vehicles are only exempt from the rules governing other vehicles if the officer utilizes audible and visible signals (*Mayor and Alderman of Town of Morristown v. Inman* 1960; *Moore v. Travelers Indemnity Co.* 1977; *Herron v. Silbaugh* 1970; and *Cornwall v. Larsen* 1977).

Some pursuit policy provisions have been developed in response to litigation while others developed in response to the research literature. In either case, administrators wish to shield their departments and jurisdictions from the increased use of litigation resulting from negative pursuit outcomes. Police agencies wishing to guide their officers' behaviors should address factors of liability, negligence, proper emergency responses and the use of emergency equipment in their pursuit policies. While some courts have evidenced sympathy for injured third parties resulting from pursuits, the liability to the fleeing suspect is somewhat diminished. Some courts held that the fleeing driver was negligent as a matter of law noting if the plaintiff is negligent and is the proximate cause of his own injuries, he is barred from recovery (*Silva v. City of Albuquerque* 1973).

Pursuit Policy Research

Auten's (1990) revealing study involved requests to municipal departments throughout Illinois and provided interesting pursuit policy data. Volunteer respondents provided data relative to the absence or presence of sixteen specific policy related elements. Sixty-one (20.6 %) of the agencies surveyed had no guidelines at all covering pursuits and more than half of the departments' policy statements failed to address the use of or authorization for roadblocks, limits on number of units involved, caravaning and whether chases were limited to marked police cars. All agencies reported officers were required to consider their safety or that of others when deciding to initiate or continue a pursuit. Over ninety-three percent of the departments required officers to consider the seriousness of the offense prior to initiating or continuing a pursuit and ninety-three percent required the officer to notify a dispatcher when initiating a pursuit. Though eighty-three percent indicated that supervisors had the authority to discontinue pursuits, only sixty-two percent required supervisors to monitor pursuits and sixty-two percent gave their officers the responsibility to discontinue pursuits. Ramming was prohibited by sixty-nine percent of those agencies responding and the use of firearms was prohibited by fifty-six percent of the agencies (Auten 1990).

Falcone et al. (1992) examined the role and impact of formal policy on departmental and officer behaviors in pursuit activities after completing a study of pursuit policies among fifty-one Illinois police agencies. Though the survey return rate was twenty-eight percent it did yield rich information relative to policies in theory and policies in practice. Findings were very similar to those of Payne (1992) in which officers and administrators were uniformly unfamiliar with the content of pursuit policy and distinctions were not made between formal and informal policy. Overall, Falcone et al. (1992) found that among many agencies, the pursuit policies were either non-existent or perceived as too complex to be useful by patrol officers. Additionally, survey results indicate that the actual number of pursuits is five to fifteen times higher than reported by police supervisors.

Charles et al. (1992) and Falcone et al. (1992) suggest it is the type of policy and training that affects officer behavior rather than its existence. Moreover, an important recommendation is that police agencies should have well developed, highly restrictive and discouraging pursuit policies with clear and simple procedures for regulating pursuits. Several others suggest the need for sound policy, close supervision and appropriate training for police conducting emergency responses. Though not always explicit, it is always implied that officers start the cycle of policy application by reporting the initiation of pursuits (Goodwin 1992; O'Keefe 1989; Koonz and Regan 1985; Scafe and Round 1979; and Hannigan 1992).

Because policies frequently synthesize the essential points of statutes and court decisions it is imperative that officers understand and comply with them. Conformance with policy guidelines is likely to be stronger when officers are in agreement with the basic tenants of that policy. Nonetheless, for uniform policy implementation to occur, it seems reasonable to assume that there should be a continuity of thinking among all members of the department. In the absence of such agreement, adherence to policy can only occur through close supervision or discipline. Very little is known of the officers' perceptions. Yet, officers' opinions and perceptions can affect pursuit decision making. Similar to policy development, training should also be based on the results of sound empirical research (Charles et al. 1992). It would appear unless all pursuits are reported and tabulated sound empirical data will remain ellusive.

Pursuit policies vary considerably among departments. In fact, pursuit policies ranged from non-existent to highly defined and restrictive. As a case in point, Auten (1990) reported that nearly twenty-one percent of all police agencies studied did not have written guidelines governing the activities of their personnel during pursuit driving operations. Furthermore, it was suggested that departments operating with written policies had serious gaps in their existing policy statements (Auten 1990). On the other hand, a more select pursuit policy specified the importance for officers to weigh the seriousness of the situation against the hazards to the health and welfare of other citizens, generated by high speeds or maneuvers (Cincinnati DPS 1980).

The Connecticut Safety Commission (1978) suggested three categories of police pursuit policies. The most common type of pursuit policy was labeled an officer judgment policy. This allowed the individual officer the discretion to begin a pursuit and decide what tactics to undertake. The second type of pursuit policy, though more restrictive, also allowed for individual officer discretion but it stipulated what pursuit measures the officer could undertake. Finally, the third type of policy was very restrictive and generally discouraged pursuits for minor violations or those not deemed absolutely necessary.

Pursuit Defined

Nugent et al. (1989) define key elements of pursuit as an active attempt by a law enforcement officer on duty in a patrol car to apprehend one or more occupants of a moving motor vehicle, providing the driver of such vehicle is aware of the attempt and is resisting apprehension by maintaining or increasing his speed or by ignoring the law enforcement officer's attempt to stop him

Other Views

In a BNA (1993) report examining a Section 1983 lawsuit, the Third Circuit U.S. Court of Appeals asked the question: How bad does an officer's conduct during a chase have to be in order for it to violate the 14th Amendment's Due Process Clause? The majority determined that the officer can be liable if he was recklessly indifferent to the safety of the public. Courts have determined that a police officer is not liable for damages caused by mere negligence. The reckless indifference standard tolerates a lot of mistakes that negligence would not; however, it is not as forgiving as the shocks the conscience standard. In examining *Searles v. Southeastern Pennsylvania Transportation Authority* (1993), as an example for reckless indifference, the court determined that initiating a high-speed pursuit is an affirmative act and is a governmental action. Thus, high-speed pursuits are an affirmative governmental oppression that, if conducted with reckless indifference to the public safety, is prohibited by the doctrine of substantive due process. In a case analysis of the Houston Police Department, O'Keefe (1989) indicates that the most comprehensive way to resolve the issues regarding high-speed pursuits is to expand the scope of responsibilities involved in pursuit situations. More specifically, there should be pre- and post-pursuit responsibilities in addition to the actual pursuit situation. Pre-pursuit responsibilities include public information campaigns informing citizens of traffic stop procedures, and tactical training for officers. Meanwhile, the actual pursuit situation should be supported with workable pursuit policies and statements which concisely define a department's values and parameters of discretion. Post-pursuit guidelines include constructive feedback to the officer and the completion of a uniform departmental pursuit form to include all relevant information.

Hannigan (1992) takes the position that high-speed pursuits are necessary for the swift and efficient apprehension of violators, indicating that the California Highway Patrol can successfully carry out pursuits with proper training, enhanced supervision and a comprehensive, consistently applied written policy. Hannigan cites the CHP study which indicated that seventy percent of those involved in CHP pursuits were wanted for felonies or serious misdemeanors. Likewise, the CHP study found that the most common pursuit involved vehicle code violations, with the officer not knowing anything about the driver, and in thirty percent of the cases the drivers were under the influence. It is reported that in 1989, twenty percent of those pursued were wanted for felonies, thirty-one percent were wanted for other crimes, twenty-six percent were driving stolen vehicles and twenty-nine percent of the drivers were under the influence. Furthermore, a policy should include the number of departmental units to participate, coordination with other jurisdictions, the use of aircraft, determining when a pursuit is justified and writing a pursuit report after the pursuit. Training should also be stressed and should include familiarization with departmental policy and the relationship and balance between and officer's mission and the risk to the citizenry.

Whetsel and Bennett (1992) call for attitudinal changes in pursuit policies, where compliance should be anchored in the cognitive, emotional, physical and spiritual dynamic of every individual. Those authors opined, regarding leadership, the following tenants should be followed: (a) you don't always have to get your man, (b) third party injuries may result in punitive damages, (c) traffic violators are just traffic violators, (d) emergency runs and pursuits are first cousins, (e) the rule should be first do no harm, (f) the media and court have high expectations of the police, (g) the agency will terminate your employment for reckless driving, and (h) police are entrusted with a vehicle for which they have had marginal training. Potential solutions against pursuits could include civil forfeiture of the fleeing violator's vehicle, making the crime a felony, using road spikes, educating the public that pursuits will result in harsher sanctions, rewarding responsible drivers and working with insurance companies to make simulators available.

Gallagher (1990) calls for departments to have an established risk management system. Some of the basic concerns include basic training, because in the post *Canton v. Harris* period it would appear that chiefs could be deliberately indifferent to the adequate training of their personnel. Likewise, departments should consider if the minimum standards imposed by the state would meet the standard of care required by courts in liability cases.

Another topic discussed was that chiefs are responsible for providing direction through policy. These written standards should affirm that wrongful actions by officers are contrary to established policy; thus, they must be developed to cover officer activities, especially that tasks that might generate lawsuits.

Since Appellate and Supreme Court decisions are constantly changing, in-service legal training should continue for all officers. Such training should address tasks, policies and new court decisions. Supervisors' responsibilities were also discussed in Gallager (1990). In designing the new management plan, it was recommended that one officer should be designated and entrusted as the departmental liaison, the agency should respond quickly to incidents, command shoud meet early with legal counsels and the department should consider initiating a form of liability assessment, consistently review high risk critical tasks and consider applying for accreditaton through CALEA.

In *Fiser v. Ann Arbor* (1983) Court examined the issue of governmental immunity, which had been held applicable by the Court of Appeals, in conjunction with the general standards of negligence and he statutory expectations relating to the operation of emergency vehicles. This case dealt with a high-speed pursuit after the suspect, Lehman, had run a flashing red light. Speeds reached a maximum of one hundred miles per hour through residential and business areas on wet pavement. After losing Lehman and reinstituting the chase, Lehman's car collided with Fiser's vehicle. That Court determined that governmental immunity does not apply in this case because the operation of emergency vehicles constituted the negligent operation of motor vehicles. Since governmental immunity does not apply, the next issue was if the officers were negligent in the pursuit. Citing *Lingo v. Hoekstra* (1964), the Court stated that the pursuit of an offender does not necessarily constitute an emergency situation. Thus, in determining whether the statutory exemptions created for emergency vehicles is applicable to any given situation, the initial factor is that the vehicle must be responding to an emergency call. Other factors considered by the Court included the speed of the pursuit, the area of pursuit, the weather, the road conditions, the presence of pedestrians and other traffic, the presence or absence of audible and visible warnings and the reason the officers were pursuing the fleeing vehicle. The question of whether or not the officers were the proximate cause of the plaintiff's injuries was left to the determination of the jury. As indicted earlier *Fiser* was overruled by *Robinson v. City of Detroit* (2000).

Reed v. City of Winter Park (1971) examined the failure of a police officer to use his siren continuously during the pursuit so as to provide other motorists a reasonable warning of the chase. In failing to do so, the vehicle being pursued struck another automobile not involved in the chase which resulted in the death of two individuals. The issue involved was if the officer used due care considering he did not continuously use the siren during the chase. The Court, citing the case, *City of Miami v. Horne* (1967) used three principles. First, police officers may drive at high speeds and take such steps as may be necessary to apprehend the offender, so long as the officer neither exceeds proper and rational bounds nor acts in a negligent, careless or wanton manner. Second, a police officer in pursuit is entitled to have any alleged conduct determined by a standard of care different from that normally imposed upon individuals, giving due regard to the types of duty which is required to be performed by the officer in the public interest. Third, in a pursuit a police officer who operates the vehicle with due care is not responsible for the acts of the pursued offender, although the pursuit may have contributed to the reckless driving of the pursued, since the officer is not obliged to allow him to escape. The Court reversed and remanded this case.

Court Opinions vary on Liability and Pursuits

In *Baily v. L.W. Edison Charitable Foundation* (1978) the court said if officers practiced due care and were not the proximate cause of the accident and were not negligent, then there are no legal grounds to hold them liable. The Court stated that if the officers did not chase "they would have been derelict in their duty" and "police cannot be made insurers of the culprits they chase." Police should do what they must do as long as they are not negligent or careless. This provision only applies when police are in an emergency situation.

Earlier cases did not hold police officers liable in pursuit cases. In *Roll v. Timberman* (1958) the court said the police department was not liable for injury to a third party because the duty of the officer is to apprehend those who are reckless. The road is safe if officers go after those individuals that drive recklessly. The proximate cause of the accident is reckless driving of the pursued person. Police in this case are seen as having a duty to act.

The court ruled in *City of Kalamazoo v. Priest* (1951) that statutes relieving drivers of emergency vehicles only from those duties which relate to observance of speed limits, heeding traffic and stop signs and yielding right-of-way, contain no exemption for drivers of emergency vehicles from duties inherent in the exercise of due care. This decision was based on the Compiled Laws of 1948 256.310 and 256.321(b).

Due Care

Courts universally recognize that police officers have a duty of care when operating emergency vehicles. Stated simply, an officer operating an emergency vehicle must drive with due care for the safety of every person using the public roadway (Kappeler and del Carmen 1990). Some jurisdictions have specific statues that state the standard. Others adopt the standard from common law. The primary focus on improper officer behavior in addressing the duty of care involves action that may indicate careless, reckless or wanton disregard for the safety of others using the roads. The true test in applying the standard involves the concept of reasonableness. That is, an officer's conduct must be that of a reasonable and prudent emergency driver. Keppeler and del Carmen (1990) said if an officer's behavior is less than what is considered reasonable than a breach of the duty of care can be found. A key concept in assigning liability to a police pursuit is that of proximate cause. An officer's driving behavior may be viewed as "a" proximate cause in some jurisdictions or "the" proximate cause in others. Officers must continually weigh the hazard originally created by the offender against future hazards created by initiating or continuing a pursuit, (Payne and Corley 1994).

The case of *Lee v. Omaha* (1981) stated the officer has a duty to balance the need to apprehend violators with due care to the general public. Such determinations are included within the concept of foreseeability. To be sure, a police officer faces a paradox when conducting a pursuit. The Court in *Jackson v. Rauch* (1969) ruled that a police officer who was driving a police cruiser, with siren, flashers and headlights in operation, and who was stopped at an intersection was legally bound to observe motorcycles approaching an intersecting street to determine their speed and whether they were attempting to stop before the officer drove his cruiser into the intersection.

In *Marion v. City of Flint* (1976) it was ruled that the officers evidenced a proper regard for their duty and proper vigilance for the safety of innocent third persons when the city was not liable to occupants of a third party vehicle which was struck by an intoxicated driver fleeing the police at a high rate of speed, where the police vehicles had their lights and sirens operating, where officers slowed at the intersection, although the pursued vehicle did not, and where the officers were still within statutory limits at the time of collision. This decision was based on M.C.L.A. 257.603 (b) and 257.632.

The issue in *Placek v. City of Sterling Heights* (1979) was whether the operator of a police emergency vehicle exercised due care in proceeding through a stop sign with lights and a siren, at which point the vehicle was struck broadside by a motorist proceeding on the through street. In this case there was disagreement as to the speed at which the police officer was driving as well as whether the officer's failure to observe the plaintiff's vehicle was negligence because the officer was focusing his attention on a vehicle which was turning right in front of the plaintiff's vehicle. The Court determined that the driver of an authorized emergency vehicle has the duty of due regard for the safety of others and does not have the right to blindly proceed through a red light or stop sign. This was based on MCLA 257.603, 257.649 (f) and 257.653.

Arizona courts viewed due care somewhat differently. In *Simkins v. Pulley* (1977) they stated that the driver of a police vehicle does not have the absolute duty to give warning via the use of a siren in their approach to other drivers or pedestrians on the highway. Instead, the language of relevant statutes sets forth the parameters of duty "as may be reasonably necessary." This was based on ARS. 28-6214.

A Utah court in *Lee v. Mitchell Funeral Home Ambulance Service* (1980) stated that even with an emergency vehicle and the use of lights and sirens, the driver must use due care for the safety of others. That court specified due care circumstances as: (a) keeping a look out ahead, (b) driving at a reasonable speed and (c) keeping the vehicle under such control as to guard against collisions and injuries.

A Kansas court in *Thorton v. Shore* (1983) determined that the due care requirement of the emergency vehicle statute applies only to the police officers physical operation of their own vehicle, and not the decision to chase or continue to chase a law violator. An officer operating an emergency vehicle in compliance with the statute while pursuing law violators is not liable, as a matter of law, for reckless and negligent acts committed by the fleeing law violator he is pursuing. An officer in such circumstances has breached no duty owed to persons injured by the fleeing violator's own negligence or wanton conduct, and, as a matter of law, the officer has not committed a tort upon such injured persons. KSA 8-1506(d) Id.

A California court in *Stark v. City of Los Angeles* (1985) held that police officers had a duty to activate their siren during an ongoing vehicular pursuit of a traffic violator, where the pursuit caused a traffic violator to engage in conduct creating a danger to other motorists. The *Stark* court also held that it was the legal duty of the police to not impose an unreasonable risk of harm to others. *Selkowitz v. Nassau County* (1977) gave judges instructions to the jury as to the obligation of the officer to accord to due care. Several other cases provided judge instructions for the jury as to the obligation of police officers to accord due care to the other motorists on the road include: (*Green v. Millsboro Fire Co. Inc.* 1978; *Casey v. Williams* 1979; *Lee v. City of Omaha* 1981; *City of Sacramento v. Superior Court in and for Sacramento County* 1982; *Tetro v. Town of Stratford* 1983; and *Maple v. City of Omaha* 1986).

Environmental Concerns

Officers conducting pursuits must consider several conditions that exist along the route of a pursuit. Such conditions can change rapidly from one point to another. The conditions that should be considered apply to the decision to initiate a pursuit, as well as, the decision to continue or abort a pursuit. They include the speed of vehicles involved, the surface of the road and weather such as ice, snow or fog. Officers must also consider light conditions, artificial lighting, the presence of pedestrians, the number of roads and driveways intersected, stops signs and stop lights, and whether the area is rural, ubran or residential. Schools must be considered as well as the number of other vehicles on the roadway. Officers should be familiar with the area covered, the condition of the patrol car, the time of day, and their abilities and physical condition.

When considering that these variables may appear and disappear frequently throughout the course of pursuit and that most pursuits are less than three miles in length and three minutes in duration, it is easy to see the seriousness of task an officer has in a pursuit situation.

Policy may be Problematic

At least three states have enacted pursuit statutes that contain model policies for police pursuits. Some issue the policy to be followed by all police agencies in the state. Others offer a model policy for use or allow a police department to construct its own policy providing the constructed policy covers each issue in the model policy. Those departments that do not have such a policy or fail to adopt the model policy are considered prima facie liable in the event they are sued. Many police chiefs resist being forced to adopt model policies preferring to construct their own. Some view such legislative action as an infringement on their autonomy or view the entire process as a turf issue. Most states do not have laws requiring the police to have a particular policy, but police executives are well advised to have a reasonable policy. The existence of a policy is of little value unless officers and supervisors are well trained in its meaning and disciplinary action is imposed for those who violate the policy. Moreover, periodic retraining in the meaning of the policy and testing of officers on its contents has been shown to be a strong deterrent to the success of plaintiffs' attorneys. With the exception of those communities that have banned all pursuits, the initiation of a police pursuit is viewed as a discretionary decision. Policies exist to provide officers guidance in discretionary decision making. They provide officers with the agency philosophy on the subject. Most policies also contain procedures for conducting pursuits and include these instructions in the departmental policy.

The police frequently amend their pursuit policies after reviewing court decisions that affect such police operations. As a result of such reviews and amendments the policies become very lengthy. It is not uncommon to find twelve to fifteen page pursuit policies.

The pursuing officer's driving behavior is of the utmost importance in establishing reckless disregard for the safety of the public. When there is no evidence of reckless operation, a frequent tactic used by plaintiffs' counsels is examine the policy in minute detail. If one or more facets of the policy were not adhered to, the opposing counsel may be able to convince a juror that the police were in fact "a" proximate cause of the fatality by such omissions. For example, many policies require that the officer who initiates a pursuit inform the dispatcher of the pursuit, provide a description of the vehicle being chased, the number of persons in the vehicle and the location and direction of travel. If just one of these elements if omitted counsel for plaintiff will exploit this omission and attempt to describe the officer as incompetent and trust the jurors to make an inferential leap.

Frequently, policies require periodic updates as to the direction of travel and speed during the course of a pursuit, but there is no way of determining how many updates are reasonable. The purpose of such policy elements is for the administrative control of the pursuit, and this has little or nothing to do with the pursuing officer's driving behaviors. There is no standard to apply in determining whether the officer called in enough or not enough, but when the officer does not call at all or calls just once it provides an opportunity to confuse and sway a jury.

On one particular case of a pursuit that was just over one and one half miles long, the officer called in the initiation and then two more times over the short course of the pursuit. The opposing counsel tried to convince the jury that each time the officer passed another road he should have notified his dispatcher. Fortunately for the community, the judge ruled that the policy was not the prime concern, but only the officer's driving behavior should be examined.

Other policies allow low-speed pursuits for minor traffic violations, moderate-speed pursuits for misdemeanors and reckless driving and high-speed pursuits for serious felonies. Such a policy provides very little guidance. Determining what is a low, moderate, or high-speed leaves a great deal to conjecture and provides fertile ground for a confusing cross-examination. The author contends that the appropriateness of a pursuit depends on the conditions presented to the officer at the time of the pursuit and the variable conditions throughout the route of the pursuit. Pursuing someone at eighty miles per hour may be moderate to high-speed on a clear, dry, four lane expressway under light traffic conditions. Pursuing at twenty miles per hour on an ice covered road in darkness may be an extremely high speed. Furthermore, there is no way an officer can know for sure what crime(s) the offender has committed.

Most polices require a dispatcher to immediately inform the duty supervisor of the pursuit and its nature. The supervisor is obliged to make some administrative decisions as to whether the pursuit should be allowed to continue or be aborted. More often than not, the supervisor is in another part of the building and may not be immediately notified. Such conditions are amplified in court to convince jurors that the police don't follow their policy. The premise is if they disregarded their own policy they must have been negligent in some manner. Thus, while a pursuit policy is considered necessary it has become a burden for the police. This is particularly problematic when the police are faced with a microscopic examination of its contents and their absolute adherence to its content. The author recommends confining the pursuit policy to active pursuit elements and conduct and placing the administrative requirements in standing operating procedures for internal use. In short, the policy is often put on trial.

Pursuit Case Issue

Most of the cases that follow involve the deaths of innocent third parties who were struck by drivers fleeing from the police. In many cases the eluder was charged with homicide or manslaughter with a motor vehicle and was in prison at the time of the civil suit. Though the pleadings of both plaintiff and defense are not addressed in the brief analyses of cases, a common focus of plaintiffs' attorneys is whether the police jurisdictions have policies and customs on high-speed pursuits that amount to deliberate indifference. A basic thrust is that most departments do not conduct a pursuit driving course per se. The majority of police officers have been exposed to precision driving courses. The course curriculum usually includes vehicle dynamics, breaking, turning, sliding and so forth. They also teach attendees the laws on pursuit and the environmental conditions to consider when deciding whether to initiate, continue or terminate a pursuit. There are very few formal pursuit driving courses that actually provide officers with opportunities to drive at high speeds and attempt to stop other vehicles. The closest thing to such courses are those used by the Secret Service or Executive Protection Programs designed to thwart terrorists.

The standards for liability vary from negligence to gross negligence. Some of the cases that follow were brought under state tort law, some under Section 1983 and others under both. More often than not, the officer was named in the suit as well as the jurisdiction he or she worked for at the time of the pursuit. Generally, municipal defendants can be held liable under Section 1983 only for constitutional violations that occur as a result of policy or custom, and the standard is usually deliberate indifference. For example, a policy or custom of failing to train staff to respect the constitutional rights of citizens could justify liability as in *Canton v. Harris* (1989). In that case the court noted that for a municipality to be liable for failure to train it must be shown that the failure to train reflects deliberate indifference to the constitutional rights of citizens.

Case Preparations

Once retained, for either the plaintiff's or defendant's side, there are certain steps that should be taken prior to making a decision to testify on behalf of a client. One should read all the police reports and depositions from both sides. Though rarely experienced, a particular attorney may attempt to keep an expert from reading certain documents that are damaging to his or her client. In such cases an ethical expert would demand the documents or drop the case. Particular attention should be given to any discrepancies discovered. Such differences may be explained by oversight, untruthfulness or greed. In pursuit cases it is advisable to drive to the scene of the pursuit and traverse the entire route of the pursuit. Unless this action is taken a person has no way of knowing the environmental conditions the officer faced during the pursuit. The pursuit route should also be measured, and all conditions should be noted. Videotaping the pursuit route is very helpful in assessing the conditions faced by the pursuing officer. If representing the defense, it is wise to have the officer being sued accompany the expert and attorney so that critical questions can be answered. Generally, there is a audiotape of the pursuit. The tape should be listened to several times. Particular note should be made of the entire time elapsed. Once time and distance are determined, the average speed of the pursuit vehicle can be determined. Miles and tenths of miles are converted to feet.

The overall time is converted to seconds and that number is divided into the overall feet providing the feet per second traveled. This number is then divided by a factor of 1.47 and will provide a very close estimate of the average speed traveled throughout the course of the pursuit.

For example, an officer may report his speed as no faster than sixty miles per hour. The computed average speed will be helpful in verifying or disconfirming such statements. If an officer states a speed of sixty miles per hour and the test reveals an average speed of ninety-eight miles per hour further investigation is warranted. Listening to the pursuit tape provides one with some feel for the level of excitement or calm in the officer's voice. Though not scientific, such information can be useful in combating plaintiff's claim that the officer was experiencing an adrenaline rush and thus was out of control. Their inference is usually that had they been in control, they would not have pursued, and an the innocent third party, their client, would still be alive.

A tactic frequently employed at trial is to get an expert to agree to a theory that this author has termed, "the cat and mouse phenomenon" That argument holds if the police would have just stopped pursuing the offender, the offender would have returned to normal driving practices and thus would not have endangered anyone on the roadway. This position is not based on any empirical research. Though also not empirical in nature, conventional police experience has shown that most eluders will not stop immediately, often get into an accident by running off the road and frequently attempt to escape on foot.

Another position taken by plaintiffs' attorneys holds that the majority of police pursuits are conducted for mere traffic offenses and, as such, the need to apprehend is far outweighed by the unreasonable risk of harm presented to the public by the pursuit. This position can be countered with presentations of research data on the percentage of felony arrests made as a result of pursuits. In many states fleeing and eluding is a felony. Moreover, a good deal of research indicates that while the initiating factor may be an observable traffic offense a considerable percentage of pursuits end in felony arrests. The reckless driving of the eluder and the obvious danger to the motoring public also are factors to be considered by the police. The infamous serial killer Theodore Bundy was captured as a result of his attempt to flee the police in Florida for a traffic offense.

In conjunction with the other positions, almost all plaintiff attorneys hold that all pursuits are inherently dangerous. In some cases the unscientific and methodologically flawed Physicians for Auto Motive Safety Report (1968) has been presented as a standard. A few attorneys have argued that a pursuit is a violation of one's 4th Amendment rights because in a pursuit the fleeing driver is at the very least psychologically seized (Urbonya 1991). This position posits if the police have violated some constitutional right of the eluder then they should be considered "a" proximate cause of an injury or fatality suffered by an innocent third party who was struck by the offender.

Charles et al. (1992) contend that the police may be under-reporting pursuits by a factor of fifteen. Payne (1997), in his research of the Michigan State Police, found officers under-reported pursuits in a year long study by a factor of fourteen and one half. The impact of under-reporting by the police is significant. Reported accidents are public in nature and they provide a record. However, pursuits that end in escape or when apprehended the offender is ticketed and released can easily be under-reported. Several reasons exist for under-reporting. Officers do not want to do the associated paper work, do not always trust their supervisors, may have violated a facet of their policy and fear law suits resulting from pursuits (Payne and Corley 1994).

The pursuit policy of the police department involved should also be reviewed for comprehensiveness and detail. Though an officer's driving behavior is the more crucial consideration, in pursuit cases attorneys frequently attack the policy. At trial they also question officers extensively as to their knowledge of every detail of the policy. An officer's personnel file and training file should also be examined closely. If representing the police, it is advisable to interview the officers regarding the pursuit. Police have a tendency is to omit important facts in their official reports that they take for granted. This practice enables an expert to probe and perhaps get a different perspective on exactly what took place. Once these actions are completed, then, and only then, should an expert make a decision regarding his/her opinions. The author feels that it is best to be convinced to a moral certainty before deciding to testify in a matter. As such, one has an obligation to inform clients of the perceived strength and weaknesses of a case and to leave the decision of going forward up to them. In one particular case, an attorney was advised of several faults with his position and was advised not to call the author to testify, as his testimony would be damaging to the police department. Disregarding that advice, the case went forward and the plaintiff in that matter was awarded one and one half million dollars in damages.

Pursuit Cases

Case 16: Pursuit of an Armed Robbery Suspect

Facts

This pursuit resulted as result of an armed robbery of a store at 10:00 p.m. in good weather in light to moderate traffic. The total length of the pursuit was 4.75 miles and it lasted three minutes and thirty-three seconds. The pursuit started in one jurisdiction and continued through two other jurisdictions. It ended in a broad side collision with another vehicle after the eluder ran a traffic light. The course of the pursuit crossed forty-seven cross streets and included eleven stop lights, four of which were red when run by the eluder. The police said they slowed for all of the traffic lights, and witnesses supported their contention.

An officer responding to the robbery call noticed a vehicle and driver that fit the description in a gas station parking lot. The officer pulled into the station and checked the driver's license and registration. The officer noticed a small baseball bat in the front seat. As such a weapon was reportedly used in the robbery, the officer ordered the man out of his car. The suspect put his vehicle into gear and sped off.

During the course of the pursuit another area police department held traffic at intersections as the speeding vehicles passed. Using a formula for determining the average speed of the vehicles revealed an average speed of eighty miles per hour. Witnesses confirmed that the police had all of their emergency equipment activated. Two officers from other police agencies joined in the pursuit and reported during the course of the pursuit their speeds varied from a low of sixty to a high of one hurdred miles per hour. The first mile of the chase was on a five lane road. The second mile was on a four lane divided roadway and the last two miles were on a one-way road that varied from three to four lanes. The offender sped through a traffic light on a down grade and hit the victim's car broadside, driving his vehicle into a telephone pole. The suspect only suffered minor injuries.

When the eluder was arrested at the scene he said, "You got me, I'm drunk and on cocaine." He admitted to having four or five forty ounce beers and smoking five twenty dollar rocks of cocaine. Both the offender and the victim had extensive police records, and both had served prison terms. Though injured, the victim's injuries were not life threatening. Aside from asking for compensation for medical bills, his primary claim was a loss of consortium. He testified at deposition that he had sexual relations five to six times per week prior to his injuries, but was now limited to once or twice a week.

Issues and Factors Considered

Determination of the proximate cause and environmental road conditions were examined. Factors relating to termination decisions were also considered. A major issue was whether the nature of the crime should make a difference in the officers' decision making processes to continue the pursuit. The officers' driving and the records of the culprit and victim were examined in detail. Other factors included how close the police car was to the fleeing vehicle, and whether the primary pursuing officer's report of his speed matched the computed speed. Because the officer disregarded traffic signals, the issue of whether the conditions amounted to an emergency was also considered. According to state law the police could not disregard traffic signals unless an emergency existed.

Commentary

The proximate cause of the accident was determined to be the driving of the suspect attempting to escape arrest for an armed robbery. The roads were clear and dry, devoid of pedestrians, and traffic was light to moderate. The police testified the crime was serious enough to pursue the offender and the emergency lights would provide a warning to motorist along the route.

Had this pursuit occurred earlier in the day, when traffic would have been heavier and several pedestrians in the area, it would have been too hazardous to conduct. The criminal record of the accident victim was of no concern in determining the proximate cause of the crash. The primary officer admitted to reaching eighty miles per hour at one time during the pursuit. Witnesses estimated the officer's speed from sixty to eighty miles per hour.

Nearly five miles in length, this pursuit was longer than most, and the officer would not have been criticized if he had chosen to terminate the chase, but he felt that the conditions were ideal and the nature of the crime boded against termination. Although several courts have said that a speeder or other traffic violator does not create an emergency, the nature of the crime in this matter could rise to that level. The officer felt it was an emergency. Prior to trial and after a mediation panel viewed the facts and depositions, a settlement was agreed to by both parties.

Case 17: A Protracted Twenty-Five Mile Fatal Pursuit

Facts

This pursuit began in a metropolitan area after an officer attempted to pull over a motorist for speeding ten miles over the speed limit and running a red light. The eluder fled soon after the officer got out of his patrol car. The officer and a back-up officer from his department gave chase and broadcasted the pursuit on the multiple department radio network. In the next twenty minutes and twelve seconds, six police jurisdictions got involved in part of the pursuit which covered over twenty-five miles.

The pursuit terminated when the chased suspect ran a traffic light at a busy city intersection killing an innocent third party going through the intersection. This protracted pursuit involved police cars changing positions from primary to secondary chase cars on several occasions. In the last four miles of the pursuit two officers, from the sixth department to be involved, used their patrol cars to block two eastbound lanes of a four lane divided roadway. The suspect drove around them on the shoulder at sixty miles per hour. Those last two officers gave chase and became the final primary and secondary cars.

Eight tenths of a mile west of the accident scene, one of the two officers terminated the pursuit because his department's orders disallowed chasing outside their city limits. Though he testified that he also terminated, the second officer continued into the neighboring city. That officer accompanied by three other police cars, who had caught up to the chase, was within ten car lengths behind the eluder when the crash occurred.

The driver of the pursued vehicle had no outstanding warrants, but was driving on a suspended license. Both he and his passenger admitted to being on marijuana and having used cocaine. He testified that he fled because he was afraid of the police. The route of the pursuit involved a portion on two different expressways, three lane roads, county roads, rural roads and four lane divided roadways.

Issues and Factors Considered

A primary issue was whether the traffic violation was sufficient reason to continue a protracted pursuit over such a long distance. The probability of an accident occurring over such a long distance, with so many police cars involved, was also an issue. One officer clearly violated his agency policy by leaving his jurisdiction. It was also learned that he was advised on the radio to discontinue, and he lied by telling his dispatcher that he had terminated. The primary issue here, as in most cases, was what could be said of the proximate cause of the accident in which a motorist lost his life. One should attempt to determine if the officer's violation of policy and proximity to the accident scene had any bearing on the proximate cause.

Commentary

All of the polices of the six police agencies involved provide for a limit of two cars on pursuits. One is to be primary and a second is to be secondary car available to take over in the event the primary car has to drop out. In this case, the primary chase car was changed on three occasions, and the originating two police cars from the first jurisdiction remained in the line of cars involved until the accident occurred. Too many police cars were involved and the general safety of the public and the officers was jeopardized. The officer who failed to terminate his pursuit was disciplined by his agency for failing to abide by orders. He was told over the radio to terminate on two occasions. The chief of that agency dropped the disciplinary charges, ostensibly concerned over liability. As it turns out, failing to discipline under such circumstances is far more likely to bring a law suit. Though the originating police officers were behind the eluder throughout the twenty-five plus miles of this chase and were not immediately behind the speeder, they did arrive within seconds of the crash.

It would be an inferential leap to conclude that the officers' driving was the proximate cause of the fatality. Surely, the eluder had several opportunities to stop and a duty to do so. The fact that the police engaged in such a long and hazardous pursuit, based only on the knowledge of two traffic violations, does not speak strongly for a general concern for the safety of the motoring public. Moreover, due to such a long span of time and distance, most reasonable officers would conclude that an accident would be foreseeable. A jury could easily conclude that the police were "a" proximate cause of the accident though not "the" proximate cause. At the time of this pursuit, case law allowed for a determination of "a" proximate cause by a jury .

After considering the length and duration of this pursuit, the violations of policy and the exposure to danger to motorists, the mediation panel's suggestion was accepted. Plaintiffs were given an unspecified amount of money. The last mile of the pursuit was in a busy residential and business district and four credible witnesses estimated the police car speeds between eighty and ninety miles per hour just a car's length behind the eluder. When police driving can be shown to be reckless or likely to be reckless, it is instructive that several jurists have advised jurors they can consider the officers actions as contributory and "a" proximate cause of the injury. New case law in the year 2000 has since overruled such determinations. Regardless, it is likely a jury would have held the agencies liable considering the speeds involved, the protracted nature of the pursuit, and the police proximity to the eluder at the time of the crash.

Case 18: Police Pursue a Shooter in a Commandeered Vehicle

Facts

An off duty narcotics detective was having breakfast at a fast food restaurant in late November in a large metropolitan city. This incident occurred during rush hour traffic. A woman ran into the restaurant screaming that a man just stolen her car and he had a gun. When the detective exited the establishment, the suspect , who was in the woman's vehicle, saw him and fired shots at him through the closed window of the car he was stealing. The officer returned fire with three shots. All three shots hit the suspect's stolen vehicle, but missed the suspect. The suspect sped away, but within one hundred feet he crashed the woman's vehicle. He got out and ran to a parked dump truck loaded with hot asphalt. The keys to the ignition were in the truck and the suspect sped off again.

The officer hailed down a citizen, asked to use his car and was given permission to use it. The driver of the commandeered vehicle asked if he go along for the ride and was allowed to do so. In the next several minutes the officer, in a private vehicle without benefit of a police radio, chased the driver of the dump truck over several busy surface streets with congested traffic and traveled briefly on an expressway. The truck exited the expressway, rolled over at the end of the exit ramp and spilled its load of hot asphalt. The asphalt fell on a young girl who was waiting for a school bus - seriously burning her. The suspect got out of the truck and held a gun to the girl's head when confronted by the arriving officer. The officer fired a shot in the direction of the suspect, but did not strike him or the young girl. During the course of this private vehicle pursuit the officer stated he never drove more than ten miles over the speed limit and stayed to within four or five car lengths behind the dump truck. He said his intention was to wave down a passing patrol car.

Issues and Factors Considered

One question was whether the officer's initial response to the report of a stolen car and a man with a gun was reasonable. Another question was whether the firing of the officer's weapon on both occasions was within the guidelines for the use of deadly force. The commandeering of a private vehicle was also a question to be resolved, as was allowing a citizen to ride along during such a pursuit. Alternatives to the officer's action had to be examined. A question of the pursuit of the truck and endangerment to the motoring public also was an issue. Lastly, the question of proximate cause of the girl's injury was addressed.

Commentary

The officer's initial response was acceptable. It would have been better had he called in the report prior to going outside, thus affording a uniformed police response. However, once outside and being fired upon the officer's return fire was appropriate, as long as there were no innocent bystanders nearby. There were no citizens reportedly endangered. He was within his rights to return fire when fired upon. Legally the officer had a right to commandeer a motor vehicle. In this felony situation however, it was foolish to allow the citizen to accompany him on the pursuit. In doing so, the officer unnecessarily endangered a citizen. The officer might have better called in the incident by phone to the nearest precinct, given a description of the suspect, the dump truck, and the commandeered vehicle if he had chosen to follow the truck.

The proximate cause of the roll-over accident was the driving of the suspect in the stolen dump truck. The officer's decisions in this incident endangered himself, the owner of the commandeered vehicle and the life of the young girl who was close to the suspect when the officer fired. Ironically, the young girl was the daughter of another police officer from the same department. The officer claimed he just followed the suspect in the stolen dump truck, but due to his reported speed it was an active pursuit. If he was in fact below the speed limit it could be conceived as just following the suspect to keep him in sight. None-the-less, the officer's actions did not indicate sound judgment, but rather a reaction to a crisis. The detective was not driving an emergency vehicle, therefore, exceeding the speed limit during his self-described "moving surveillance" was illegal. By statute, in order to be afforded protection from exceeding the limit, the officer must be in an emergency vehicle. The father of the injured girl sued his own department in this matter. In spite of the dangerous descriptions described here the officer was supported by his superiors and the case was settled out of court. Not surprisingly, that same department was recently reported to have paid over forty-one million dollars in civil settlements in the past ten years.

Case 19: A Double Fatality Motorcycle Pursuit

Facts

This pursuit began at 2:15 a.m. in a small village with a population of 2000. A part-time township police officer observed a motorcycle with no headlights driving through the village. The officer turned around and came abreast of the motor cycle and activated his overhead emergency lights. At that time he noticed the cycle did not have a registration plate affixed. Neither of the two young men on the cycle was wearing a helmet, as required by law. The driver of the cycle did not stop for the police, but sped up through a thirty miles per hour zone, then a forty mile per hour zone, and turned onto a two lane paved country road. The road was curved with several dips. A short distance down the road, at an intersection, the driver of the cycle lost control while attempting to turn right. The cyclist and his passenger were thrown off the cycle. The officer stopped behind them and got out of his patrol car. The two fifteen year old youths righted the cycle and sped away.

At a point .2 of a mile further down the road the driver of the cycle lost control again, ran off the road to the left into some brush and struck a tree killing himself and his passenger. The total distance of the pursuit was 3.4 miles. The officer called in the pursuit to his dispatcher after the first .8 of a mile and called for assistance after 1.1 miles. He maintained a speed of no more than fifty miles per hour throughout the pursuit, and that speed was born out by tests of speed and distance. It was later alleged that the driver's father had taught him to drive a motorcycle at nine years of age and that the driver never applied for a driver's license. The officer said that had he been able to recognize the driver or obtain a registration plate number he would have terminated. As it was, he merely kept the motorcycle in view and did not attempt to overtake it.

Issues and Factors Considered

The issues here are the nature and scope of the department pursuit policy and whether the officer was trained in and following the policy. Another issue was to determine whether the officer's driving behavior was in any way contributory to the fatalities. A last issue was whether the officer should have pursued the motorcycle in the first place.

Commentary

The department had a good policy and it is so constructed as to inform officers of the considerations to take into account in such circumstances. The officer weighed the environmental factors and drove at a moderate speed throughout, just to keep the fleeing cycle in sight. The proximate cause of the fatality was that of the driver of the cycle who chose, for his own reasons, to disregard several attempts to stop him. He could have stopped immediately or could have ceased his attempted escape after his spill at the intersection.

The officer operated his vehicle consistent with the law and a police officer is not obliged to allow the driver of a motorcycle to leisurely escape because he chose not to obey the law. People in some quarters maintain that police should not pursue juveniles. This argument is fallacious. First, it is very hard to determine age of a driver under these conditions. Second, errant drivers whatever age, can kill others by their manner of driving. In this case, that is exactly what happened. If the officer had recognized the driver, a termination would have been wise, but this was a valid pursuit regardless of the assumed age of the eluder. No improper actions were observed on the part of the officer. The plaintiff did not prevail.

Case 20: A Multiple Department Pursuit Ends in a Million Dollar Settlement

Overview

The complexity of this pursuit requires an overview. This was a protracted pursuit that began when officers of the originating police department confronted two seventeen year old youths in the process of stealing a vehicle. That action started a pursuit that lasted over ten minutes, covered twelve miles and ended with a broadside collision accident that killed one man and seriously injured another. The first two miles of the route were on a four lane road. The next ten miles were on a four lane road that had a turning lane in some places. The entire route was clear and dry and traffic was very light to non-existent throughout the route. Three police agencies were involved (A, B & C) in portions of the pursuit, and each of the officers from those departments terminated their pursuit after reasonably short distances. Two other police agencies (D & E) had officers who only witnessed the driving of the eluder and followed for short distances, but they were not actively involved in the pursuit. A sixth uninvolved agency (F) had a police officer on patrol at the accident location who witnessed the fatal accident.

A command officer was the last officer to see the eluding offender, and he terminated the pursuit 1.5 miles north of the fatal accident scene. The pursuit started in jurisdiction A, went through the four other jurisdictions of B,C, D and E, and ended in a fatal crash in jurisdiction F.

A trial was held in circuit court and a jury dismissed claims against all of the departments except jurisdiction C which was the last to report seeing the eluder's vehicle. That agency had a judgment of 1.25 million dollars assessed against it because the jury did not believe that they terminated. A half mile south of the termination point of agency C, an all night gas station attendant testified that he definitely saw a red Camero go by at one hundred miles per hour. Shortly thereafter, he testified a white police car with blue lettering on the door with overhead lights operating went southbound at a high rate of speed. Proofs were introduced at trial showing that none of the agencies involved in this pursuit had white police cars or blue lettering. The only nearby department that had such markings was agency F. Their department had a no pursuit policy and though defendants' attorneys investigated thoroughly, they could not find any officers from agency F who would admit being involved in this pursuit.

Facts

In late October at 4:20 a.m. three officers from department A responded to an apartment complex in their jurisdiction to a report of two young males attempting to steal motor vehicles from the parking lot. On arrival, two officers in separate cars drove into the complex at 4:28 a.m.: another remained at the main road to block any possible escape. The roads were dry and the weather was clear. On entering, the officers found two young males who appeared suspicious near two vehicles. One vehicle was a black Mustang and the other a red Camero. The driver of the Camero fled the scene and turned west on the main road at the complex entrance. The officer waiting there pursued the vehicle as did one of the two officers from within the complex. The driver of the black Mustang attempted to evade the officer who remained in the complex, spun around a few times and then drove directly at her. His vehicle careened off the patrol car and hit a tree, and he was arrested in the stolen vehicle.

At 4:32 a.m. two officers from department A began the pursuit of the red Camero westward for two miles. Both officers believed the vehicle to be stolen and knew that one of the two vehicles in the complex had attempted to run over one officer. One was a primary car and the second stayed back several hundred feet. The driver of the primary car reached speeds of eighty miles per hour but said that the Camero was pulling away from him and was far ahead of him. He observed that driver run a red light at ninety miles per hour. The pursuing officer slowed to forty miles per hour to negotiate that intersection. Arriving at the next intersection and only seeing the vehicle's tail lights in the distance, he terminated the pursuit.

An officer from department B was waiting at that intersection and observed the Camero turn south on a four lane road at a high rate of speed. He noted that the cars from department A could not be seen in the distance looking eastward. He had heard the radio traffic from department A officers at 4:32 a.m. when they initiated the pursuit. He turned south to follow the Camero and activated his emergency lights. He followed the vehicle for five miles only to terminate because the vehicle continually pulled away from him. At his point of termination, five miles south of the west bound road, he noted the Camero was at least one mile ahead of him. The road was straight and had only one slight curve in it over the ten mile southward course. Another officer from department B had momentarily followed the Camero route for a mile, but disengaged and continued to drive in the same direction at lower speeds in the event the driver of the stolen Camero crashed and would run from the vehicle. A third officer was behind him, but he said he never saw anything of the Camero.

At approximately 4:36 a.m., officers from department C got involved as the Camero approached and entered their jurisdiction. Five miles south of the westbound road from which the Camero turned on to the four lane southbound road two officers from department C attempted to pursue the Camero. They continued for two miles to no avail. They did observe the driver of the Camero run a red light at over one hundred miles per hour. The closest they got to the stolen vehicle was one half mile.

Two and a half miles north of the accident scene a Lieutenant from department C got involved in the pursuit. He was the southern-most police vehicle and nearest to the Camero. He pursued for a short distance, and at an intersection 1.5 miles north of the accident scene he terminated the pursuit. His termination was broadcasted on the radio, and he ordered all of his agency officers to do the same. He testified he heard of an accident further south on the inter-city radio so he told the dispatcher that he was going to head in that direction to see if it was the Camero. He proceeded to the scene at the speed limit without emergency lights. He was driving a dark blue semi-marked vehicle. Two officers from departments D and E were only involved momentarily and did not actively pursue.

Upon his arrival at the accident scene the supervisor from department C found the driver of the Camero outside his car, uninjured, and laughing about the pursuit. He was arrested by officers from department F. One officer from department F witnessed the Camero run a red light, cross a divided eight lane roadway, and hit the victim's vehicle. That crash killed the plaintiff and seriously injured his passenger.

Both of the seventeen year old young men involved in this incident were arrested for stealing a vehicle. The driver of the Camero was originally charged with manslaughter with a motor vehicle, but that charge was subsequently dismissed. He offered the fact that he had learned to steal cars by attending classes in someone's basement who had a mock up of a vehicle that allowed him to "hot wire" a car and learn to break into a door quickly.

Issues and Factors Considered

The response of the officers from department A to the initial complaint and their conduct of the pursuit was examined. The responses and behaviors of officers from departments B and C were also examined. How they pursued the stolen Camero and the environmental conditions were closely examined. The actions of the supervisor from department C were also an issue in determing what, if any culpability, these officers had. The policy of each department was examined and the officers' actions were compared for adherence or violation of the policies.

Commentary

All three officers from department A conducted their actions in a professional manner. Once injured, the driver of the Mustang was given treatment at the scene prior to incarceration. The secondary car in the originating pursuit remained at a reasonable distance from the primary car per their policy. The decision to terminate by the primary officer was sound under the conditions at the time. He slowed for one light and after determining that to continue would be futile and dangerous considering the speeds involved, he terminated.

All officers involved used good radio procedure by calling out their locations, and all used their emergency lights and sirens, slowed down for cross street and remained at reasonable distances from the pursued vehicle. After seeing they could not catch the Camero each officer made a sound decision to terminate. The supervisor of department C radioed his intent to terminate the pursuit by putting this information out to all departments. His decision to continue southward to investigate possible involvement of the Camero in the reported accident was reasonable and consistent with sound police practice. The policies of all three involved departments were found to be complete and provided sound guidance for discretionary decision making. Each department administration conducted internal investigations. To a person, officers felt they could not catch the Camero, but wanted to use their emergency equipment to warn other possible motorists along the chase route.

The jury in this case clearly disregarded the facts presented at trial. One department has since amended their pursuit policy to ban pursuits unless the case involves a serious felony and then only when based on probable cause. That department, who in the opinion of the author, suffered a severe financial loss with a judgment of 1.25 million dollars was a victim of jury nullification. Some jurors later revealed that they felt that someone had to pay for the victim's injury. The proximate cause of the victim's death was clearly the result of the Camero driver's action. The author has serious reservations as to honesty of unknown officers from department F.

Case 21: Officer Uses Faulty Judgment during Rush Hour Traffic

Facts

This pursuit at 6:25 a.m. traversed 2.5 miles through morning rush hour traffic in a medium sized industrial city. This case in an example of an over zealous officer who used poor judgment in commencing a pursuit and continued to pursue even though he knew the identify of the juvenile he chased.

The incident began when the officer was called to a home earlier in the morning for the report of a stolen vehicle. The complainant, the father of the pursued person, reported that his step-son had stolen his Monte Carlo vehicle again, and he was tired of it. He was prepared to prosecute. He identified his son and his car in detail. He told the officer he thought his stepson might be with friends and gave him his friends' addresses. The officer drove to the location and started searching for the suspect. At 6:14 a.m. the officer advised his departmental dispatcher that he located the Monte Carlo vehicle and he was stopping the driver. At his deposition, the officer said the vehicle had three youths in it. He exited the patrol car and approached the Monte Carlo with his weapon in hand. The officer's report states he noticed the youths all crouched down inside the car attempting to hide from him. As he reached the vehicle the driver sat up, started the car and sped off .

Over the next two and one half miles the officer chased the vehicle through residential areas, made several turns and drove down two one-way streets the wrong way. One of the one-way streets was fifteen blocks in length. Traffic was heavy and the officer and the pursued person had to continually dodge other vehicles. During the pursuit the officer radioed he was chasing a "kid". He also radioed to other officers "he won't stop for you" and "he doesn't care about a police car."

The chased car ran several traffic lights during the course of the pursuit as did the officer. The pursuit ended in the death of an innocent third party that was struck by the driver of the Monte Carlo. The driver and friends were not seriously injured, and they all ran from the crash scene. A short time later the driver was arrested.

Issues and Factors Considered

Several questions were posed as issues in this pursuit. Does the policy have restrictions in pursuing juveniles or persons known to the officer? Did the officer slow down as necessary for traffic signals? Did the officer consider the seriousness of the offense, the age of the driver, and the fact that he knew who it was that was fleeing? Did the officer's driving contribute to an already dangerous situation? Was the officer's driving and continuing the pursuit likely to endanger others on the road? Should the officer have terminated the pursuit? Did the officer have alternatives other than pursuit?

Commentary

Prior to taking the author's deposition, the city settled with the plaintiff's family for one million dollars after consultation with the plaintiff's counsel and the author The officer was subsequently separated from the department. The policy of the department is restrictive and gives sound guidance for terminating a pursuit under the conditions present in this case. Notably, the policy states that safety outweighs apprehension. According to the policy, officers shall discontinue a pursuits when the risks outweigh the benefits, when the roads and traffic indicate futility, when the identification of the driver is known, when the offense is not life threatening and when the driver is a juvenile or the crime is not a serious felony. Though the proximate cause of the fatality was the driving of the juvenile, the officer's actions and manner of pursuit would provide most triers of fact to include the police as "a" proximate cause. The officer in this pursuit not only violated at least two sections of his policy, but he used poor judgment in conducting the pursuit under the circumstances. He also violated the law because he could not run a red light or go the wrong way on a one-way street unless he had an emergency. A stolen vehicle is not considered an emergency. The manner of the officer's driving clearly endangered other motorists.

Case 22: Cyclist Killed after a Short Pursuit

Facts

Shortly after midnight on a summer evening in a small village of less than twelve thousand population, the police chased a motorcycle when it was observed speeding past the police station. The motorcycle had a driver and passenger. This typical pursuit lasted three minutes and traversed ten blocks in a residential neighborhood. The motorcycle driver lost control at a T-intersection, ran off the roadway, struck a telephone pole and killed the passenger. The passenger was the driver's brother.

As the officer was leaving the police department parking lot he observed the motorcycle driving ten to twenty miles over the limit. He immediately turned on his overhead lights and gave chase. The cycle went two blocks then turned left and sped another eight blocks before running off the road. During the last eight blocks the cyclist, driving on the wrong side of the road, passed two motorists on the street. The closest the police car got to the cycle during this short chase was three hundred feet. The highest speed attained by either vehicle was fifty-five miles per hour. Two independent witnesses testified that the police were not right behind the cycle, but two friends of the cyclist said they were very close. The police arrived at the scene ten seconds after the crash. One alleged witness testified that the police officer was directly behind the motorcycle and forced it off the road into the pole. He was later exposed as having a bias against the officer from several previous arrests and exposed as a liar in the community by two other witnesses. He later recanted his testimony. A trial was held and a no cause for action was rendered on behalf of the police.

Issues and Factors Considered

One issue was whether the policy of the department was comprehensive and instructive. It had to be determined if the chief investigated the alleged charges against the officer, if the officer was trained in and followed the policy, if the officer's driving was contributory and whether the environmental conditions were positive or negative.

Commentary

The policy of the department on pursuits was general in nature and lacked many specifics, however, it did provide advice consistent with the law, and transmitted the idea of safety and balancing the need to apprehend against the need for public safety. On balance the policy was poor, but sufficient. The roads were clear and dry and the weather on this morning was clear. There was one traffic signal in the final eight blocks, and cyclist failed to stop for it. The officer slowed to almost a complete stop for the signal.

This was a low-speed pursuit and the highest speed attained was fifty-five miles per hour. The posted speeds on the route were thirty miles per hour for the first two blocks, thirty-five miles per hour for the next five blocks and twenty-five miles per hour for the last three blocks. At the point of impact, an on scene investigation revealed the police car was three hundred feet behind the cycle when it crashed. There was no damage to the police car. The chief failed to counsel the officer, did not investigate the accident and did not have any notes available. He did not remember ever speaking to the officer regarding the policy. In spite of these conditions the case was won by the defendant at trial. This type of pursuit suit is not uncommon in small communities where people harbor biases toward the police for an aggressive enforcement policy. It is not uncommon for such so-called witnesses to come forward with negative testimony. Thorough investigation by defendant's attorney into such witnesses' backgrounds was crucial in developing a trial strategy for cross-examination for the jury's consideration in determining causality.

Case 23: Pursued Driver Drowns in a Creek

This pursuit involves a drunk driver with a blood alcohol level of .25 who ran off the end of a country road, turned his pickup truck over in a drainage ditch and drowned the passenger. The victim's family attempted to connect the pursuit to the victim's death, claiming the officer should have made attempts to enter the overturned submerged vehicle in an effort to save the victim.

Facts

The driver of the pursued vehicle had just left two taverns in a small village at approximately 2:50 a.m. in the morning. He was observed by the officer attempting to pass a vehicle in a no passing zone, tailgating another vehicle and running off the edge of the roadway. The officer, who suspected a drunk driver, attempted to stop the vehicle by activating his overhead lights while driving northbound on a paved two lane road leading out of the village. The total distance from the attempted stop until the pursued vehicle crashed was 3.5 miles. The driver of the pickup truck failed to stop when signaled to do so, and he turned east on a country road. Speeds did not exceed fifty miles per hour on this road and the officer did not attempt to overtake the vehicle. The pickup truck was at least one quarter mile ahead of the police car. The driver of the pickup then turned north on a gravel road. The officer continued north attempting to get the vehicle to stop by following the vehicle with his overhead lights activated. One mile from the accident scene the officer actively pursued the vehicle. The officer reported being in pursuit of a vehicle at 2:56 a.m and at 2:58 a.m. he reported on the radio that he had lost sight of the vehicle. He disengaged his overhead lights and did not use his siren.

The pickup truck had reached a jogged T-intersection. The road jogged to the left and then north again over a culvert and a flooded drainage ditch. At this juncture, the pickup overturned and settled into the water upside down. The officer did not see the vehicle when he arrived at the intersection so he drove further east, then west, and then north. On returning to the T-intersection he noticed the vehicle in the ditch inverted in the water. At 3:00 a.m. he reported losing the vehicle at the jog in the road. At 3:01 a.m. he reported finding the vehicle in the ditch and called for a wrecker. Time and distance calculations revealed the officer's average speed to be near forty miles per hour. The total elapsed time from the first attempt to stop the vehicle to finding the vehicle in the water was seven minutes and five seconds.

Issues and Factors Considered

One factor was to determine if the officer had reasonable grounds to stop the pickup truck. Other factors examined were the use of emergency equipment, the environmental conditions, the pursuit policy and the officer's familiarity with the policy. A major question raised by plaintiff was whether the officer had a specific duty to the plaintiff and an obligation to enter the water to save the victim. The distance between the two vehicles during the short pursuit was also a relevant factor.

Commentary

The officer had a right and a duty to stop a suspected drunk driver. The driving behavior of the pickup driver would reasonably indicate operating under the influence. The officer used his overhead lights, but not his siren, except intermittently. State law does require the use of emergency lights, but the siren is only required as needed. The siren would have been of little value with no other vehicles on the road to warn. Moreover, the distance between the two vehicles would have negated any value of the siren.

With the exception of one small rise on the northbound gravel road the route was straight, level and unremarkable. The officers estimated speed of forty miles per hour was appropriate for a gravel road. The officer was well trained having just completed an advanced precision driving-pursuit training program. The policy of the department was comprehensive. The policy requires termination if an officer loses sight of the target vehicle or pursues more than five miles without a back-up vehicle. It also requires lights and siren and notification to dispatch. The only violation of policy was the lack of consistent use of the siren, but that action was consistent with state law. The policy also requires disengagement if there is a risk of loss of life, the identification of the fleeing person is known or when the roads or traffic are dangerous. None of these conditions existed.

The crashed vehicle was found upside down in the water and the officer could not see a driver or a passenger. Had he gotten wet and attempted to extricate someone it would have been to no avail as the victim was pinned under steel and could not have been extracted in any case. The driver was partially out of the vehicle but could not be seen.

The officer called for the jaws of life equipment to extricate the persons in the vehicle. Both this author and another expert testified that the officer did not violate any professional standards in not attempting to get into the submerged vehicle. Experts on both sides of this case agreed it would have looked good and more humane had the officer attempted a rescue, but it would have been to no avail. The author found no wrongdoing on the officer's part and concluded this was a very short, slow speed pursuit which was properly conducted. The officer's distance from the accident scene and his disengagement from an active pursuit precluded any finding of proximate cause. The cause of the death of the victim was the intoxicated driving of the pickup truck driver. The defendants were relieved of any liability.

Case 24: Pursued Driver Tackled by the Police

Facts

This 1.5 mile long pursuit ended when the offender ran the third of seven traffic lights at a T-intersection and side-swiped the plaintiff's vehicle causing him slight facial injuries. The offender ran his vehicle off the end of the roadway into a field and then ran from the scene. He was tackled by the officer a few hundred feet from his vehicle. The entire route of 1.9 miles included five city residential streets at 9:30 p.m. with no vehicular or pedestrian traffic on them. The officer noticed the chased vehicle weaving and attempted to stop the driver in the second of five residential blocks. The driver pulled over momentarily and then sped off. After negotiating a right and left turn through the five block neighborhood and running three stops signs, he ran a traffic light and turned left. The officer activated his overhead lights and the pursuit was initiated. At that time the officer called his dispatcher with the license plate number. The entire length of the pursuit route was 1.5 miles on a four lane street bordered with factories and businesses. Only two businesses were open. The route traversed six traffic signals. The offender ran two additional lights including the last one at the crash scene. A moment after the officer called in the pursuit he was told the vehicle was stolen. Another officer advised the pursuing officer that the vehicle had been involved in a strong armed robbery. The average speed of the officer and offender was fifty-five miles per hour, and the officer maintained a distance of 250 feet behind the chased vehicle. While waiting for the last light to change to green, the plaintiff, who was facing the same direction the eluder was driving, was sideswiped.

Issues and Factors Considered

The officer followed his policy by calling the dispatcher and gave three location broadcasts during the pursuit. Traffic was light to non-existent . The offender ran three red lights. He ran one of the three at fifty miles per hour. All of the evidence indicated the officer slowed down prior to going through the lights. Those actions are factors to be considered. The issue of due care on the part of the officer was examined. Other factors included whether the officer had a duty to pursue the offender, and whether the officer's driving was in any way a proximate cause of the injury to the plaintiff. The overall issue in this minor case was the reasonableness of the officer's driving behavior.

Commentary

Maintaining a speed of fifty-five and slowing for three red traffic signals indicates the officer drove with due care. Maintaining a distance of 250 feet behind the eluder was also good judgment on the officer's part. The officer had a right to pull the offender over for weaving. He had a duty to pursue a reckless driver after he observed the offender run three stops signs and a traffic light. Once he learned of the felony, he had a duty to make every reasonable effort to arrest a probable felon.

A question posed on many pursuits is whether the officer was confronted with an emergency. Whether the attempted capture of a serious life threatening felon is an emergency remains within the purview of a judge who comments on matters of law. The issue is important in one respect. The statute in the state in which this pursuit took place allows officers to disregard the speed laws when attempting to capture criminals or traffic violators. They may disregard the speed laws as long as they drive with due care. Interestingly, that law does not allow the officer to proceed through traffic signals without stopping, go the wrong way on one way streets or run stop signs. Those privileges are limited to emergency conditions. In order to avail themselves these privileges, officers must be in an emergency vehicle, have the emergency light operating and use a siren as needed. The officer must also reasonably believe an emergency exists. As to the answer of whether chasing a felon is an emergency, case law previously provided offers some guidance. If the officer believed it to be an emergency, even though it may later have been found to be a non-emergency, then some courts would support the running of the red lights and stop signs.

Under these circumstances it is probably wise to have all officers comment on their justification and determination of emergency status when pursuing. Nothing is stronger in the defense of a police officer on the stand for his or her actions than documented articulable facts outlined in a police report. In Case 20 of this work, one officer, when asked if he thought he had an emergency to justify his speed, said, "Yes, it was an emergency because two thousand pounds of steel careening down the public road at one hundred miles per hour presents a danger to everyone in its path" The author concluded and testified at deposition that the officer's actions were appropriate. Weighing the costs associated with a trial and the minimal injury to the plaintiff, the jurisdiction paid the plaintiff a token amount for his medical costs.

Case 25: Pursuit by Officers in Unmarked Police Vehicles

Facts

This case illustrates a problem for big city police departments. The question posed in this case is whether a so-called moving surveillance by several plainclothes officers in unmarked cars without sirens or grille lights is a pursuit when the officers are driving over the speed limit to keep a criminal suspect in sight.

In a suburban city of a large metropolitan area five plain clothes officers in unmarked cars were working in a special operations unit as a surveillance team. A criminal suspect had been robbing women of their purses by grabbing them through their open car windows in mall and super market parking lots. This crime is an unarmed robbery and classified as a serious felony.

On the day of this incident the five officers received information on the description of the robbery suspect and his car. They spotted the suspect and vehicle but were within the city limits of the large city at the time. They called for back-up from that police department for a marked car to make the felony stop, and followed the suspect on a long and complex route through the city on what they termed a moving surveillance. The officers' average speed was computed and found to be at least fifteen miles per hour over the posted limits most of the time. The policy of their department does not allow them to pursue in unmarked cars and neither does the state law. The officers contended that they were just following the suspect to keep him in sight while awaiting for a marked car to make the stop.

Although they were driving over the speed limit, their chief determined that it was not a pursuit according to his understanding of his policy. Over the course of a 3.4 miles the team located the driver, boxed him in and lost him on several occasions. During the course of this pursuit on two occasions the suspect pulled to the curb as if to shake a tail. On both occasions the officer's attempts to box him in failed. At the end of the 3.4 mile route over many side streets in residential neighborhoods, the suspect ran a traffic light and killed an innocent motorist. He was charged and convicted of manslaughter with a motor vehicle.

The officers nearest to the eluding driver maintained they were at least one block behind the suspect when the accident occurred. Other officers were paralleling the chase on other streets. The suspect maintained that the officers were directly behind him. He identified two officers behind him by describing the color of their car, the clothes they wore, and that they both had mustaches. The incident took place at 1:00 p.m. on a sunny day with medium vehicular traffic and some pedestrian traffic.

Issues and Factors Considered

The first issue was to determine if the officers were conducting a pursuit. Another issue was whether the officers had other alternatives. A third issue was whether they violated their policy and the law. The final issue was whether their manner of driving was a contributing factor in the fatal accident.

Commentary

After reviewing the policy of the department, it was determined the officers were in fact in a pursuit. The term "moving surveillance" is a misnomer. Without the benefit of a siren and grille lights the officers could not legally drive over the limit. The officers appeared to have had solid identification from another police department on the identity of this suspect. As such, they would have had probable cause to make a felony arrest. One alternative would have been to box him in along the curb tighter than they did and make an arrest. They also had good information on who he was and his address. They could have set up a surveillance of his residence and arrested him there. They could also have obtained a warrant and arrested him at a later time.

Once the alleged robber pulled out from the curb after his first pullover, the officers had to make a decision. Their choices were either chase him and violate their policy or attempt to tail him at the speed limit and hope the home jurisdiction police responded with a marked car to make the stop. Clearly, the officers were paralleling in this incident and that too is disallowed in their policy. A recommendation was made to defendants' counsel that this case had many weak points for a trial, even though it was not felt that the officers' actions were contributory to the fatality. The case was settled out of court for an undisclosed amount. Several jurisdictions have chosen to install sirens and emergency grille lights in their unmarked cars to avoid such complications.

Case 26: Passenger in Pursued Vehicle Sues the Police

Facts

This fatal accident occurred after a one mile, two minute pursuit, during five o'clock rush hour traffic, in a mixed residential-business area. One of two passengers in the pursued vehicle was killed. The pursued driver and his two passengers were not wearing seat belts. The officer had left his rear window flashing lights on in his semi-marked police car while out of his car handling a larceny complaint. On his return he noticed a red vehicle stopped near a railroad track nearby. He turned off his lights and then noticed that the red vehicle sped off. He gave chase and reportedly activated his grille lights and rear window deck lights. The pursuit traversed a few residential streets and then on to a main four lane road. One mile after the pursuit started, and after just two minutes, the red vehicle sped up to forty miles per hour and ran a red light. The eluder's vehicle was struck broadside by another vehicle.

The pursued driver ran from the scene and was caught a block away by the responding officer. Three witnesses said they did not see the police car flashers on, but an officer following the officer said his deck lights were on. If they were on then his grille lights were also activated. Two witnesses thought the officer was very close to the pursued vehicle when it ran the light. Another witness did not hear any siren but did hear the patrol car tires squealing to a stop. The driver of the second vehicle was not injured.

Issues and Factors Considered

One factor to consider was whether the willing passenger in a pursued vehicle has a right of claim against the police for her injuries. The police officer's driving was also an issue. A third issue was to determine if the pursuit was warranted, considering the risk of harm presented to the general public by conducting a pursuit during heavy traffic conditions for unknown reasons beyond speeding.

Commentary

The officer had a right to pursue the red car as he observed the vehicle speeding. The speed limit was thirty miles per hour and the officer testified he was going forty miles per hour. Although this is only ten miles over the limit the officer had a right to stop the vehicle. Some question is raised as to the officer's proximity to the pursued vehicle, but there was no concrete evidence that he was directly behind the eluder. To the contrary, the officer and his associate officer both said he was several car lengths behind him. In rush hour traffic the pursuit of a low level speeder of ten miles over the limit is not recommended. The issue becomes one of foreseeability. The driver of the pursued vehicle was charged with manslaughter, fleeing and eluding, and leaving the scene of a personal injury accident. Case law exists that precludes recovery by a willing passenger in a fleeing vehicle. The case was settled out of court for a small, but undisclosed amount. Had the author testified he would have recommended against such a pursuit due to the traffic, time of day and low speeds observed.

Case 27: Witnesses with Damaging Testimony

Facts

This is a case of conflicting witness statements on a pursuit, some of which were very damaging to the police. In such incidents, even if the police were not negligent, had conducted the pursuit properly, were not reckless and were not a proximate cause, the risk of going to trial is considerable. The jurisdiction in this matter, in consultation with their insurers and attorneys, and after taking numerous depositions, went along with the mediation panels recommendation and paid a very high six figure settlement rather than go to trial.

At 1:00 a.m. in January an officer observed a Camero with three people in the car in a large grocery store parking lot. He was patrolling the parking lot due a recent rash of larcenies from motor vehicles. When the driver of the Camero spotted the police he began to speed out of the lot, fish tailed his vehicle and ran a stop sign when entering a main thoroughfare. The officer followed the car out of the parking lot and activated his emergency overhead lights as the suspect sped up to sixty miles per hour. The officer advised his dispatcher, activated his siren and started a pursuit. The pursuit was conducted over a 2.5 mile course. The first mile of the chase was on a four lane divided highway. The last mile and a half was on a four lane undivided roadway with cross traffic. During the course of the pursuit the suspect ran three lights at speeds up to eighty miles per hour. The officer testified that he slowed at the first two traffic lights, thus opening the distance between them. The officer claimed he ended the pursuit one half mile before the crash at the third red light, but left his overhead lights on and continued in the same direction to warn other motorists. He stated his speed was close to sixty miles per hour and estimated the speed of the eluder at eighty miles per hour.

The second light was run by the suspect and the officer as another officer was already there and blocking cross traffic. At the third light the suspect swerved around traffic waiting for the red traffic signal, spun out and hit the plaintiff's vehicle. The total time of the pursuit was less than two minutes providing an average speed of the pursuit at eighty-one miles per hour. The plaintiff suffered injuries requiring surgery. The officer also said that he was one half mile behind the suspect at the time of the crash.

A passenger in the stolen car testified he told the driver to stop, but he would not. One witness said the suspect was traveling seventy to eighty miles per hour after the first mile of the pursuit, and the police car was one hundred feet behind them.

Another witness estimated the speed of the Camero to be 110 miles per hour and said the police were thirty yards behind the pursued vehicle. At the accident scene the father of this witness said, "another high speed chase and another innocent victim." Another witness said the Camero was doing 120 miles per hour and the police car was one car length behind it. That witness further claimed that the officer was in full pursuit when the crash occurred. A passenger in the stolen car stated the police were one half block behind them at the start, but after one mile the police were only twenty feet behind. He said when the driver of the stolen vehicle ran the second light, the police were right behind them. The driver of the stolen vehicle said when he ran the second light the police ran the light with him. He also said he did not want to drive that fast, but the police would not back off. In the officer's favor another witness stated the police car was less than a city block behind the stolen car.

Issues and Factors Considered

The first issue was to determine if the initiation of the pursuit was warranted. Another issue to resolve was whether the officer's speed and manner of driving was reckless. A third issue was to determine whether the officer in fact terminated the pursuit, and if so, whether he should have terminated it sooner.

Commentary

The officer had a right to investigate and pursue the speeding vehicle from the parking lot. Once out on the main road and observing the stolen car speed away, a pursuit was warranted. There was moderate to light traffic on the four lane expressway, but when the road was no longer divided the traffic was described as moderate. If, as some witnesses testified, the officer was directly behind the fleeing vehicle or very close to it at the speeds involved, he should have terminated the pursuit. If the officer pursued the vehicle right up to the collision then he could be considered "a" proximate cause for failing to back off and resume a more normal speed. On the officer's side is his testimony that he did in fact terminate some distance from the scene. Continuing in the same direction with his overhead lights would not be inappropriate under those circumstances. Having driven the route with the officer and questioning him as to his performance the author felt his actions were warranted and that he did in fact slow down.

However, the onus upon him and his department was extreme. Two witnesses were clearly opposed to all kinds of police pursuits. Three others in the stolen car, though considered self-serving, could also provide damaging testimony. Two reliable witnesses supported the officer's contentions.

Regardless of the potential merit of the officer's behavior, the negative testimony from the other witnesses was such that the department paid a six figure settlement rather than test the matter in the courts. It is a common practice for officers to disengage from an active pursuit and continue in the same direction with lights on at reduced speeds. While this practice is designed to possibly warn other motorists, it is often interpreted by others as an active pursuit because the emergency lights are in operation.

This author has maintained that it is not the equipment status that makes a pursuit, but the driving of the officer. It is impossible to determine whether this accident would not have happened had the officer turned off his emergency lights and slowed to the legal limit. Police face this paradox in all pursuits. The advisable termination point is that point where the state's need to apprehend is off set by the unreasonable risk of harm presented to the other motoring public. This is a movable and elusive point, and one that must be determined in a matter of seconds. The proximate cause is somewhat more clear. Had the driver of the stolen car not fled or had he stopped after being summoned to do so by the police, the accident would not have happened.

Case 28: A Relentless High-Speed Pursuit

Facts

A police chief from a small village started to follow a motorcycle with a passenger at 11:30 p.m., six miles from the fatal accident scene. The cycle passed his observation point in the village and the female on the back of motorcycle yelled, "Whoopee." The chief said he saw the cycle weave back and forth toward the centerline, but he did not feel he had probable cause to stop it at that time so he just followed them. For the first two miles he followed the cycle, he said he was driving ten to twenty miles over the limit. During that period he was not using any emergency lights and the closest he got was two to three blocks behind the cycle. When asked what speed he was traveling he said he did not know as he was not watching. When asked if it could be up to one hundred miles per hour he said it could have been. After two miles, the motorcycle accelerated and the chief turned on his overhead lights and began a pursuit. He called his dispatcher and attempted to alert the police in the next village, but no one was on duty. He testified that he was driving "flat out" and probably 120 miles per hour. When he entered the second small village he said he was not watching his speed when he ran the single traffic light of the village. The speed limit in the village was twenty-five miles per hour and the chief admitted that he was doing at least three times that speed but countered, "so was the motorcycle and then some." On the last four miles of the chase the road is a straight, two lane road with an eight foot ditch on either side, and runs through a farm area.

When asked if he thought that a motorcycle at those speeds could easily spin off into a ditch he agreed and said that he realized someone could be killed but he did not think of it at that time. It did not bother the chief to drive through the village at one hundred miles per hour and he justified his speed by saying that he did not initiate the pursuit. The chief testified that he used due caution and care. The cycle did in fact run off the road and the driver was killed. When asked if he would have terminated the chase if told to do so on the radio he said, "No, because they don't have the authority to do so," referring to being dispatched by a department other than his own. The average speed of the pursuit was calculated at 106 miles per hour. The violation was for suspected drunk driving which escalated to fleeing and eluding. At that time, fleeing and eluding the police was a misdemeanor.

Issues and Factors Considered

Several issue questions can be raised in viewing this pursuit. Was the officer pursing prior to putting on his overhead lights? Was the officer violating the law by failing to engage his overhead lights in the first two miles of the run? Did the officer drive with due care during the four mile pursuit? Did the officer follow his own policy? Was the officer's driving "a" proximate cause of the accident?

Commentary

The chief's speed in the first two miles of this route was in excess of the speed limit so he was legally required to engage his emergency lights. He was in violation of the law. His apparent intent indicates he was pursuing in the first two miles. It was felt the chief wanted to get as close as he could get before activating his emergency lights. The speed and manner in which this officer drove, particularly through a small village and by running a traffic light at such a high speed is likely to endanger himself and others on the roadway. The officer's driving was deemed to be reckless. Moreover, his cavalier attitude as to speed and his logic for his actions provide a basis for a jury to determine that he was at least "a" proximate cause of the accident. A relentless high-speed pursuit at night under these conditions gives rise to liability.

The agency policy was weak and ambiguous. The justification for a pursuit leaves the initiation and continuance up to the judgment of the officer. The policy also requires officers to consider the seriousness of the offense when making pursuit decisions. Officers are advised that they are never justified to willfully or wantonly disregard safety in accomplishing goals. Emergency lights and sirens must be used at all times. If, in an officer's opinion, the seriousness of the reason for the pursuit is outweighed by the likely potential for death, the pursuit should be discontinued. The policy also indicates that pursuits that are too long in duration or distance are not warranted. Prior to taking the author's deposition, but after his review of the case, settlement negotiations were held and the plaintiff prevailed.

Case 29: A Thirty-Five Second Pursuit Injures a Driver

Facts

This very brief pursuit lasted just thirty-five seconds. Two officers in a small village at 2:00 a.m. in the summer received a dispatch that young persons were drag racing in their community. The officers took up a position to observe traffic on the twenty-five mile per hour zoned main street. They noticed one black and one white Camero racing east out of town. They pulled out, turned on their emergency lights and siren, and attempted to stop the white Camero, which was the closest vehicle to them. Both vehicles sped up to over eighty-five miles per hour as they left the town. Just after reaching the city limits, and in accord with the departmental pursuit policy, the police driver said he was not going to be able to catch them at the city limits, so he terminated the pursuit. The police car slowed down after turning off the emergency lights. Both officers saw the lights go off on the camero as it rounded a small curve ahead them, and then saw sparks and observed the vehicle go airborne. The vehicle had run off the roadway and struck a utility pole seriously injuring the passenger. Officers did not see the black camero again. The plaintiff charged that the officer had a duty to the passenger plaintiff, that he failed to follow his policy, and drove recklessly. Plaintiff also complained the officer caused the driver of the camero to speed, and the village failed to provide pursuit driving training or issue a policy.

Issues and Factors Considered

The primary issues in this case were whether the police department had a reasonable pursuit policy, if the pursuit caused the driver of the white camero to speed, and wether the policy was obeyed by the officers. The question of whether the department was obliged to train its officers in how to conduct a pursuit was also at issue.

Commentary

From depositions it was learned that there were no other vehicles on the roadway. At the accident scene, the driver of the camero said the reason he did not stop was because he knew the police were behind him. He also said the passenger told him the "Cops are behind you, don't stop, go, go." The driver of the police car stated that he knew the pursuit would be futile so he stopped it at the village limits.

The small police department did in fact have a policy and that policy was adapted from the state police policy. It offers officers sound guidance on pursuit decision making. It also requires officers to abort pursuits at the city limits if to continue would be dangerous or there was little hope of apprehension.

It would be an inferential leap to assume that the speed of the fleeing vehicle was caused by the police. The driver had ample opportunity to stop, and he was aware of their presence behind him. He chose to turn off his headlights, and he later stated he did not realize how dark it was at the time. Once he turned off his lights he attempted to turn them back on as he could not see and that is when he ran off the road.

At trial the circuit judge said the jury did not need an expert to testify on the efficacy of policy. He said the policy was not the relevant issue. In pursuits, the court said, the only issue to address as to liability of the police is whether their driving was reckless or proper. After a four day trial a jury found no cause of action for the defendant. The short duration of this pursuit, the officer's decision to terminate for safety reasons and the driving of the camero were the salient factors considered. As minimal as this pursuit appeared to be, it is a good example of a seemingly reasonable police action leading to the high expenditures of a defense

Case 30: High-Speed Pursuit Ends in the Death of Two Cyclists

Facts

This pursuit was 2.6 miles in length on a two lane paved country road at 2:15 a.m. during the summer months. The road was clear and dry, but it was a narrow, bumpy, crowned road with soft narrow shoulders. Several large trees were located at the edge of the road. There were many road repair bumps along the road and the maximum fifty-five mile per hour state speed limit would have been at the outer limits of safety.

Two city police officers noticed a motorcycle with a passenger driving slowly past a gas station. They suspected the persons might be checking out the location for a future break-in and decided to follow the cycle long enough to get the registration number for future reference. The officers also noted that the passenger on the cycle appeared young and they could see long hair from under the helmet. After following the cycle for seven blocks through the city they activated the overhead lights to stop the driver and get his/her identification at an intersection stop sign. The intersection was one half mile from the city limit. When they turned on their emergency lights the driver of the cycle wheeled his vehicle on to one tire and sped away. At this point the officers called in a pursuit. The officers both testified that they still did not want to do more than obtain the license number. For the next 2.6 miles they pursued the cycle on the country road.

Six tenths of a mile into the pursuit the police driver testified, at his first deposition, that he got behind and to the left of the cycle to see the license plate. At that time both vehicles were traveling at 100 miles per hour. He said he was seven to ten feet to the left and rear of the cycle in the passing lane. The cycle continued to speed and ran a stop sign at a high rate of speed 2.1 miles into the pursuit. The police admit running that same sign, but said they slowed to fifty-five miles per hour to do so.

At a point 2.35 miles into the pursuit the road curves sharply to the right. The police stated they slowed at this point and decided to terminate the chase because they knew the curve could not be negotiated at a high speed. The police driver said on the radio, "Its out of hand!" They continued with overhead lights for some distance, but did not see that the cycle had run off the roadway to the left on the curve. The cycle crashed, injuring the driver and killing the passenger. The officers drove for another mile searching the shoulders for the cycle, but to no avail. The officers testified they drove along both shoulders at twenty miles per hour for some distance looking for the cycle, but found nothing. Prior to reaching the location of the stop sign, 2.1 miles into the pursuit, the officers received the registration information from their dispatcher on the cycle. The driver and the passenger were found after daylight when noticed by a passing motorist .

Issues and Factors Considered

This case presents several issues. First, was whether the officers had reasonable suspicion to stop the cycle. Second, was the content of the departmental policy. Third, was whether the officer violated the policy. A fourth issue was the manner of the officer's driving. Fifth, the environmental conditions had to be examined to see if they boded for or against a pursuit. Finally, an issue of reckless driving had to be addressed.

Commentary

The chief of the police, after reviewing all the reports and depositions, testified that the officer should have terminated the pursuit as soon as he had the license plate number. The policy in force was sufficient to provide officers sound guidance. After the chief's deposition the police driver went back over the pursuit route and changed his testimony in his second deposition. He said that he made an error, and after re-driving the road he estimates his speed when immediately behind the cycle was more like seventy-eight miles per hour rather than the one hundred miles per hour he had previously testified he was driving. More importantly, he said it was not .6 of a mile into the pursuit when he got the license number, rather it was 1.8 miles into the pursuit.

On scene observations and measurements were made. It was determined that the police officer could not have terminated where he said he did, but had to be no less than 1,320 feet behind the cycle when it ran off the curve to the left. In order to see the tail lights of the cycle, the officer had to be that close. There is no doubt the driver of the motorcycle was reckless. The road could not support safe speeds over fifty-five miles per hour, and in some places that is doubtful. The cycle driver had a blood alcohol level of .125 and did not have a valid driver's license.

The police driver's behavior was imprudent, reckless and unreasonable. His actions violated accepted police standards. The author supported his attempt at an investigatory stop of a suspicious circumstance. He could have stopped the cycle sooner and obtained identification. The practice of closing to within seven and twelve feet at such speeds with a motorcycle is reckless and likely to result in an accident. Along the entire pursuit route, under the physical conditions present, any reasonable driver should conclude that an accident was likely to occur.

The original attempt of escape by the cycle driver provided the officer with the grounds to attempt to stop him. It is the protracted high speed and reckless manner in which the pursuit was conducted that should have been terminated. Driving through a stop sign at fifty-five miles per hour under the conditions presented violated a reasonable standard of care. After documenting the facts in a police report to an outside investigative agency and in a sworn deposition, the officer in this case changed his version of those facts. No one can show that the officers' attempt to locate the cycle after it had crashed was not reasonable. It was clear that they believed that the cyclist had escaped. The terminal point of the motorcycle was fifteen feet to the left of the road in some brush, and such that it could only be seen if one were on foot walking the shoulder with a flashlight.

The motorcycle driver's insistence on driving recklessly and under the influence of alcohol was the proximate cause of the death of the passenger. If this case had gone before a jury the author is convinced the police would have been considered contributory and determined to be a proximate cause. When asked to assign an estimate of culpability to the police, the author considered it was fifty percent. The matter was settled for the plaintiff prior to going to trial . In the state in which the accident occurred the standard for liability was comparative negligence, thus if an agency is found to be fifty percent at fault by a jury, a judgment of one million dollars would cost the jurisdiction one half million dollars.

Case 31: Emergency Response Results in Liability

Facts

Though technically not a pursuit, the following case of purported emergency driving provides some insight into the potential for liability resulting from a lack of knowledge of policy and the law. The injury accident between a motorist and a speeding police car took place shortly after midnight in early summer on a forty mile per hour posted business loop of a U.S highway that traversed a college town of 45,000 population. Traffic was light to medium and many pedestrians were out frequenting fast food businesses. A county officer, who was parked in a hospital parking lot checking other vehicles, overheard a city police radio transmission from an officer requesting a second unit and a supervisor at the scene of a domestic call. Though not assigned, the officer decided to respond on his own. He was aware of the address and had been there in the past on domestic trouble.

Driving southbound through the city, in a business and restaurant district, the officer stated he was driving somewhere around forty-five miles per hour. He stated, as he neared a lighted intersection, he slowed to get around another vehicle then sped up continuing south. A short distance further the officer noticed a vehicle attempting to make a left hand turn in front of him. That driver pulled back over to avoid the oncoming police car. The police car veered, but hit the motorist broadside injuring the driver of that vehicle. The police car did not have its emergency lights or siren activated.

The city police had five patrols out that evening and did not request the officer's aid. The officer said he felt the run was urgent. He said he was southbound and saw the other vehicle in the northbound inside lane. He looked in his rear mirror, and when he turned around the vehicle was right in front of him. The parent agency investigated the accident. The supervisor noted that it was not a pursuit, but he felt it was assistance and in the officer's mind it was an emergency. He recommended three days suspension for the officer's failure to have his emergency equipment activated. Interestingly, the supervisor in his deposition said, "The officer was technically speeding, but ninety percent of the people do it, so what." Moreover, the supervisor indicated that individual officers develop policies for themselves. A fellow officer testified that he did not think it was an emergency and felt that no one was in danger.

The officer said whoever is driving makes the decision to activate the emergency lights. When asked if he had to put the light on if he were over the speed limit he indicated he would look at each situation from its own perspective because every situation is different. The officer said when he is on a run he is not thinking about speed. An accident reconstructionist determined the speed of the injured motorist's vehicle to be fourteen miles per hour at impact. The police car pre-impact speed was sixty-three to sixty-seven miles per hour.

Issues and Factors Considered

The first issue was whether the officer's self initiated response could be considered an emergency. Another factor was the officer exceeding the speed limit without activating the emergency equipment. One has to consider whether the officer's driving was the proximate cause of the injury to the driver of the other vehicle. The disciplinary action taken by the department was also considered a factor in forming opinions and conclusions.

Commentary

Based on the testimonies of officer and his supervisor, supported by six outside witnesses to the accident, the emergency lights were not on. In order to be afforded protection, in response to an emergency or when pursuing a criminal or suspect, the police are required by law to activate their emergency equipment. As to whether his response was in fact an emergency is a matter of conjecture. One other officer who followed him did not think it was. Case law indicates it does not have to be an actual emergency, but only has to be so in the mind of the officer. Facts must be considered to determine if his view was correct. Whether it was or was not an emergency, the police officer violated the law in making the response that he did, and his driving was the proximate cause of the injury. This case illustrates a need for further training of officers and supervisors of the agency involved as to the law, good judgment and justification for tactical decisions. The fact the agency gave the officer three days off indicated they felt he was culpable. The police department was held liable and paid an undisclosed amount to the plaintiff.

Case 32: Youthful Eluder Killed after a Ten-Mile Pursuit

Facts

The primary claim in this case was the police demonstrated negligent operation of the police vehicles. The case went to circuit court for trial and a jury determined no cause for action against the defendants. They determined the officers' driving was not negligent.

At 10:00 p.m. on a July evening a deputy sheriff had just turned on to a state trunk line highway, and he was driving eastbound when he noticed two vehicles coming westbound about one mile ahead. He noticed that after one vehicle passed the other, the passing driver rapidly narrowed the gap between himself and the deputy. The deputy felt the driver of the sports car was exceeding the fifty-five mile per hour limit. Utilizing his radar, he obtained a clock on the oncoming vehicle at ninety miles per hour. The deputy activated his overhead lights and attempted to get the vehicle to stop, but it sped by him going west and increased its speed.

The officer made a U-turn and pursued the vehicle westward. He radioed his dispatcher that he was in pursuit of a small sports car and was east of a small village to the west. In that village another deputy heard the radio traffic and turned his vehicle to face west. He began to drive westerly hoping to stop the vehicle as it entered the village. The second police vehicle had all of its emergency lights activated, but the speeding sports car did not slow down. The second officer confirmed that the first deputy's emergency lights were activated as well as his siren.

Leaving the village, the second deputy took over as the primary vehicle. The highway is a two lane road, was dry and has a few up and down grades. In the village the 35 mile per hour posted road was a four lane road, but was reduced to two lanes west of the village. The road had edge markings, a painted centerline and gravel shoulders. The sports car traversed the village at over eighty-five miles per hour, according to the second police driver.

West of the village the primary police vehicle got to eighty miles per hour, but the sports car was pulling away from him. One and one half miles west of the village the sports car made an abrupt turn to the south on a gravel road. The primary car could not negotiate the turn and ran off the road to the left. The original pursuing officer again became the primary car. One mile south of the highway the sports car overshot an eastbound gravel road, turned around and then drove easterly. The gravel road was rough with no definite shoulders, and it was bordered with trees and shrubs. It was open country and no residences were observed.

After driving east for one mile there is another gravel road controlled with a stop sign for east and westbound traffic. The officer lost sight of the pursued vehicle as it reached that intersection. He felt the vehicle turned at that intersection. Arriving at the intersection he searched northward and the second deputy searched southward.

On their return to the intersection the officers located the sports car in the northeast quadrant. It had gone airborne over a drainage ditch and hit a telephone pole head on. The driver was dead at the scene. The total distance of the pursuit was 9.6 miles. Seven and one half miles of that length were on the paved state trunk line roadway.

Issues and Factors Considered

One issue was to determine if the officers' driving was reasonable under the conditions. Another issue involved determining whether the officers had a right or duty to apprehend the speeding motorist. In light of the length of the pursuit it had to be decided whether the officers should have terminated the pursuit. As in all pursuit cases, the policy and the officers' driving behaviors had to be examined.

Commentary

The officers remained at a respectable distance behind the sports car throughout the chase. Neither officer ever got close enough to obtain a license number or identify the actual make of the vehicle. There were no other vehicles on the road at the time of this pursuit, and both officers advised they were aware of the conditions and were evaluating the conditions throughout the pursuit. Both officers testified they felt the conditions of the pursuit warranted continuance.

The officers stated that due to the excessive speed of the sports car and the fact that the driver was aware of the two police vehicles and chose not to stop, they may have had a serious crime incident. They did not endanger any other drivers on the road because there were none. The officers' tactics revealed they attempted to keep the vehicle in sight, but did not attempt to overtake the sports car. The proximate cause was determined to be the driving behaviors of the sports car driver. He chose to fail to stop for two marked and lighted patrol cars. His speed, reckless driving and inability to negotiate a turn at the intersection caused his death. It was learned after the fatality that the victim's mother, the plaintiff, had recently purchased the sports car for her son. He was an inexperienced driver having only recently obtained his license to drive. A jury trial was held and the defendants prevailed.

Case 33: A Terminated Pursuit Results in Liability

Facts

This pursuit began in one jurisdiction when a police supervisor working the road attempted to stop a driver at 5:00 a.m. in the morning for suspicion of driving under the influence of alcohol. After a short and low-speed pursuit, through the first community, the eluding driver ran into a curb at a right angle. The originating officer and a back-up officer from a neighboring community attempted to box-in the vehicle at the curb. The offender rammed the two police cars, got away and sped off through two more jurisdictions. After 10.6 miles, the eluder hit an oncoming vehicle head on. That vehicle was crossing a narrow bridge at the time of impact. The eluding driver and the other driver were killed instantly.

The first agency officer followed the vehicle at thirty-five miles per hour. He testified the driver was weaving back and forth and hitting curbs. He called for assistance to make a stop and a second agency officer assisted. When the eluder's vehicle came to a stop perpendicular against a curb the officer from the first and second agency blocked his vehicle. The offender then put his car in gear and rammed his way out of the block and sped southward. At this point the pursuit was initiated. The road at this point was a two lane road that was dry and in an industrial area, and there was no other traffic on the road. The first police officer followed the speeding vehicle for another mile and then terminated his pursuit. The officer from the second jurisdiction got up to one hundred miles per hour, but he could not get close to the escaping vehicle. He too terminated his pursuit.

The speeding vehicle traversed another jurisdiction and finally entered a fourth. An officer from the fourth jurisdiction was able to get behind the speeder. During his pursuit another officer from his department, at a stationary position, clocked the speeder on radar at 105 miles per hour as he passed his point of observation. Shortly after this clocking, and another mile down the road, the driver lost control at a bridge, hit a northbound vehicle coming across the bridge and drove that vehicle one hundred feet backwards killing himself and the innocent motorist.

A one week trial was held in circuit court. Plaintiff's primary position was the police officers chasing the fleeing car were the cause of his client's speed. The theory provided to the jury by plaintiff was had the officers all stopped the speeder would have resumed normal driving.

It should be noted that he was intoxicated and a resumption to normal driving would likely had ended in the same manner. After lengthy trial and fifteen hours of expert witness testimony, the jury absolved the second and third police departments, but awarded plaintiff 3.5 million dollars in damages against the originating department. The original officer, who had terminated the pursuit much earlier, arrived at the accident scene over three minutes after the crash.

Issues and Factors Considered

Several questions are posed here in the form of rhetorical questions. Did the first police department officer act reasonably in attempting to stop an intoxicated driver? Was the intentional damage to police department property a felony ? Should the officers have pursued the driver after he rammed their vehicles and sped off ? Did the officers from the first and second department act responsibly by terminating their pursuits? Was the officer from the original department the proximate cause of the deaths of two persons several miles distant from his location?

Commentary

This case was puzzling. The first officer clearly terminated his pursuit. The termination was documented and supported by the other officers. It is reasonable, and even a duty, to stop a suspected drunk driver. Causing intentional damage to police property is a felony, and both officers were warranted in attempting to capture such a driver who was also fleeing. Both the first and second officer showed responsible thinking when they aborted their portions of the pursuit. The first officer terminated because he lost sight of the speeding vehicle. The second terminated because he did not wish to drive over one hundred miles per hour.

The original officer was several miles to the north when the crash took place. Interestingly, the fourth department officer was one quarter mile behind the speeder when the crash took place, but this was not a factor in the jury's deliberations. It was clear to the author that the jury bought the idea that had the police slowed down the speeder would have also slowed down. This so-called cat and mouse theory was heavily pressed during the trial. For their own reasons, the jurors disregarded clear evidence presented that the originating police driver was not culpable. This case points out the pitfalls of going forward with a trial.

Summary

The general attitudes of some police officers, and their lack of knowledge and preparation have often worked against their own agencies' defenses. Some officers have been observed to just lie about details such as how close they were to the pursued vehicle or how fast they were driving. Others have claimed to have their emergency lights activated only to have credible witnesses refute their claims. Some few have a misguided view of their authority. Others do not bother to review their own pursuit policy and have testified that the last time they saw the policy was during their early trainee days. A few have not understood the law on pursuits. However, the majority of officers encountered in law suits have done a credible job

A few administrators have overlooked obvious violations of policy by their officers to avoid the appearances of having been in the wrong. This tactic is apparently employed to avoid litigation when in fact it works against the agency for failing to take appropriate remedial action.

The most common problem observed in pursuit cases is the failure to fully document detail in the police reports. Those reports are the official record of the police department. When an officer's court room or deposition testimony differs substantially from the report a tremendous burden is placed on the agency to settle a case.

Most officers do not intentionally write a report to be ambiguous or incomplete. Some do so because they are familiar with the conditions, and they assume others are as well. They do not think that there may be others, beyond the police audience, that will read the report later. Others do not write a complete report because of their general disinterest. Others yet may fear discipline because they violated one or more elements of the policy. Plainly, some officers are not properly trained to write a detailed police report. The majority of these practices are supervisory and training problems. Most of them can be rectified by responsible management.

There is no bright line test to know exactly when to pursue or exactly when to terminate a pursuit once one has been initiated. Statutes provide some guidance, but they are not always specific. A lot is left to conjecture when deciding what driving with due care means. Some police agencies may opt for a no pursuit policy, but this posture, when carefully examined, does not make much sense or provide adequate protection for society. If a person injured someone in an accident and left the scene, is the officer not to attempt to capture the person if he or she is able to do so? Is a message sent to violators that one need only drive over the limit to avoid capture?

Might such a policy lead to several dangerous drivers on the road-ways? These and similar questions continue to plague the police.

Some departments address the pursuit problem by limiting pursuits to felonies; others limit pursuits to serious life threatening felonies. It is seldom possible for an officer to know when the driver of a fleeing vehicle is involved in a felony. Some police department policies are discretionary, but this does not offer the officer guidance on what to do either. That one position on the continuum fulcrum of the state's need to apprehend and the citizen's right to be protected from the unreasonable risk of harm is very difficult to pinpoint.

The question as to whether a majority of pursuits are inherently dangerous is still a matter in need of further study. Those that end in the injury and death to others are certainly dangerous. However, to espouse that the majority of pursuits end in injury or death is not empirically supported. Moreover, it is not clear that the police involvement in pursuits necessarily means they are a proximate cause of resultant injuries or deaths.

Successful pursuits that are conducted without accident or injury, but go unreported, have been referred to as the dark figure of pursuits. If all pursuits conducted were known and factored into the calculus perhaps they would be considered no more dangerous than many other police practices.

Because many pursuits have ended in fatalities police departments must train their officers for such practices. Police departments should also have reasonably sound policies that are realistically restrictive. Moreover, administrators must review these activities and hold errant officers accountable, regardless of their fears of future litigation. Though costly, departments would be wise to install video cameras in patrol cars and consider not allowing a pursuit unless a vehicle is so equipped, except in extreme cases.

Perhaps technology will provide some help. Though not empirically evaluated to any degree, the conventional wisdom is that stop strips work well in stopping pursuits. These too have limits and work best only when there is advance notice of an ongoing pursuit and officers equipped with the technology are in a position to utilize them. The technology to electronically stop a vehicle engine and bring a fleeing vehicle to a safe stop is already available. Studies are underway to evaluate this system. Costs may prove to be prohibitive and there are few guarantees that such a system could not be neutralized.

One location in the northeast United States actually tested a mobile harpoon system that the officer activated to impale the speeding vehicle. As the patrol car slowed down the impaled speeding vehicle would also be forced to slow down. That futile effort seems doomed from the start for a host of reasons, the least of which is its potential for deadly force.

Several states have training programs to teach officers how to force a vehicle off the road. This practice is designed to prevent a collision with an innocent motorist, but in fact it is a police initiated collision that may result in the death or injury of the pursued driver. Ramming a pursued vehicle is a 4th Amendment issue, and it would appear to have its sole application in cases where deadly force could be legally employed. Recent court decisions appear to be favoring police officers in pursuit so long as they have a sound policy and have followed the policy.

Observations made by the author in reviewing over fifty-five pursuit litigations reveals a growing tendency on the part of police departments to administratively terminate a pursuit if it is determined that the only known violation for which the pursuit was initiated was a traffic offense. This is particularly so among departments that have been successfully sued for past pursuits. Only a few states have legislation providing for mandatory uniform police pursuit policies. Attempts to legislatively place caps on liability judgments have been met with stiff resistance from trial lawyers associations in the past.

The police in America are fragmented. There are 18,760 police agencies in the United States employing 695,378 sworn officers (Source Book 1997). There are forty-nine state police organizations with over 54,000 sworn officers. Some have general police powers and others have a more limited focus such as highway patrol agencies. A few states have the uniform patrol units in one sub-organization and the criminal investigative in another. There are 3,088 county sheriff departments with 174,673 officers. Some are small and limit their role to running the county jail and serving papers, while others are full-fledged general police agencies. Some others are county-wide departments that handle all crimes in every jurisdiction within the county.

The 13,540 local police agencies account for 420,152 sworn officers. There are township police departments and municipal police departments. Some township police departments just enforce traffic regulations while others are broad based. There are town marshals and small village police departments. Texas alone has 751 agencies employing 1,038 officers. Most of the police agencies in the United States are small in the number of officers employed. Considering such fragmentation and the variations of policy, training and administrative variances, it is logical to conclude that police pursuits will continue to be a problem area for police administrators, their jurisdictions and the public at large.

Chapter 4

A Brief Review of Police Orders and Directives and Case Analyses

Police Orders and Directives

Departmental orders or directives should be a standard feature of every police organization. Official orders become the administration foundation of all programs and operations in that they specify the parameters of organizational behavior through policies, procedures, rules and regulations. Such orders outline the authority, responsibility and duties of each position in the agency (Carter 1986; Leonard and More 1974).

Unfortunately, it is common for a smaller law enforcement agency to have limited directives, orders which are dated, orders which are non-functional or, in the worst case, no written directives at all. The need for written, comprehensive and clearly written directives cannot be over emphasized. This is particularly important in light of the recent history of litigation against police departments of all sizes. At the outset of this chapter it is important to stipulate the meaning of several critical terms (Payne and Carter 1997).

Policy

The principles and values which guide the performance of the departmental activity is a policy. A policy is not a statement of what must be done in a particular situation; rather, it is a statement of guiding principles which should be followed on activities which are directed toward the attainment of departmental objectives. Policies are formulated by analyzing objectives and are based on police ethics and experiences, the desires of the community and mandates of the law. A policy is articulated to inform the public and the departmental employees of the principles which will be adhered to in the performance of the law enforcement function (Los Angeles Police Department 1982).

Objective

An objective is a desired end for which an agency effort is expended. An objective contributes to the mission of the department and, if attained, contributes to the fulfillment of the department's defined purposes.

Procedure

A procedure is a method of performing an operation or a manner of proceeding on a course of action (e.g. how to conduct a liquor inspection). It differs somewhat from a policy in that it directs action in a particular situation to perform a specific task within the guidelines of policy. An example of a procedure would be departmental handcuffing procedures. Policies and objectives are both objective oriented. However, a policy establishes limits on action while a procedure directs responses within those limits (Carter and Dearth 1984).

Rule

A rule is a specific requirement or prohibition which is stated to prevent deviations from policies and procedures. Rules allow little deviation other than for stated exceptions. A violation of a rule typically involves an internal investigation and may result in disciplinary action. Regulations are synonymous with a rules.

General Order

A general order is a written directive that pertains to permanent policies and procedures for general departmental operations and exists for an indefinite future. The general order is the medium by which policies, procedures and/or rules on a specific issue or entity are presented to departmental members.

Special Order

A special order is also a written directive of a policy or procedure, but it is designed for a specific unit, as opposed to an entire department. A special order may also apply to a specific event of a temporary nature. Most special orders are self-canceling.

Written Directive

Written directives are terms used to collectively describe policies, procedures, rules, regulations, orders or memoranda (Payne and Carter 1997).

Most police departments have a book that is known as the manual. This is a book or series of books that contain all of the agency rules, regulations, policies and procedures. Some agencies refer to the manual as SOP or standard operating procedures. Carter and Dearth (1984) feel that such directives are essential for police agencies in order to maintain organizational control and accountability and to ensure compliance with a myriad of legal stipulations. In short, such a manual states the departmental philosophy, and gives members information as to their role and anticipated behavior in the agency.

Though procedures and policies differ somewhat, they are often combined into one directive. Most departmental rules and regulations stipulate the duties of each rank of the department and provide information so officers know what they are responsible for and who they must report to (e.g. the chain of command).

No rule, regulation, policy or procedure is of much value unless the members are thoroughly trained in the meaning of the document and administratively held accountable for their actions. McCoy (1985) observed in her analysis of police liability cases that the failure to train officers properly or the failure to supervise them so that they adhere to constitutional standards are sufficient grounds to bring supervisors, the agency as a whole and the governing body of the department into liability. As cited by del Carmen (1986), a significant and consistent number of cases have been settled in favor of plaintiffs at costs of millions of dollars to law enforcement agencies because proper direction was not given to officers for performing their tasks. As stated earlier, though all departments are sued smaller departments, typically those without effective orders, training and supervision suffer the greatest number and propensity for lawsuits.

The assigned duties and tasks confronted by police officers in the course of their careers are too numerous to list. It is impossible to develop policies and procedures for each potential incident an officer confronts. Based on their training, education and experience police officers have to make decisions on the appropriate action to take under any given set of circumstances. The overall general policy of a department may provide some guidance, and specific objectives provide some insight into the desired end state to be achieved, but this still does not provide specifics for the host of variable situations encountered on the street.

Education for the police is critical and must be a never-ending process. Much of an officer's professional education comes from the experience of other officers and testing by trial and error the decisions made by themselves or others in similar incidents.

Emotional stability, maturity and intuitiveness all play a role by assisting the officer in making decisions on the street. Maintaining high entrance standards, recruiting only the best and conducting thorough detailed background investigations on future officers all have a bearing on the quality of the decision making of police officers. A police officer's world view should, ideally, be compatible to the ideals of the ethical police agency.

In many law suits brought against the police there may not be a specific rule, policy or procedure that applies to the facts of the incident. In many cases the only defense may be that the officers conducted themselves consistent with accepted conventional police wisdom or standards. That is, they acted in a way that it is recognized by police professionals everywhere to be the right thing to do. Some standards are written such as standards of CALEA, the American Bar Association or the President's Commission. More often than not, however, the act is judged against accepted police practices. Another test of appropriate police action is to ask oneself what would a well trained, ethical, reasonable police officer have done under similar circumstances and why?

Higher Standards Required

The police are the only social control agency in the United States that are provided the discretionary use of coercive power. These powers are granted to the police by the public to maintain an orderly society within the constraints of the law and the Constitution. The police may detain and question a person, make arrests, and use necessary force up to and including deadly force under certain conditions. Such awesome power was not bestowed to be misused, but it is held in the public trust and exists for the general good and safety of the body politic. Providing the police with the authority to deprive a person of liberty, as in an arrest, or to take one's life, as in the application of deadly force, would be ludicrous without appropriate controls in place. Such awesome authority should be carefully circumscribed by responsible management, appropriate legal safeguards, rules and regulations, codes of ethics, and higher standards than those imposed on the general public.

Police officer violations of laws, rules or standards require police executives to take definitive action to ensure organizational integrity and to uphold the public trust. The high standards apply not only to issues of force, but include how officers investigate crimes, respond to calls for assistance, and provide their day to day services.

Some jurists have said that violations of the law by those appointed to protect instead of destroy personal security deserve no favor. Skolnick and Woodworth (1967) support the concept of the need for internal discipline in police departments and the necessity of organizations to be able to detect infractions prior to imposing sanctions. Accountability is absolutely necessary in police departments. It applies to improperly performed police responses just as strongly as it applies to extra-legal police activities. Police administrators must therefore have systems in place to monitor and contend with not only violations of rules, regulations, policies and procedures, but also to receive citizen reports of improper behaviors. The efficacy of a police department varies directly with its capacity to observe and receive reports of transgressions (Skolnick and Woodworth 1967).

A case that has application to higher standards for the police is *Parker v. Levy* (1974). In that case, the court upheld different and higher standards of the military as opposed to that of ordinary citizens. The issue was conduct unbecoming an officer and a gentleman. The Supreme Court upheld a court martial because of the differentials between the military and civil society. Such differentials have obvious application to policing. The court noted that Congress is permitted to legislate with greater breath and flexibility when prescribing rules for the military.

The rules for the police should be no less stringent. Justice Black-man once emphasized that articles of conduct are not only to pun-ish potential criminal conduct, but also to foster an orderly and du-tiful fight force. This is not unlike the need for a chief or sheriff to require an orderly force.

Payne (1988) noted the different character of the police force, as a semi-military organization, as described by rules, regulations, rank structures and discipline requires the application of standards that are quite different than those applied to the public. This higher standard is frequently referred to in the context of the public trust.

Sellars v. Lamb (1942) regarding contracts relative to the perfor-mance of duty or trust, noted if a contract of a public officer inter-feres with the unbiased discharge of his duty to the public, in view of his official position, or if it tends to induce him to violate his duty to the public, the contract is against public policy and void. The Michigan Compiled Laws, for example, have statutes covering the wilful neglect of duty and the failure to uphold and enforce the law. Other cases related to the topic of higher standards for the po-lice include (*O'Dell v. Civil Service Commission of Flint* 1950; *Ri-naldi v. Livonia* 1976; and *Royal v. Ecorse Police and Fire Commis-sioners* 1956).

Delegation of Authority

In a properly organized police department, the chief executive of-ficer delegates authority for decision making to people at all levels in the agency. Such delegated authority provides the power to make decisions and perform tasks. The ultimate authority lies with the chief executive who must wisely delegate his/her authority so that sound decisions can be made and business can be properly con-ducted.

Those to whom such authority is delegated are expected to use the authority responsibly in the public's best interest. Only by such delegation can the executives be assured that their organizations will continue to function when they are not physically present (Sheehan and Cordner 1989). Souryal (1976) posits that delegation refers to conferring of a special authority by a higher authority. In essence, delgation is a dual responsibility. The principle of the dele-gation of authority remains at the center of all formal organiza-tions.

Accountability

Executives should be aware that there is always the possibility that those who have been delegated authority may misuse or abuse it. Systems must be in place for monitoring all activities. Such systems include a readiness to receive citizen complaints, internal investigations, disciplinary systems, rules and regulations, inspections, and official reporting systems. This system is based on the concept of accountability.

Police Procedure Cases

Case 34: Unattended Police Car is Stolen: Subsequent Chase Results in Injury

Facts

A 2:20 a.m. during the summer a woman called the police department dispatcher and requested officers arrest her husband on several outstanding felony warrants. Her husband, she reported, had previous arrests for assaulting police officers. She provided a description of the vehicle she would be driving and requested the officers make the arrest as a result of a routine traffic stop. Officers verified the wanted status of her husband and assigned units. Officers assigned to the task observed her vehicle traveling on a main artery in the large metropolitan city. They observed a woman driving with a male passenger. The vehicle was stopped, despite attempts by the man to commandeer the vehicle from his wife. The police boxed the car in to the curb, arrested her husband, handcuffed him, and placed him in the rear seat of a semi-marked police car.

The semi-marked car was not equipped with a prisoner cage. The man was left unattended though several officers were within view. The man managed to free himself from his restraints, jumped over the seat, and took control of the police car which had been left running. He then escaped by driving off at a high speed through a business district and then into a residential area. The man in the stolen police car drove for over two miles. He ran two stop signs and then ran through a Yield Right of Way intersection. The pursing police car, directly behind him, followed the stolen car through the controlled intersection without slowing down. The driver of the police car hit a vehicle broadside injuring a woman and himself. A command officer near the scene terminated the pursuit. The felon was later captured in the general area. An accident reconstructionist determined the patrol car speed, at the time of impact, to be a minimum of fifty-nine miles per hour in the twenty-five mile an hour posted zone.

Issues and Factors Considered

Though ostensibly retained to determine the liability of the police on the pursuit and resultant injury, the precipitating events had to be considered. The response to the call to arrest the man was examined as was the method of boxing him in. The placement of the arrestee in an uncaged patrol car and the method used in handcuffing him was also viewed to determine if any of those tactics had any bearing on the subsequent pursuit crash.

Commentary

The original response to the woman's call for help was positive. Five officers were assigned to this task. Warrants were verified prior to assigning officers to make the stop. Once stopped, the husband of the woman jammed his foot on the gas pedal and attempted to leave the arrest scene. He crashed into a road construction barricade a few feet away, and the officers appropriately boxed him in without colliding with the vehicle so the arrest could be made.

The decision to place the man in an uncaged and running police vehicle was a poorly thought out procedure. At least three other cage-equipped police cars were on the scene. The officer's explanation for doing this was he did not want the other officers thinking he was pushing the arrest off on them by putting the man in one of their marked-caged cars. That justification was not sound. The officers handcuffed the struggling man, but he complained the cuffs were too tight. Reacting to concerns of a complaint of excessive force, three officers assisted each other in reapplying the cuffs. It is believed that the man used a finger to keep a wide gap on the cuffs during this confusing procedure to later facilitate his own release. A visual check of the secured cuffs should have been conducted.

Leaving a police car running at the scene unattended is poor police procedure. Had the keys been removed the worst that could have happened would have been an escape on foot. The officer directly behind the fleeing man was too close and driving too fast for the conditions. His running of the yield sign was the proximate cause of the injury to the innocent woman. A series of procedural errors compounded this situation and contributed to the end result. An after action review of the arrest and hand cuffing procedure was recommended. There was no specific policy requiring all arrestees to be placed in only in caged cars. Had the officers properly handcuffed the man or placed him in a secured patrol car this incident would not have occurred. The author recommended the department settle the suit.

Case 35: Interfering Arrest in a Volatile Situation

Facts

Two police officers were called to a trailer park at 12:30 a.m. by a woman who reported suspicious youths hanging around her trailer. Officers advised her they would check the area, but she was irate over their apparent lack of concern, and she said if the kids came back she would get rid of them with a baseball bat. Less than a hour later the same two officers responded to the same park to a domestic dispute. The call was described as a man with a knife. The arriving officers located the trailer, knocked, and entered the trailer. On entering the trailer the officers observed over ten young people in various states of intoxication. All of the people were excited and yelling.

One officer located the potential assailant, searched him, and placed him in cuffs. The other officer identified the would be victim of the assault and ordered the rest of the group out of the trailer. After they all went to the attached porch the second officer took the victim to the porch to question her out of sight of her drunken boyfriend. Once on the porch, the officer asked everyone to get off the porch and wait in the yard so he could do his job. As he was starting to get the potential victim's side of the story, the woman from the first complaint ran up on the porch and began shouting orders to the officer. She was an aunt and had heard the call over a police scanner.

The officer asked her to get off the porch three times, but she insisted on interfering. At one point she put her finger to his nose and pushed him backwards knocking him off balance. At that point the officer told her she was under arrest for interfering with an officer in performance of his duty and for assaulting a police officer. She was placed face down on the porch, handcuffed, and taken to his patrol car. During the arrest process the intoxicated crowd out front yelled at the police officer who made the arrest shouting, Gestapo! Rodney King!, but none of them attacked the officer.

The investigation revealed the intoxicated boyfriend did not have a knife but did tell two other participants that he had one and was going to cut her up. Eventually, he was taken home and released to his parents. As soon as the arrest was made and it was determined that the so-called man with a knife call was not factual the officers went to their patrol cars.

In the patrol car, the woman who was arrested was crying and apologizing for assaulting the officer. A third officer came to the scene and interviewed her to get her side of the story. He supports the arrest as she did in fact admit her role and apologized again. As she was not intoxicated and partly because of the potentially unruly crowd, the arresting officer released her with a notice to appear ticket. She thanked him and the following day filed a law suit for excessive force claiming she was kicked when on the ground, cursed at by the officer, and had her head banged on the porch. She also had photos taken of bruises she received during her arrest.

Issues and Facts Considered

One issue was whether the officers were responding to a potentially dangerous call. Another was whether the officers followed good police procedure by ordering the persons out of the trailer and securing the alleged assailant. Ordering the persons off the porch was also a factor to consider. The legality and appropriateness of the woman's arrest was also an issue. One should examine whether it was a sound police procedure to release the arrested woman after she calmed down. Lastly, the wisdom of taking the intoxicated alleged assailant to his parents' home should be examined.

Commentary

Over fifteen depositions were reviewed prior to a circuit court trial on this matter. All but one of the deponents supported the officers account of what happened. No one saw the officer kick the woman or bang her head on the porch, but most were shocked at her arrest. The majority of the ten participants admitted to being somewhat intoxicated at the time. The third officer interviewed the arrestee in the patrol car and told the woman's husband he did this to avoid a law suit. Such remarks are very damaging and make the police appear over reactive. His statement may have prompted the law suit. The officers' conduct in separating the crowd was sound. The officers were in an unknown and potentially explosive environment. Ordering the remaining participants off the porch afforded the officer privacy to interview the victim as well as security from assault from a loud and drunken crowd. The officer's arrest of the woman was legal and proper. Police are not required to be assaulted, and under the conditions at the scene her presence and demeanor not only interfered with his ability to interview but could have acted as a spark to incite the crowd.

The officer's release of the penitent woman was allowable and humane, but such action could create a doubt in the mind of the person arrested that there was no legal basis for the arrest in the first place. In this matter, she later pled guilty to the charges. The release of a drunken youth to his parents is also a humane act, but such releases can often backfire. He could have gotten out of the house and driven or assaulted his parents. The officers used their best judgment based on the circumstances they confronted. Most of the decisions that were made were not covered by a policy, rule, or procedure. A trial was held in circuit court and the defendant police officers prevailed.

Case 36: Deliberate Indifference to Medical Needs Results in Suit

Facts

The plaintiff in the case sued a police department and its officers for a serious head injury he allegedly sustained in a fight he had with another individual in front of that person's residence. The plaintiff's claims were based on Section 1983 and state tort law under the concept of negligence. The plaintiff had been driving his car erratically down a street and he appeared to be out of control by the alleged assailant. The assailant was raking his yard. As the plaintiff passed his residence he threw a rake at plaintiff's vehicle to "wake him up." Plaintiff stopped and got out of his car and met with the assailant. A neighbor who said she witnessed the fight said that the assailant beat the plaintiff senseless, and she saw the plaintiff fall backwards on the street. She said she heard his head hit the pavement with an audible thump. The assailant believed the plaintiff to be unconscious. Another witness said after she saw the plaintiff fall on the ground he rolled over on his side, began to snore, and appeared to be sleeping.

The police arrived within minutes and found the plaintiff sleeping in the road in a pile of leaves with his head cushioned in his arms, and a bunch of leaves pushed under his head. A third witness told the officers that the plaintiff was drunk. One officer testified he smelled a strong odor of alcohol on the plaintiff. Both responding officers testified under oath that they did not observe any head injury that the plaintiff might have sustained. After the officers moved his car off the street the officer woke the plaintiff who rose and stood up and, with an officer holding each of his arms, he was walked to the patrol car.

There was some testimony from other witnesses that the officers laughed because this was not the first time he had been involved with the police for drinking. En route to the police station the plaintiff asked to lay down in the back seat of the car . He was told it was allowed as long as he did not get sick. He said that he did not feel sick.

At the police station a breathalyzer test revealed a blood alcohol level of .12 in his blood. In that state a level of .10 level or greater prohibits driving a motor vehicle. The plaintiff was placed in a cell at the police department where he spent an uneventful night. At 8:30 a.m. a janitor was required to clean up vomit in the plaintiff's cell. He was found sleeping on his cot. Plaintiff was told to wake up and did so just prior to his release. The supervisor on duty called plaintiff's father to come pick him up. In the meantime, the plaintiff went back to his cell to rest. The plaintiff returned home with his father and remained there for the next five days.

Plaintiff's parents testified they had no reason to suspect any illness or injury to their son over the next four days. They also testified there was no reason to believe that he needed medical treatment. On the fifth day after his release his parents called an ambulance to take him to the hospital, because he was having trouble breathing and was sweating profusely.

Plaintiff was diagnosed with skull fractures and several areas of hemorrhage in his head and brain. Surgery was performed and the blood clots were removed. His attending physician said plaintiff suffered multiple head injuries causing permanent brain damage which will affect his ability to communicate normally, result in memory loss, and cause him to experience personality changes. The doctor also offered that the injuries were consistent with falling backward on a street and hitting one's head on the pavement.

The plaintiff charged the police were deliberately indifferent to his medical needs in violation of the 8th and 14th Amendments. He further said that their failure to locate his injuries and tell his father of the fight caused his injuries. The plaintiff's position revolved around the officers not concluding that he was injured and thus needed medical treatment. The officers responded to a drunk call and were not told at the scene that he had struck his head on the pavement. The officers held the plaintiff never complained of any injury or illness.

Issues and Factors Considered

The first issue was to determine if the officers acted with deliberate indifference to the plaintiff's condition. Another issue was the officers' failure to interview potential witnesses at the scene. Other factors examined were the officers knew the assailant had a reputation for fighting and they should have conducted a broader investigation at the scene. Another issue was whether the police department had adequate policies or procedures to insure that officers conduct thorough investigations.

Commentary

Plaintiff denied being in a fight on two occasions. Though the polices were sufficient on their face, the chief testified that he has all the policies in a manual and the officers are supposed to read them. This is less than close supervision. The 8th Amendment did not apply because it applies to cruel and unusual punishment and is only applicable to sentenced criminals, whereas the Due Process Clause of the 14th Amendment does apply to citizens who have not been convicted of crimes (*Baily v. Andrews* 1987). The law in the judicial circuit in which the trial took place was that negligence or gross negligence of police officers is insufficient to establish a deprivation of life without due process (*Jackson v. City of Joliet* 1983).

The court held that unintended injuries to life, liberty or property by government officials does not violate a persons right to either procedural or substantive due process. If officers failed to notice an injury, but should have, it would be negligence and mere negligence is not sufficient in 1983 suits. The officers asked plaintiff on several occasions if he was ill or needed treatment. One jail officer checked the plaintiff's cell at 3:00 a.m, 3:30 a.m., and 5:30 a.m That officer testified the plaintiff was sleeping and he did not see any injury. Another jail officer checked on his status at 1:45 a.m., 2:00 a.m., 4:30 a.m. and 6:30 a.m.

What was problematic in this case was the fact the plaintiff was in a stupor with a blood alcohol level of .12 percent. The official orders require a person found unconscious or incapacitated be taken into protective custody due to that condition and then be taken to a hospital. The rule is somewhat ambiguous because it does not specify that being intoxicated is the same as being incapacitated. The officers should have investigated the details of the fight. The assailant was known to the officers as a combatant. He later came to the station and asked what the police were going to pin on him now. This statement should have alerted the officers to investigate further. The officers viewed the plaintiff as a typical drunk. While the officers may be considered to have been negligent in terms of not taking the plaintiff to the hospital, they were not deliberately indifferent to his needs.

Just prior to the trial, the court ordered a summary judgment for the defendants. Several weeks after the decision the attorney for the defendant officers advised that an investigation was underway. The plaintiff's father, irate over his son's continued drunkenness, was alleged to have pulled him out of his bed and thrown him on the floor. It is possible the father injured his son.

Case 37: A Failure to Fingerprint Results in Arrest of Wrong Man

Facts

The police of a metropolitan city received a radio call of an assault. When they arrived they found an unconscious woman lying on the ground with an obvious injury. They learned from a witness she had been beaten with a shovel. The victim awoke and she and a witness said they knew the assailants. The names and descriptions of both assailants were given to the police by the victim and her witness. One suspect was identified as Clarence Doe, a black male, twenty-five to thirty years of age, six foot and two inches tall , medium complexion with thin short hair. The second suspect was identified as Lorenzo Doe, a black male,thirty to thirty-five years of age, with a heavy build who is also known as Lionel. The victim said she knew about where they lived. The police took the report, but there was no indication they did any follow up with the information they had received.

The supplementary police report listed the names of the two brothers with ages of twenty-six and twenty-eight respectively. There were no records of photos taken of the victim's injuries or any description of her injuries in the police report. For reasons unknown to the author, and not obvious by reading the police reports, a warrant charging James Doe with assault with intent to commit murder was issued and placed in the police statewide computer network. No efforts were made to locate the suspect.

It appeared that Clarence Doe was arrested a few years earlier and gave the name of his younger brother James at the time. He was fingerprinted under the name of James. A second set of finger prints for Clarence Doe were in the police files and those prints matched those of the person previously printed as James Doe. Mug shots of each of the two brothers were also in the police files. There was little or no follow-up investigation by the police department, and no attempt was made to have a photo show up using police records. No active or documented attempts were made to arrest Clarence or Lorenzo Doe.

Seven months later James Doe was stopped in an adjacent city for a traffic violation and when the police ran a record check of him they learned he was wanted on a warrant for assault with intent to commit murder. He was arrested and, after spending four hours in the local lockup, he was transferred to the originating police department. He was not fingerprinted at the time of this arrest for the felony, although it is a misdemeanor in the state not to fingerprint a person arrested for a felony. James Doe was subsequently arraigned and released on bond.

A few weeks later he failed to show up for the preliminary examination and the court issued a bench warrant. He later came to the court with his attorney and showed proofs of being at a funeral, but the court rejected his excuse. His attorney met privately with the victim, out of sight of James Doe, and she identified him by name only as her assailant. As a result of this identification the attorney had James waive his examination and he was bound over for trial. James Doe remained incarcerated in jail for forty-six days while awaiting his trial.

On the day of the trial Clarence Doe was in the back of the court room. The victim saw Clarence Doe in the court room and identified him as her assailant. The prosecutor dismissed the charges against James Doe, and he subsequently brought suit against the police for false arrest and imprisonment. Not to his credit, and suspiciously, Mr. James Doe did not complain vociferously that his brother Clarence was using his name. The police had three sets of prints in their files on these persons. One set in 1986 are those of Clarence Doe. Another set taken in 1987 bear the name of James Doe, but are the same as those of Clarence. A third set of James Doe were taken in 1991 for a crime that was dismissed when it was learned once again Clarence was using his brother's name. The police contended that James Doe, with his brother Clarence, were in collusion, were obstructing justice, and were scamming the police for the purpose of bringing a law suit for false arrest. It should be noted that the physical description of James is very different from that of either of his two brothers.

Issues and Factors Considered

One factor was whether a reasonable effort was made to identify and arrest the suspects. Another issue was whether the investigative methods used by the police were consistent with accepted police standards. Failing to fingerprint an arrested felon, as required by law, is an issue to be considered. The nature of the police follow-up and any impact it may have had on the arrest of James Doe was also a factor to consider. While it is possible that the plaintiff was part of a conspiracy to dupe the police and thus provide a basis for a law suit, this factor should not be considered unless there was evidence indicating it was probable.

Commentary

It is quite possible that James Doe was part of a ruse to fool the police. It is particularly worrisome that he did not speak up to either department that he was the wrong person. That aside, the police in this case did a very poor job of investigation and there is little evidence the officers or the follow-up detectives were under any supervision or case supervision.

The victim identified both assailants by name and description and was willing to show the police where they lived. Had the police checked their records they would have found the fingerprints and other records on Clarence. If they picked up the suspects, the victim could have participated in a line up, but none was conducted. She also could have been asked to do a photo show up, and perhaps the false arrest could hve been avoided. After the original police report was taken, the case was assigned to the detectives and there is little evidence they did anything other than obtain a warrant for the wrong person and place it in the state computer system.

State law requires the fingerprinting of felons. The detective said that their practice was once a person has been fingerprinted they do not do it on subsequent arrests. This self-initiated practice is illegal. The officers conducted an inadequate investigation and, in this author's opinion, the content of the police report did not support the elements of the crime charged. After being identified in court, Clarence came into the police station and said, "I am Clarence Doe." At that time the police checked their files and learned that he had been previously arrested and printed in 1987. If the three brothers conspired to dupe the police, a sound investigation could have uncovered that attempt, and all of them could have been successfully prosecuted. In this particular case the police were lucky. Regardless of the poor job the police did in investigating, reporting, and following, up the court dismissed the plaintiff's action.

Case 38: False Arrest and False Imprisonment

Facts

In the process of obtaining the wrong name of a suspect, and based on a computer hit, the police obtained a felony warrant. Without the benefit of a solid investigation the originating police department had another department arrest the wrong person for First Degree Criminal Sexual Conduct (CSC) which is a serious felony. As a result of the errors made by the police the plaintiff brought suit for false arrest and false imprisonment . The plaintiff's claim was based on his view that the police investigation was poorly done and his arrest and incarceration was the direct result of their errors, negligence, and non-detailed investigation.

On June 14th at 11:00 p.m., the thirteen year old daughter of an Hispanic woman reported to her mother that she had been sexually violated by finger penetration by a man who was at their house earlier in the day. The victim was able to get away from the assailant and told her mother that he had already left the scene. The police were called and the victim was checked at an area hospital where her assault was confirmed.

The mother, who spoke English with difficulty, told the police the suspect was her 5th or 6th cousin and was at their house earlier that day. The complainant told the police the suspect's wife's name was Estella, provided a good physical description of the suspect including the fact that he had long hair, wore a pony tail, had a birthmark on his nose, drove a red car, and lived in the states largest city some 110 miles away. She also told the police he was married and had three children. She said she was not sure of the spelling of his name, but offered Fidel Casio or Fidel Ramirez. The police ran a computer check on the names given and got a hit on Fidel Ocasio Ramirez with an address in a city forty-five miles from the city given by the complainant.

Based on the above information the detective requested a warrant from the prosecutor who in turn issued a warrant for CSC First Degree for the plaintiff. The police entered the warrant into the statewide computer system and notified the department in the city in which Fidel Ocasio Ramirez lived. They requested he be arrested on the warrant. The detective from the original department failed to tell the serving department that the suspect was married, had three children, wore a pony tail, had a birthmark on his nose, and drove a red car.

On June 25th the police from the second department arrested Fidel Ocasio Ramirez at his place of employment. He was read his Miranda rights in front of his fellow employees. He immediately told the arresting officer he was not the person sought. He told them they had a mistaken name. Nonetheless, he was placed in handcuffs, taken to the city lock-up, and was not allowed to ask any questions. He was lodged in jail awaiting pick up from the originating agency. That same day he was picked up and transported to the originating jurisdiction some forty-five miles distant, and lodged overnight in jail. On June 26th he appeared before a judge. On July 3rd the charges against him were dropped.

The actual suspect was later arrested. His name was Fidel Casio Ramirez. His physical description was similar to the plaintiff's, but the plaintiff was single, lived in a different city, did not have a pony tail, did not have a birthmark on his nose, and did not drive a red car.

Prior to the plaintiff's arrest the police attempted to get a phone number listed to Estella Ramirez, but were refused the number without a court order. The detective later said that he did not think it was right to try to call her. He also said that the department procedure requires an interview with a suspect prior to arrest when possible.

Issues and Factors Considered.

The first issue was whether the police were liable for the false arrest of the plaintiff. Another issue was whether the police had other alternatives open to them before asking for a warrant for the plaintiff. The level of completeness of the CSC investigation was a factor. The level of supervisory oversight of the detective's work on this case should also be examined. The fact the second police agency failed to allow the plaintiff to ask questions or act on any of the plaintiff's statements may be a factor.

Commentary

Once the police noticed the language barrier of the complainant they could have easily obtained the services of an interpreter. The complainant lived in an area with a large Hispanic population. The police should have provided the second police agency with the physical description, marital status, and vehicle description of the wanted suspect. The information the police had describing the distinctive birthmark on the suspect's nose would have been crucial information to provide the second police agency. Had that information been given to the arresting department, in all liklihood the plaintiff would not have been arrested.

Before requesting service of the warrant, the originating department could have made an attempt to locate suspect by checking out the computer generated address of the suspect's wife. Had the police followed their policy and interviewed the suspect before seeking a warrant, they would have had a stronger case for probable cause.

The complainant could have positively identified the suspect in person or by photo. The police were also advised by the complainant that the suspect was unemployed. A quick check with the state unemployment commission or the public assistance agency might have been helpful. A court order could have been obtained to get the suspect's phone number by contacting the telephone company security personnel. Had they wished, the police could have gone to the address they developed on the suspect and interviewed neighbors to confirm the description of the suspect.

In short, the officers acted too quickly and made an honest, but avoidable mistake. The false arrest could have been avoided if the police took their time and did more background work. If an experienced supervisor had reviewed the work, prior to the issuance of the warrant, the detective could have been given proper direction as to how to proceed.

A check of the state's sex motivated crime files would have, in hindsight, been beneficial. The correct suspect, who was later arrested, had previous convictions for sexual related crimes and his name was in that system. The prosecutor authorized the warrant for the serious felony based on minimal information, however, prosecutors cannot be sued.

The detective never talked to the police officer who completed and filed the original police report. The serving department could have interviewed the suspect, but they relied on the validity of the warrant on its face. If they had any doubts, based on the plaintiff's vociferous denial, they could have called the originating agency and asked for a physical description and other identifying information. This case did not go to trial. Once the process used by the detective was disclosed the police agency and its insurers settled with the plaintiff. Had fundamental police practices been adhered to the plaintiff never would have been arrested. This case points out the importance of responsible case supervision, attention to detail, and the need for clear communications.

Case 39: Police Responder's Reaction Leads to Woman's Death

Facts

At 1:30 a.m. on a two lane road in a suburban community the plaintiff was killed in a motor vehicle accident. Her vehicle was struck broadside by a police officer who claimed he was responding to an emergency. The officer did not have his overhead lights or siren operating at the time of the collision. The officer on patrol overheard a call being given to a fellow officer to check out a suspicious person in an apartment complex. The call was not in his assigned area. The caller said the person was in a hall and did not belong there. There was no crime in progress reported to the police. The officer in this case decided on his own to go to that location and inferred that the call was an emergency for him. After hearing the call, the officer turned from a main highway and turned east on a two lane road reaching speeds of eighty-two miles per hour. This speed was maintained without the benefit of his emergency lights or siren. After driving nearly three miles at that speed he testified he noticed a vehicle attempting to make a left turn ahead of him. He also testified that he felt he could make it around the vehicle, but the vehicle slowed, and he hit the plaintiff's vehicle almost broadside resulting in her immediate death. An accident reconstructionist computed the officer's impact speed at a low of sixty-seven and a high of eighty-two miles per hour. The accident occurred in a forty-five mile per hour zone.

Issues and Factors Considered

A first question was whether the officer had a real emergency or if he had a basis to assume his response was an emergency. Another more troublesome issue was he did not have his emergency equipment operating. If the officer had, or thought he had, an emergency he did not have the option to decide when to use his equipment. Another issue was the officer's speed prior to the accident. Critical issues in determining culpability were the high speeds driven , forty-five zone, and the fact it was dark and a two lane road. The chief testified as to his policy and his interpretation of the law. An issue here was whether his policy was appropriate and whether his knowledge of the law was accurate.

Commentary

If this call was an emergency the police are required to use both the overhead lights and the siren as needed and there is only one partial exception. The emergency driving statute provides an exception for officers responding to some emergencies where stealth is required. The statute allows the siren to be deactivated, but not the overhead emergency lighting. In either case the officer was violating the provisions of the statute.

The officer testified the reason he did not activate his emergency equipment was he did not want to scare away the so-called person in the apartment basement. There was no basis for his conjecture that the call was a burglary. As it turned out, the person was using the apartment halls to walk to his residence behind the complex. In his deposition testimony the officer said if he were going to an accident, for example, and he did not know if it was an emergency, he would assume it was and make it an emergency. Such thinking and conjectures are dangerous. The chief of police testified the emergency lights and sirens are optional with the officer. He also testified their use is dependent upon whether or not the officer is endangering life or property. His testimony indicated a lack of understanding of the law. The officer also testified that at first he thought the call was a non-emergency, but when he heard the other officer check out at the scene, it heightened him to an emergency. It would appear, based on the officer's testimony, he made an inferential leap from a suspicious person to a burglary in progress. He was not assigned to support the second officer nor did he report his actions to the dispatcher. Two minutes and twenty seconds elapsed from the officer's decision to make the unassigned run to the time of the accident. The case was referred to the prosecutor for possible criminal charges, but that office declined to initiate prosecution against the officer.

Under the conditions at the time and considering the motivation of the officer, the author concluded his driving was reckless. The policy of the department was ineffective and inaccurate. The department settled the case for an undisclosed amount. As is often the case, the police department ran a record check on the victim. Ostensibly, it would appear that the police would infer some culpability on the part of the victim if she had a criminal record. An examination of a plaintiff's behaviors during the incident is always relevant in attempting to establish a level of culpability, but depending on a plaintiff's former record in the criminal justice system to infer some level of current negligence is foolish and inappropriate.

Case 40: A Questionable Accident Investigation Leads to a Law Suit

Facts

On a clear day on dry pavement in a large metropolitan residential area, a ten-year-old girl riding her bicycle into the street was struck by a police car and severely injured. The young girl suffered a fractured skull, broken ribs, and a collapsed lung. One year after the accident she was completely incapacitated. The street was posted at twenty-five miles per hour and was a narrow one-way street which had cars parked in both curb lanes. There was only one full lane open to travel. The officer was responding to a missing person complaint, and thus he was not in an emergency status. Several children were playing on the sidewalk. The girl entered the road from between two parked cars.

The officer said he was driving at twenty miles per hour, and he could not avoid striking the child. Two hours after the accident investigation the officer's superiors determined the accident was nonpreventable. That conclusion appeared reasonable on the surface; however, the plaintiff's family brought suit after a review of the way the case was handled.

The accident report indicates the police officer's speed to be fifteen miles per hour. Two witnesses said he drove between twenty and thirty miles per hour. Two other witnesses, who were not contacted by the investigators, said he was driving between forty-five and fifty miles per hour. Respondiong police officials included a deputy superintendent, two local precinct officers, the department's accident investigation team, and an evidence technician.

The accident investigator did not arrive until forty minutes after the accident happened, and he obtained all his information for the report from the police driver. The investigator said they always go to the hospital first and therefore arrive at the scene much later. The vehicle and the bicycle were removed from the scene prior to the accident investigator's arrival. Scene photographs revealed the front wheel and handle bars of the bicycle was badly bent and twisted.

The officer said the girl ran into the left front tire well of his car and hit the tire. The officer completing the accident report said she hit the side of the car and the spot light. However, two eyewitnesses said she was hit by the police car from the front, flew over the hood, and finally hit the windshield. Damage to the spot light and dents on the hood support the witnesses' account. The evidence technician did not measure the skid marks, but said he just paced them off by foot. He did not run speed tests or coefficient of friction tests to determine the speed of the car.

At their depositions each officer present said the other officers from the other units were responsible for the investigation. There was no coordination of police activities at the scene, and several witnesses were overlooked. One officer said he only interviews those people who identify themselves as witnesses. The department policy on near-fatal accidents involving patrol cars require the evidence be secured in the property room, but the officer in charge of the property room said he did not know if there were any general orders covering the handling of property.

Days after the accident, family members went to the police station to view the bicycle. It was stored in a police garage, but not protected. For reasons unknown the wheel and handle bar had been straightened. The patrol car was also there and had, what appeared to be, blood on the license plate. One year after the accident, and immediately after being sued, the police sent the license plate to their lab to see if the smear on the plate was in fact blood. No lab test were discovered in the police reports.

The accident investigator said that he did not know if the scene was protected or not prior to his arrival. The accident investigators volunteered that the nature of a person's injuries determines the scope of their investigation. The deputy superintendent said it is the duty of officers to protect the scene for location of evidence, but said it was the job of the local precinct officers to protect the scene. He then said, "We believe we knew what happened and we collected evidence to support what had happened. We look for crimes not negligence or civil suits." He then said, "We are lucky if our beat officers know how to preserve evidence." The evidence technician of the accident team said that the bicycle was not physical evidence. In their depositions, members of the accident team said there were no manuals for conducting such an investigation. The investigator from the precinct said there is a policy against taking a statement from the police driver, but the superintendent said there was no such policy.

Issues and Factors Considered

What appeared on its face as an unavoidable accident was faulted by a poor, uncoordinated investigation. Ranking officers at the scene are in charge. The police did very little to reconstruct how the accident occurred. The accident investigators did not act responsibly. Though the police response was far less than one would expect, a determination as to proximate cause had to be determined.

Commentary

The sloppy manner in which the accident scene was handled and the investigation was conducted gave rise to this law suit. There is no doubt as to the proximate cause of the accident. The plaintiff ran into the street from between two parked cars without looking, and the officer could not avoid striking her. Family members became suspicious after seeing how the accident was handled. The victim's family sued because they suspected a cover-up of some kind. The only way the officer could be held partially liable would be if there was some proof that he was speeding. No efforts were made to determine the officer's speed.

The fact the bicycle appeared to be altered raises serious concerns. The method used by the police led to the suit which tied up agency members for two years and resulted in unnecessarily high costs for defense. Though one may never know what actually happened this form of police work is counter-productive and procedurally poor. The case never went to trial and was eventually dropped by plaintiff. Definitive answers from the police were never forthcoming. It appeared the police at best were incompetent and at worst shaded the facts as best they could to reduce chances of liability. Such police practices erode police community relations.

Case 41: Failure to Protect Results in a Murder

Facts

In a large metropolitan city in 1993, three officers responded to a call from a woman who wished to remove her personal property from her home. The woman had an Order of Protection signed by the court. That order was issued to protect her from her abusive husband who resided in the home. After a minimal contact with the husband the officers allowed her to enter the house and, with the help of some of her relatives, she started removing her property. The police remained outside on the sidewalk. After a few trips in and out of the house the officers heard shots fired from within the house. It was later learned that her husband had obtained a rifle, shot and killed his wife, and then shot himself. The murder-suicide in the house was witnessed by the plaintiff's sister. Shortly after the plaintiff entered the house to retrieve her belongings a third officer arrived and stood by outside with the other two officers.

The plaintiff's relatives brought suit in her name for a failure to protect the plaintiff. The plaintiff's sister stated she was directly behind her sister when she showed the officers the Order for Protection. She was resolute that her sister told the officers that her husband had up to ten weapons in the house. The officers said they saw the order but did not read it. An affidavit supporting the order indicated that her husband was abusive and assaultive. The officers denied being told her husband had weapons.

What was not disputed was the officers went to the door, knocked, and met her husband. The officers informed him of his wife's wishes and the Order for Protection. They asked him if they were going to have trouble with him to which he answered no. At that point, the officers testified they felt the husband was amicable, and they asked the plaintiff if that was fine with her.   The officers admitted they never asked the plaintiff if there were weapons in the house, of her previous relations with her husband, or about the basis for the Order of Protection. Once the plaintiff began removing her property, the officers, later joined by a third officer, went to the curb and had a conversation, the subject of which they did not remember. After hearing shots fired, the three officers took cover behind their patrol cars and called for assistance. When they entered the house they found the plaintiff and her husband shot to death in an apparent murder-suicide. The official orders, in place at the time, relating to such incidents were vague and ambiguous. All three officers testified that they had not received any domestic violence training in the preceding ten years.

Issues and Factors Considered

A primary question in this matter was whether the police had a duty to protect the plaintiff. Another question was what were the alternatives the police had at their disposal to prevent such an occurrence. The dispatcher for the department testified that after she received the plaintiff's call for assistance she did not ask her any questions, but only assigned officers to assist her while she got her property under an Order of Protection. Two major questions in this case were: (1) should the police have taken some preventive actions at the scene prior to allowing the plaintiff and her sisters to enter and (2) were the two officers grossly negligent in the manner they handled the case.

Commentary

If the officers had questioned the plaintiff or read the affidavit of the Order of Protection, they would have learned the husband had a history of abuse and weapons were in the house. They clearly had a duty to protect the plaintiff in this matter. Officers should have checked the house for weapons or they could have entered with her and stayed between her and her husband until she could peacefully remove her property. They could have asked the husband to wait outside during the transfer of property and stayed with him.

When asked whether they asked about weapons, the officers said they did not have evidence of weapons and had no probable cause for arresting him. Though the officers made some erroneous assumptions regarding the amicability of the husband, no experienced officer would allow a plaintiff to enter a house without police protection. That issue is basic. It was not clear if the affidavit for the Order of Protection was attached to the Order. If it was, the officers were grossly negligent by their inaction. Plaintiff's focus in this suit was negligent training. If the officers were correct about not having any domestic violence training in the past ten years, there would a strong likelihood of plaintiff prevailing. There may be a question of fact as to plaintiff's sister's veracity wherein she said her sister told the officers there were guns in the house. Both officers flatly denied her statement. Regardless, good police practice would require the officers enter the house or keep the husband outside at a safe distance from the plaintiff until she cleared the scene. The best practice would have been to enter and search for other persons and make a protective sweep of the house. Such protective actions are common practices among experienced police officers, and have been so for decades.

The department dispatcher did not act responsibly. The author has done extensive research and training with emergency dispatchers. All trained dispatchers on receipt of 911 calls ask about possible weapons or other dangers and routinely pass that information on to the responding officers. Interestingly, but not surprisingly, the department rewrote their official order on the subject of Protection Orders, domestic violence, and similar circumstances after being sued. The internal affairs section of the department conducted an investigation, and shortly after doing so, they exonerated all three officers of any violation of policy or statute.

The third officer in his subsequent deposition said that he would have definitely gone into the house to protect the plaintiff, and he has done so for years. He said he learned this practice on the street. Two other officers testified they would have gone into the house and brought the husband out.

Gross negligence involves deliberate indifference to the safety of others and a total disregard of the obvious. In this case, if the officers did not see the affidavit and were not told of the guns, as the plaintiff's relatives alleged, it might be a case of negligence based on a lack of training, lack of experience, ignorance, wrong-headed inferences, or misplaced trust. What is most puzzling is why they did not ask her if he had weapons in the house for their own personal safety. The author declined to support the defense in this matter for reasons outlined here. Strong recommendations were made for the department to re-evaluate its policies and procedures, training, and internal investigations. What is so disturbing about this case is the department involved is a major police department in the United States that has long boasted of its training programs.

Case 42: A Failure to Call Paramedics Results in Judgment

Facts

At approximately 1:50 a.m. the driver of an old 1976 vehicle ran off the roadway to the right, hit a curb, and spun around 180 degrees throwing the driver out of his car. The vehicle continued over the curb and slid over the body of the driver pinning him under his vehicle.

At rest, the vehicle had three wheels on the lawn between the curb and sidewalk, and one wheel on the pavement. The engine was running and the radio was playing loudly. A nearby resident, who heard the noise of the radio, came out of this home and walked to the car. He found the driver's door opened about thirty degrees. He reached in and turned off the radio and the ignition. He also noted a jacket on the ground. He did not see any person near the vehicle. He called the police at 1:59 a.m.

The first officer arrived at 2:05 a.m. and said the driver's door had been held shut with a bungy cord, and he confirmed the resident's story that the door was ajar. He turned off the lights of the vehicle. He stated the car was on the grass with the right rear tire on the pavement. He also noted the left front tire was flat. The officer felt it was a typical drunk driving situation in which a driver, not wanting to be arrested, ran off the road, and left the scene on foot to avoid an arrest.   The officer called a wrecker service. The officer and the wrecker driver looked under the vehicle. The officer said the vehicle was resting so tightly on the grass that one could not get a knife under the vehicle. The wrecker driver also testified he could not see under the vehicle. They both noted the driver's door was stuck in the sod. The officer, who had been to an accident investigation school, said he interviewed a few people nearby, but no one reported seeing anyone walking.

In preparation of hooking up the vehicle, the wrecker driver put a chain on the rear of the vehicle and pulled it out backwards into the street. When the car was pulled over the curb a body rolled out from under the rear bumper area. The car had been pulled fifteen to twenty feet before the body rolled out. The wrecker driver said it is routine to check under a vehicle to see if it was hung up on a sprinkler or something before attempting to hook up. He said he checked the vehicle from both sides.

The driver of the wrecker said the car was not bottomed out. He pulled it approximately four feet off the grass and the vehicle lifted about six inches from the ground. He then pulled it forward fifteen feet before the body fell out. At 2:55 a.m. a detective was called to the scene. The original officer checked the body visually for vital signs and made an assumption the person was dead. He did not call a paramedic or make any attempt to transport the person to a hospital. To the contrary, the officer reached a decision, absent any medical certification, that the son of the plaintiff was in fact already dead.

In his deposition, the detective was asked, according to their departmental procedures, who should pronounce a person dead at an accident scene. He testified that it is practice for the officer to call for paramedics, who would in turn hook a person up to life lines and then transmit data to the hospital for interpretation. The detective testified that only a doctor pronounces someone as dead. As it turned out, a doctor at the morgue signed the death certificate after pronouncing the man dead. He testified that this action was a break from traditional practice. Morever, he said, it was not conventional. The detective also testified that he assumed the paramedics had already been summoned.

The detective was a deputy medical examiner and thus was authorized to pronounce someone dead under extreme conditions. When asked if he believed the first officer should have summoned an ambulance or paramedics to the scene, he answered yes.

The mother of the victim filed suit against the police. She alleged her son's death was caused by the dragging of the vehicle over her son's body. She felt it was negligent not to have run an EKG and further alleged he should have been taken to a hospital. She held it was wrong for the officer to assume he was dead. She also alleged the driver's door was locked in place.

Issues and Factors Considered

There were very few photos taken at the scene. The victim's body came to rest next to the curb and there was a blood stain at that point. Photos were not taken of the blood stain. Dead bodies, of course, do not pump blood, so it would have been good to have taken close-up photos. A large amount of blood was located on the grass seven feet from the curb, but no mention was made as to whether it was a spot or a pooling. Again, no photos were taken. The under carriage of the vehicle was given a perfunctory examination. Some blood was located near the muffler, and the rest of the underside of the vehicle was crusted with sod.

The detective said that he had a theory as to what had happened and examined evidence that fit that theory. Perhaps if evidence such as marks, blood, flesh, photos, measurements and so forth, had been examined and/or collected such an examination may have led to an inference as to what had happened. In other words, the evidence might lead to a theory of what had happened, and not the other way around. Because no foul play was suspected, the crushing, dragging, and other injuries of the victim were not identified. Both officers said they never considered that pulling the car over the victim caused his death. The victim had a blood alcohol level of .33 percent.

Commentary

The day after the accident the victim was examined by a credible medical examiner who determined that the death was due to asphyxiation due to compression under the motor vehicle. The victim was crushed on both sides of his body. The rib cage was crushed and the lungs were torn. He said, if the person was there for any length of time before the vehicle was moved, he was dead. Overall, he felt the victim died because so much of his body was crushed. He also opined that he died rather quickly because so little blood was found. The medical examiner said that had the victim been alive after the crushing there would have been more blood. He summed up his views stating he felt the man died within thirty seconds, and thus he was dead before the towing operation. Another doctor, but not a pathologist, said he disagreed with the medical examiner's conjecture of death within minutes, but felt it was more like a fraction of a minute.

In as much as the doctors agreed that the person was dead from his injuries under the car, and dead when his body rolled out, the officer's inaction would not have made a difference in the outcome. However, if he was not dead, and had he been sent to a hospital and been pronounced dead there, the officer would have done what he could.

Because the officer took it upon himself to assume the man was dead, and because he failed to summon medical assistance as required by police practice and standards, he opened the door to this law suit. His own department agreed he should have summoned help. The final question was whether the man could have lived fifty-five minutes with the injuries he sustained. Fifty-five minutes had elapsed from the time the officer arrived until the body of the victim fell out from under the car. This issue can only be determined by qualified medical personnel and it becomes a question of fact for a jury. At best, it becomes informed speculation.

No significant effort was expended by the police to investigate and gather evidence to assist forensic medical professionals in reaching their conclusions. While the death of the victim more likely occurred as envisioned by the police, their decisions on this case gave rise to suspicions and speculation resulting in a costly law suit that could have been averted. If plaintiff's medical experts were able to convince a jury that it was more likely than not the victim was alive at the time he rolled out from under the vehicle, the police decision not to call medical assistance to the scene could well have resulted in a determination of proximate cause and liability against the police. Though it may not have had an important bearing on the outcome, the failure of the police to attempt to identify physical evidence at the scene could also affect a jury member's thinking. The case was settled prior to going to court.

Case 43: Police Raid the Wrong House

Facts

This is a case of a police raid on the wrong house to execute a search warrant for drugs based on information from a confidential informant. Five months prior to the raid on the residence, an officer, working in a multi-department cooperative force drug unit, attempted to make a drug buy at the residence in question but to no avail. The suspected dealer, John Doe, was living at the residence on 1210 Main St. A few days prior to the raid, another officer, of the same team, bought drugs from an informant. The informant had a deliverey of marijuana charge pending. The informant gave the police the dealer's name and said he lived on Main St.

The team leader contacted the local police for verification of John Doe's address. He was given the address of 1210 Main St. That verification, it was later learned, came from a registration check of the motor vehicle driven by Doe. Intelligence reports, which were later learned to be two local police officers, revealed the same address.

Based on this information the team leader filed an affidavit for a search warrant and obtained a warrant for 1210 Main St., the residence of John Doe. The officers knew Doe drove a brown pickup truck, and they had his license plate number as well.

In late November the raid team, composed of officers dressed in black and wearing ski masks, knocked and entered the home of John Smith to conduct a search on the warrant. Three officers entered and found Mr. Smith in his living room and his twelve-year—old son in the kitchen. Both persons were put on the floor and held at gun point. Other officers entered and conducted a protective sweep of the second floor. When the fifth officer entered, he told the others that Mr. Smith was not Mr. Doe, and they had the wrong house. The two Smiths were then allowed to get up and sat at a kitchen table while the team leader attempted to verify the location of John Doe. Officers checking on Mr. Smith learned he was wanted on an unrelated warrant.

When Mr. Smith's wife returned to the residence she became irate. Her son told her the officers had a gun to the back of his neck. Her husband had abrasions on the back of his neck. She provided their lease agreement to prove they were in fact the legal tenants and told the police that Mr. Doe had moved out several weeks prior. She filed a law suit claiming violation of their 4th Amendment rights and abuse of authority , including excessive force. She claimed in her suit that within months of the raid her stepdaughter dropped out of school and became incorrigible, and her son turned to the use of drugs as a result of being ridiculed at school as a member of a drug dealing family.

Issues and Factors Considered

Officers failed to confirm the accuracy of the raided residence before executing an affidavit. They could have checked utility records. No officer took the time to have the informant point out the correct house at 512 Main St., where John Doe currently resided. There was no attempt made to verify the correct residence or to check for Doe's brown pickup prior to attempting a raid. When asked in deposition whether it was a common practice to have the informant take an officer to point out the house and/or to give a description of the house,the team leader responded in the positive. He also did not recall any surveillance of the target house and testified that he "loved raids."

All of the officers on the raid denied pointing long guns at the Smiths. Though officers testified to making a protective sweep of the upstairs of the house they denied making any searches, but the plaintiff testified the rooms had things lying about indicating a search had in fact taken place. The following day a second affidavit was executed and a search was made of the correct address at 512 Main St. where John Doe lived with his girlfriend. Officers testified they did not remember pointing guns at anyone and did not remember if long guns were used.

Commentary

All raids are potentially dangerous. It is important to conduct surveillance of the target residence. Those actions confirm the correct location and provide other officers with the precise description of the raid target. Placing a suspect in and around a target is the accepted practice. Obtaining registrations of vehicle parked at such houses is a common and accepted practice. It is a standard practice to verify inhabitants of the raid target by checking with the gas and electric utilities to see who is being billed for services. It appears the suspect, John Doe, moved six weeks prior to the date of the raid. His move could have and should have been verified.

Previous intelligence reports revealed that Doe frequently used his brown pickup truck to conduct his narcotics business, but a check for his vehicle at the Smith residence was not conducted. Good police practice requires the first person through the door on a raid be a uniformed officer. The team policy only requires that a uniformed person be in sight. This is a short sighted policy. After learning they had raided the wrong residence,one officer in the house called the informant and only then learned the suspect had moved. This information should have been obtained prior to executing a raid. The day after the raid the officers made the informant take them to the house that the marijuana was reportedly growing. That house was located at 512 Main Street.

The officers' testimony on deposition was that they did not remember if shot guns were used in the raid. They did not deny they were, but only did not remember. While the psychological harm the plaintiff claims may be false, the defense is hard pressed to prove these injuries did not occur. The evasive testimony of some officers, coupled with the fact that they raided the wrong house, tends to provide a jury with a basis for inference. Though clearly a mistake, the raid of the wrong house was completely avoidable. The officers involved rushed to get an affidavit and did not take basic preliminary steps that a reasonable officer would have taken. Advise to defense counsel was to settle. Recommendations were also made to tighten up team raid procedures to avoid such errors in the future.

Case 44: Officer's Weapon Used in Accidental Shooting

Facts

This case involves an off-duty deputy sheriff, who spent the afternoon with close friends target practicing in the backyard, and the accidental shooting of the seventeen-year-old daughter of his friend with the officer's weapon. The officer involved in this case was off duty and spending the afternoon with friends at their rural home. In the back of the house there was a make-shift target range. Four a few hours the officer and his friends, including another off duty officer, took turns shooting their weapons at the targets. At one point, the fifteen-year-old son of the host was allowed to fire the hand guns under the watchful eyes of the adults.

All present were drinking some beer, but there was no evidence or claim of anyone being intoxicated. After the target practice the adults went in to the house to prepare for an evening dinner at a local restaurant. The officer took off his holster and placed his loaded .357 revolver in the holster. He then placed it on a counter top in the house. At this time, he warned his friend's fifteen-year-old son and nine-year-old stepdaughter to stay away from the holster, because the gun was loaded. The officer left the room and the fifteen-year-old boy began to handle the gun. He jokingly pointed it in the direction of his sister and the gun went off with a bullet striking his nine-year-old sister in the face. He claimed he did not know the weapon was loaded. He said he was dry firing. An ambulance was called and first aid was administered to the girl. She had a serious head wound, but did recover from her injuries. The officer immediately reported the incident to his department, investigators responded and interviewed all present, and the residence was treated as a crime scene.

An adequate investigation was conducted and documented. The investigation revealed that both officers had some beer to drink during the day, but there was no evidence of over consumption. Both the boy and his mother, who was in the living room at the time of the shooting, stated they heard the officer give the warning to avoid the holstered weapon. The boy said he heard the warning, but he must have misunderstood. The case was closed, because the prosecutor did not wish to pursue prosecution. The officer was not held responsible for the shooting.

The mother of the injured girl brought suit against the sheriff department and the officer. She claimed the officer was acting under color of law because he was on call twenty-four hours a day. She charged that the officer consumed alcohol while carrying a firearm and that amounted to gross negligence. The department was sued for failure to train.

Issues and Factors Considered

The primary issues that surfaced in the pleadings of this case were acting under color of law and gross negligence as a result of deliberate indifference. The rules and regulations of the department address accidental discharge of a weapon and state that such accidental discharges are considered to be negligent. Officers found guilty of accidental discharge may be disciplined up to and including dismissal.

Commentary

An officer who is off duty and not engaged in any police type function is not believed to be acting under color of law. Color of law and being on call twenty-four hours a day are not synonomous. Color of law means available for duty call or to act if needed as a police officer. The officer does not take his gun to bed. Being required to carry a weapon off duty does not indicate under color of law either. That requirement means one must be armed when off duty, but not that one is on duty because he is armed. If that were so, the agency would have to pay the officer twenty-four hours a day. The plaintiff claimed the officer had consumed alcohol. That was admitted, but there was no evidence or testimony of any improper level of consumption. If he was in fact under the influence it would be a different set of circumstances. Another position the plaintiff held was the officer was consuming alcohol while carrying a weapon. In order for that claim to have any merit for negligence, one must have some proof that he was intoxicated or his judgment was impaired from the alcohol. No such proofs were offered. The plaintiff also alluded to the concept of reasonable care. If the shooter had been much younger or no warnings had been given, such a claim could rise to the level of merit, but those conditions were not present.

The claim of negligent training or failure to train was discounted because that department had firearms training three times per year. The deliberate indifference standard does not apply because even if the training was less than desired, one incident is insufficient to hold an agency as deliberately indifferent.

Accidental discharge does not apply because the officer did not accidentally discharge his weapon. The weapon was fired by another. Simply, the rules do not apply to someone else who accidentally discharged the weapon. If it were so, the discipline would have to be applied to the young boy and that is nonsensical. Gross negligence denotes a level of deliberate indifference. In this case, the officer took care to warn those in the room to stay away from his holster. His action may have been imprudent. It might even be wise to counsel the officer for poor judgment, but the author was not convinced to a moral certainty that the officer acted negligently, and plaintiff's counsel was advised that their case had serious weaknesses. The plaintiff did not go forward.

Case 45: Two Officers Killed in Mismanaged Raid

In this unusual and tragic case two officers of one department were shot and killed by fellow officers in a mismanaged raid on a crack house. This case points out the critical need for administrative control and adherence to departmental policy. This happened in a large city police department. Ironically, one victim-officer's family brought suit against his own department alleging negligent training of the other police victim who had shot and killed him.

Facts

A home owner who either knew or suspected crack cocaine trafficking in her rented home called the police and made a false report of a shooting at the residence. Two two-officer marked patrol cars responded. The four officers, one of whom was one of the victims, entered the occupied house to investigate the report of a shooting. On entry, four persons were found in the living room of the house. It was dark and the interior of the house was dimly lit. Officers were in the process of separating the persons and making inquiries. The officers were making observations for drugs and their own safety, and there was a good deal of confusion in the house. Both marked patrol cars were parked in front of the house.

Unknown to the officers in the house, earlier in the day, narcotics officers of the same department had made a purchase of drugs from that residence and were preparing to raid the house.

The departmental policy on the conduct of raids requires narcotic enforcement team leaders to notify the appropriate precinct administration of a targeted raid just prior to conducting such a raid within a precinct. This was not done. Accepted police procedures also require a uniformed officer to be the first one through the door to alert occupants that it is the police that are entering. This also was not done.

The multiple member raid team drove the house, saw the marked cars, but none-the-less approached the enclosed front porch for entry. A female uniform officer brought along on the raid per their requirement, was sent to cover the back door of the house. Once inside the enclosed porch to the house, the sergeant took up a position to the left of the doorway and another officer, dressed in an army fatigue jacket with long hair and armed with a shot gun, was the first to forcibly enter the dwelling. Upon his entry into the darkened room all of the officers inside began yelling "Police" as did the undercover officer.

The youngest of the four original officers in the house saw the shot gun in the hands of the approaching undercover officer, did not recognize him as a police officer, and fired one shot killing him. The shot propelled the wounded officer backwards. He fell out the door and landed at the feet of his sergeant.

The officer who fired that shot then leapt through a window onto the front porch and was immediately shot and killed by the sergeant. Right after the sergeant shot the patrolman he was shocked to note that the person he instinctively shot was wearing a uniform. This entire incident happened in a matter of seconds. The second officer who was killed was a recent graduate of the police academy and the son of a retired officer from that department.

Issues and Factors Considered

The first issue examined was the adherence to standards of the raid procedure. Polices to avoid such occurrences were also an issue. Another issue was whether the shooting by the younger officer from inside the house was reasonable under the conditions. Likewise, the reasonableness of the sergeant's shooting was also an issue. The question of proximate cause was also examined in light of the raid team's behaviors. The method of approach and entry by the raid team was a factor to consider to see if they conformed to accepted police practices. A final issue was to determine whether there was any relevance to the plaintiff's claim that had the younger officer been trained in raid procedures while at the academy, he would not have shot the officer that entered the crack house.

Commentary

Clearly, deadly force was used by both officers who fired their weapons. The younger uniformed officer was in a crack house assisting others in stabilizing a confusing and potentially dangerous situation. He was in a dimly lit room with suspects from an alleged shooting, several people were milling around, and a bearded male with shaggy hair dressed in an army coat burst into the room armed with a shot gun. Moreover, the gun was pointed in his direction. It would appear that he fired his weapon after yelling "police" in self-defense of himself and his fellow officers in the room. His reaction to leap through a window to the porch may have been poorly thought out, if thought through at all. It can only be inferred that he was attempting to locate other possible intruders or attempting to escape from what he felt was a dangerous situation.

The case of the shooting by the sergeant poses other problems. His shot was reactionary having just seen his partner sprawled on the porch and shot dead. There is some question as to whether he was firing in self-defense or just reacting to the trauma he had just witnessed.

The policies were sound and were designed to prevent just such an occurrence. Had the raid team called the precinct, as required, they would have learned that two uniform cars were already at that location. Armed with such information they could have logically aborted the attempt to conduct a raid. Moreover, had they assigned the female uniformed officer to go in first, as required by policy and sound police practice, this incident may have been prevented.

Having a swarthy-looking officer armed with a shot gun enter the house first was very poor decision making in the raid context. Those experienced in conducting raids would suggest that it is common practice when approaching a crack house with police cars parked out front to drive past and make an inquiry as to why they are there before initiating a raid. Any experienced officer is aware that the element of surprise is lost if two marked cars are parked in front of a house to be raided.

A subsequent internal investigation did not hold the members of the raid team responsible and suggested that the policies on calling the precinct prior to a raid or having a uniform officer enter first may be ambiguous. These suggestions appeared to be ludicrous and self-serving for defense of the department's image.

Counsel representing the slain sergeant predicated his suit on negligent training. His position was had the younger officer been properly trained in the academy on raid procedures and techniques he would not have shot the officer entering the house. This position was rejected by the author who advised that the proximate cause of both shootings was the failure on the part of the raid team leader to adhere to policies on notification and entry.

Furthermore, it was suggested that experienced officers on the raid team failed to consider the likelihood of officers being in the house based on viewing the patrol cars out front. It was the opinion of the author that they not only violated their own rules, but also failed to consider conditions that would lead an experienced officer to abort the raid. The action of the department administration raises doubts as to their commitment to accountability and could likely raise public suspicion of white-washing.

Case 46: Police Sued for Failing to Shoot a Violent Man

Facts

Two brothers and their wives played games and cards and drank at the home of the younger brother from approximately 3:00 p.m. to 9:30 p.m. At 9:30 p.m. the elder brother and his wife left to go home. Sometime later, the younger brother received a call from his brother who said he was going to shoot himself. He immediately called 911 and reported his brother was going to kill himself, and that his brother was armed with a shot gun. He provided the police with his brother's address. The younger brother then left to go to his brother's house. He told his wife he could talk him out of it.

The family was well-known to the police. The older brother had shot and killed his stepfather when he was twelve-years-old, but was not charged. A sergeant, who later became a negotiator in this incident, knew the older brother well.

A sergeant and four officers initially responded to the home of the elder brother. Sometime after the police arrived the younger of the brothers arrived and pushed his way towards the house in an attempt to talk to his brother. He was ordered back and warned to stay back. The brother in the house was firing shots inside the house. At one point the brother came out of the house and held a shot gun to his chin. He then fired a shot, although the shot did not hit him he said, "It hurts." Once again, the younger brother pushed past the police to get to speak to his brother. At this point he was arrested for interfering. He was handcuffed and taken to a patrol car parked along the curb approximately 250 feet down the street from the house.

Other officers arrived and warned neighbors who had gathered on porches to go to their basements until the incident was settled. Officers took up positions in front, to the side, and to the rear of the house to keep a watch for the man inside. Over the next few hours the older brother fired shots in the house, pointed his shot gun at two officers when he exited the house, and exited and re-entered his house on several occasions.

The sergeant at the station, who knew the elder brother, called his house and engaged him in conversations. The brother was assured if he disarmed himself and let his wife and three children out he would be taken to a hospital for treatment. He told the sergeant he wanted that agreement in writing. The sergeant came to the scene with a note and left it on the porch. Eventually, the police got the wife and three children safely out of the house.

Shortly after 2:20 a.m the following morning the older brother came out of the house with the shot gun in his hands and began working his way up the sidewalk. Police officers from positions of cover behind trees and cars yelled at him to drop the gun, but he continued to walk and menace them. As he passed the plain police car, which held his younger brother, the younger brother yelled at him to let him out. Over the objection of the police he let his brother out of the car. The younger brother, still handcuffed, called out to the police, "Don't shoot my brother" and "I can handle this."

The scene was mobile and determined by the actions of the older brother. As the two of them crossed a field down the street the younger brother grabbed the shot gun by its strap. A struggle for the gun ensued and the gun went off. The younger brother was struck by the shot and suffered a collapsed lung and three broken ribs. As he fell to the ground, the elder brother started to run and was fired upon by the police. None of the seven shots fired at the brother hit him. He then dropped down, knelt on the ground, and raised his hands in the air. He was arrested and handcuffed, and the younger brother was sent to the hospital.

The injured brother became the plaintiff and brought suit against the police for Failure to Protect while in custody. Plaintiff's experts questioned the police procedures used claiming they should have established better perimeters, called in SWAT teams to handle the hostage situation, and should have taken the younger brother to the police station to avoid his being captured by his elder brother. Plaintiff also claimed the police should have shot the older brother in the legs to disable him before he got to his younger brother's location.

Issues and Factors Considered

One issue was whether the police should have called for a SWAT team to assume command of the situation. Another was the police response procedures. The plaintiff's expert's opinion that stationary perimeters should have been set up was examined as were his views that the brother should have been transported from the scene. The younger brother's insistence on being involved was also examined. The issue of whether the police should have shot and disabled the older brother was also considered. The containing actions of the officers at this mobile scene was also a factor for consideration.

Commentary

The police do owe a special duty to a person taken in to custody. The fact that they placed him in a patrol car some 250 feet south of the scene, coupled with the fact that they needed all the officers they had assigned to cover the house, does not bode against them seriously. There was no way for the police to know that the older brother, by his movements, would create a moving tactical scene. The fact remains that the older brother was walking by the car when his younger brother called out to him to open the door. The injured brother acted on his own volition and against previous police warnings when he voluntarily got out of the car.

Calling for a SWAT team was irrelevant. This was not a hostage situation and, as the chief of police testified, it was a fluid, violent, evolving situation. The officers showed restraint in not attempting to shoot the older brother. They knew the older brother was intoxicated and displayed mental problems. The older brother, on one of his forays from the house earlier in the evening, had asked the police to shoot him. He said he did not want to hurt anyone, but himself.

The idea of shooting him in the leg, while somewhat theatrical, does not make any sense. The cause of the plaintiff's injuries was his own immersion and interference into the police incident. Considering the rapidly evolving incident, the police used good judgment. They also secured the safety of the older brother's wife and children and made several reasonable attempts to get him to give up his weapon.

The older brother was charged with felonious assault but was placed in a treatment center by the court when it was learned he was not competent to stand trial. The younger brother had a jury trial on the charge of Interfering with a Police Officer in the Performance of a Duty. A jury rendered a verdict of not guilty on that charge, and it is believed that this may be motivated the law suit. The city made a settlement offer after mediation and prior to trial. The offer was accepted.

Summary

There are no valid justifications for poor police work, but there are several explanations for why such occurrences happen. This is not to say that the police should be able to solve all crimes discovered or reported to them or to satisfy all people who call for their services in other than the context of crime. In the past decade the crime solving rate for several crimes in the United States has regressed, but it is not the purpose of this work to explore that issue. What is the concern of this work are those situations in which the police do less than what they obviously could have done, or worse, do it improperly or illegally. When a person is wrongly arrested and incarcerated, they are deprived of their liberty. If not rectified, such persons may spend months to years in custody. In capital cases this may mean a life in prison. In states that allow capital punishment it could result in an error that can not be reversed. When a police officer uses excessive force in making an arrest, a person is unnecessarily injured without legal justification.

The primary concern is not that the agency may be sued for its officers' improper actions, but because it is wrong in itself and contrary to our form of government and the Constitution that guides such a government.

Police officers exceeding their authority by speeding when it is neither appropriate nor prudent may injure an innocent motorist. An investigation poorly conducted can not only lead to an erroneous conclusion, but in some cases may, when critical factors are overlooked, lead to the injury or death of a person. Not all poorly conducted police work results in injury, death, or wrongful incarceration. In some cases the result is limited to an injustice done to a citizen. It is recognized the police often have to make split-second decisions.

From time to time they make honest mistakes under the stressful conditions presented to them. Such oversights are understandable and may even be reasonable. Several courts have recognized such conditions and taken those elements into consideration. However, in cases where an officer's actions are deemed unreasonable and do not comport to established police practices or standards, the result includes the loss of the public trust.

Some of the examples given here that reflect poorly-conducted police work may occur singularly or in combination. Some may be isolated and some may be commonplace. Police administrators would be well advised to have systems in place to monitor aberrant police behaviors. A trend or an increase in police liability cases is a fair barometer of a potentially serious police department problem. When such observations are made by administrators they should consider conducting an internal audit of operational practices.

The starting point for such an audit may include a re-examination of its recruitment goals and processes, its selection criteria, and its training programs. There is no excuse for not conducting a thorough background investigation on police applicants. Administrators would be wise to re-evaluate their standards for acceptance. They should also examine their disciplinary processes to insure fairness and reasonableness.

The citizens' rights and protection must be part of the formula of such an examination. A chief administrator must be confident that his/her supervising subordinates have the moral integrity to see that appropriate discipline it is implemented when needed.

Training must be viewed as an ongoing process in policing. Police departments that do not stay current on training issues and contemporary court decisions are destined to become the focus of civil-rights-based law suits. It is not a case of if, but only when, this will occur. When complaints are made against officers, police administrators are bound to conduct fair and impartial investigations into the allegations. Bias, protectionism, or paternalism have no place in such investigations. Fear of liability should never be a bar on the decision to investigate alleged wrongdoing. All credible administrators must adopt a philosophy that public accountability is not optional.

In order to properly delegate, administrators are bound to promulgate rules, regulations, policies, and procedures to guide their officers when they are required to make discretionary decisions. Policing, by its very nature, is not a closely supervised enterprise. Officers on the street are virtually on their own much of the time, and they must have reasonable organizational bench marks to guide their thinking and action. The mere promulgation of such orders is not sufficient to ensure accountability. The individual officers must be trained and tested in the meaning of the rules and held to account when violations of those rules are discovered. A policy that is not enforced is no more than a piece of paper and is not controlling.

Many improper police behaviors can be traced to mismanagement. Several informed police agencies in the United States operate programs that monitor complaints against officers, deviations from policy and incidents of the use of force. Such programs strive to identify potentially errant officers and intercede with positive counseling and training initiatives to prevent future improper behaviors. A computerized risk management database system is no longer a luxury, but a necessity.

As should be evident in the examination of these cases, police officers are often forced to make split-second decisions and must do so under extreme and dangerous conditions. A specific policy may not exist to guide each and every action an officer takes. Moreover, in the heat of a dangerous confrontation, an officer's actions should be judged against whether he or she acted reasonably at the time. It was said best in *Graham v. Connor* (1989) when the court said that the officer's actions should be judged from the perspective of a reasonable police officer at the scene and not from hindsight months later.

Chapter 5

Police Practices in Homicide Cases and Analyses of Cases

Homicides

From time to time police officers are confronted with homicide scenes, but generally they can not turn to a specific policy or procedure that outlines the proper response and behavior expected at such scenes. Most officers apply their training and experience, but for those with deficits in this area of policing, serious mistakes can be made that can not be rectified later.

Response and Procedure

Whether an officer is called to the scene of a homicide or comes upon one on patrol, the simplest procedure is to secure and protect the scene until experienced investigators and specialists arrive. Smaller police agencies may be required to call other agencies that have sufficient personnel and capabilities to properly handle a homicide investigation.

Some first responders may be confronted with an apparent homicide scene, but may not be sure the alleged victim is dead. In those cases, a slight intrusion into the scene would be in order to check the victim for vital signs. Though emergency medical assistance is paramount to the criminal investigation some precautionary steps can be taken to preserve the scene.

In these situations an officer's knowledge of evidence, associated with a homicide scene, becomes critical. For example, an officer's awareness of potential evidence such as footprints, tire prints, fingerprints, blood spots, and other forms of evidence could reduce the crime scene contamination. Leaving one's own trace evidence at a scene further complicates a homicide investigator's efforts. Any action taken at the scene, albeit necessary to possibly save a life, non-the-less alters the scene from its original form. In such scenarios, it is critical for the officer to document exactly what action was taken.

Officers not trained or confident in crime scene handling, who have opted to secure the scene and wait for assistance, can still take some basic steps. After securing the scene, a visual check of the scene may reveal that the perpetrator is still there. Potential witnesses should be identified and contained. No matter what actions are taken, it is imperative that the officer document times, activities, and observations in a notebook. Field notes include the time of arrival, observations on arrival, description of the scene, nature and location of potential evidence, other actions taken, and witnesses identification.

Most of the field training officer programs in the country provide rookie officers with some basic knowledge on what to do and what not to do upon arrival at a homicide crime scene. In those departments that provide for a probationary period of six months or more, seasoned senior-training officers have the opportunity to give specific instructions of what to do to prevent contamination of a crime scene.

While these suggestions may seem rudimentary to the reader, it should be noted that mishandled crime scenes have led to deadend investigations, and in some cases, the loss of convictions.

It is not the purpose of this chapter to provide details of the necessary step-by-step processes involved in homicide investigation. Rather, it is to discuss a few cases in which officers were involved in homicide cases in varying circumstances. The cases that follow involve officers and departments that were sued. The complaints of the plaintiffs vary. Some plaintiffs based their complaint on the way officers conducted themselves, others for allegedly failing to properly investigate, and others for the procedures the police used when reacting to the circumstances. What the police did or did not do at the time became the focus of the plaintiffs' law suit.

Some cases involve emergency responses to volatile situations that evolved into a homicide committed by the officers. Some plaintiffs focused on whether the police did all they could have done to prevent the killing of the person. Other cases proposed the police methods were so negligent that they resulted in the unnecessary death of a person. The bases of the majority of homicide law suits are predicated on the concept of negligent training. Some cases focus on policies and procedures that direct officers to behave in certain ways. The goal of the attorney for the plaintiff is to convince a juror that there is some nexus between what the officers did or did not do and the death of their client. Each homicide context discussed here is unique, therefore the expectations for appropriate officer behavior varies with each case.

The police can, however, rely on some of their existing polices and procedures for their day to day police operations for guidance and support. A case in point might be an officer's response to a robbery in progress scene which later becomes a homicide committed by the responding officer. One might ask if the officer responded correctly by parking the patrol car so close to the building as to alarm the would be robber and thus precipitate a shoot out. Such a proposal may appear to be an inferential leap, but it is a common thrust on such cases.

Another likely approach by plaintiffs' attorneys is whether an officer should have entered the building. Many departments have policies on the proper method of entry and most recommend a back-up prior to entry. Such polices are examined very closely in court and police officers must be prepared to justify all of their actions. The majority of law suits are filed years after the incident. The importance of complete and accurate original police reporting and documentation cannot be overemphasized. In cases where officers are compelled to use their firearms the focus of a plaintiff's case will be the department's firearms training program, the officer's proficiency, and the justification for the use of deadly force.

Justifiable Homicide and Felonius Homicide

Homicide is any taking of a human life and may be felonious or nonfelonious. Murder is just one kind of homicide. A homicide may be justifiable or excusable. Justifiable homicide includes the necessary killing of another person in performance of a legal duty or right where the slayer is not at fault. Such cases may include those of self-defense, non-negligent accident, or state executions. An excusable homicide refers to death from accident or misfortune that may occur during some lawful act. Felonious homicides are treated and punished as crimes. Murder and manslaughter are examples of felonious homicide.

Homicide Cases

Case 47: Hostage Murdered after Foiled Robbery

Facts

The plaintiff in this case was the husband of a murdered woman. At approximately 11:15 p.m. in the evening, during the eleven o'-clock news, two retired persons were sitting in their township home watching television . Three male youths entered their home. One of the three was their grandson. After entry one of the two who accompanied the grandson, and who was armed with a hand gun, demanded money from the couple. They were told they would be killed if they did not give them the money they demanded. The husband said he did not have any money at the house but, out of fear, he said he would take them to an ATM machine at his bank in a nearby town eight miles away. Two of the assailants tied up the plaintiff's wife. The plaintiff went to get his coat and secreted his handgun on his person. One of the young men stayed behind to watch the wife and told the plaintiff if they were not back with the money in forty-five minutes he would kill his wife. The plaintiff, his grandson, and the other youth left for the ATM in the plaintiff's van.

On arriving at the bank, the plaintiff was able to get his gun out and there was an exchange of gunfire between the plaintiff and the armed youth. No one was struck in the exchange of gunfire. The grandson remained in the van and his accomplice escaped on foot.

The plaintiff called 911 and officers from the local and township police departments responded at 11:42 p.m. The police removed the grandson from the van and placed him in custody. At the police station the plaintiff informed the police of his wife's hostage situation and the threat to kill her if they were not back in forty-five minutes.

At 11:47 p.m. the chief of police of the township was called and informed of the hostage situation. He ordered his dispatcher to call the state police emergency response team. His decision was dispatched to all the cars in the area. At 11:50 p.m. township officers were advised of the hostage situation. Their sergeant gave them instructions to take up specific positions near the plaintiff's home to prevent escape of the hostage taker and to observe the house. All officers were told to await further instructions. At 11:58 p.m. two city officers observed the escaped armed youth in the city and arrested him at 12:08 a.m. without incident. The township sergeant assigned two additional officers to another location near the home to prevent a possible escape.

The sergeant did a drive-by of the house in a plain car and observed a Lincoln in the driveway and a green Ford Escort on the road in front of the house. This information was passed on to all the officers assigned. The chief arrived at the hostage scene at 12:20 a.m. At least six officers were stationed nearby maintaining a surveillance of the residence.

At 12:41 a.m. an officer on the radio reminded the chief of the 45 minute time limit on the threat. At 12:52 a.m., on advice from the chief, a city officer interviewed the arrested gunman and obtained a layout of the interior of the house. All cars were ordered to standby and limit their activity to surveillance of the house and the parked vehicles. One officer who had completed a three day hostage negotiation course offered to conduct negotiations, but his offer was refused by the chief.

At 12:52 a.m. the state police sergeant interviewed the arrested suspect in the city and obtained the layout for the house to pass on to his arriving emergency response team. He testified that when he was originally called and asked to activate the response team, he advised the sergeant who called him to secure the scene and set up a perimeter surveillance. He also said that he would not have used the alleged negotiator. He testified that according to his agency's policy his department had overall authority based on the request from the chief. He also said the chief was in charge of the scene until he arrived.

The state police sergeant arrived at the scene at 1:15 a.m. and at 1:20 a.m., working in conjunction with the chief and his sergeant, they called the plaintiff's residence twice. They did not get an answer. At 1:35 a.m. the Lincoln vehicle from the house was stopped by two state police officers, and the third suspect was arrested. At 1:39 a.m. the chief, his sergeant, and the state police sergeant entered the house and found the plaintiff's wife had been stabbed to death. The scene was secured and crime lab personnel were called. It appears the murder occurred while the police were setting up their perimeters for surveillance, their command post, getting the layout of the house, and prior to the arrival of the emergency response team.

Issues and Factors Considered

The plaintiff maintained that his wife would still be alive if the officers had rushed the house and entered to protect her. He also claimed the chief should have utilized the services of the officer who claimed to be trained in hostage negotiation. His primary emphasis was that the forty-five minute threat period had expired and the police should have taken a position of intervention prior to the expiration of that time.

Commentary

Rushing the house to flush a suspect is a poor police practice. Experience and training both indicate that time is generally on the side of the police under these circumstances. Seldom are such threats carried out. Setting up perimeter control is also sound police practice. It allows the police to be able to control entrance and exit of the target house. If officers had decided to enter, a layout of the interior of the house would have been necessary for safety reasons.

The idea of using a person with a mere three days training to negotiate is not sound. Most hostage negotiators have a minimum of 112 hours of training and are seasoned officers. One should not begin a negotiation until a back-up tactical unit is in place in case the talks break down. Most credible agencies require a minimum of two negotiators, and many opt for four. In early studies of hostage negotiation it was learned the average time for such a tactic is twelve hours.

A typical minimum hostage negotiation team includes the negotiator, a secondary negotiator to take notes, a psychologist to interpret, and a team leader. If the minimally trained officer was allowed to conduct a negotiation he too would have had to have background on the suspect in the house and know the layout of the interior of the house. The chief was correct in refusing his offer. Allowing an untrained person to attempt to negotiate could well have put the victim's life in jeopardy.

All preliminary steps for a hostage situation were taken. The team was alerted and steps were taken to set up an inner perimeter and outer perimeter. A command post was set up as was a staging area for other arriving officers. After all these actions were taken, attempts to contact the hostage taker by telephone were made to no avail. While it is easy to understand the plaintiff's grief and concern, the police practices evidenced in this case were proper. To have acted as the plaintiff's counsel suggested and rush the house or use an inexperienced and untrained negotiator would have in most cases increased the chances of a hostage being harmed.

The vicious nature of the three persons arrested in this case cannot be understated. It is even more disturbing that the victim's own grandson was involved. The author advised plaintiff's counsel that he could not represent his interests as the police, under the conditions presented to them, acted in accord with accepted police standards.

Case 48: Police Exonerated in Fatal Shooting

The following case took sixteen years to adjudicate and went from a state circuit court to a state court of appeals, to a state supreme court, to a U.S. District court, and finally to a state circuit court for trial.

Facts

Sometime after 8:20 p.m. John Doe was shot and killed at his place of residence by an officer of a county law enforcement agency. The plaintiff was a landlord of an apartment building. Earlier on the day of his death he was in the process of evicting a tenant who was the focus of several complaints from other tenants. The tenants had complained to the plaintiff about noise and parties from the evicted person's apartment. When the plaintiff evicted the tenant he was told by the tenant he did not have boxes in which to package his belongings. The plaintiff volunteered to assist him by using his truck and getting him boxes.

At 12:57 p.m. the plaintiff had called the police agency and reported having trouble with a tenant. It was apparent the plaintiff was somewhat fearful of retaliation from the tenant and two of his friends who were also in his apartment. He identified himself as the landlord to the arriving officers and advised them of the frequent, loud late night parties. The two assigned officers contacted the tenant and obtained his identification and that of one of his associates. According to the police reports the sergeant on duty responded to the plaintiff's address at 1:15 p.m. and talked with the plaintiff. He reported that the plaintiff had returned to the apartment. The plaintiff advised the sergeant that he was assisting the evicted tenant and his friends in their move to another location several blocks away.

Later in the day, after the move had been completed, the plaintiff and the tenant went to a tavern and returned to the second residence where a good deal of alcohol was consumed by plaintiff, the tenant, and the tenant's two friends. The tenant passed out in the second locale and it appeared he had made some threats to the plaintiff.

At 8:20 p.m. the plaintiff left the porch of the second residence, went to his vehicle, and produced a 30:30 rifle. He returned to the porch and fired one shot through the floor of the porch. Then he left to return to his apartment building. It was learned that no one was in any immediate danger and the plaintiff was apparently showing the subjects, most of whom were in various stages of intoxication, that he was not afraid of them and he was armed. The plaintiff was also intoxicated.

At 8:21 p.m. the same sergeant and another officer received an in-person report from a neighbor near the second house that a shot had been fired at the given address. The complainant reported that the police said, "Lets go" and he said, "And away they went."

Earlier in the afternoon the plaintiff on one of his return trips to the apartment building told another tenant he was scared that the evicted tenant would return and cause more trouble. He told her that the original tenant had returned once and was drunk. He asked her to call the police if she heard any noise or saw trouble, highlighting his fears.

When the plaintiff returned to the apartment building, after firing a shot into the porch at the second location, he sat on a step with a tenant in front of the apartments. While still sitting, he cocked his weapon and fired one shot into a vacant basement doorway which was filled with dirt and refuse. He uttered, "Proof, huh ?" then entered his apartment doorway. One witness saw the tenant give the plaintiff a hug. Another said she saw him stagger into his doorway.

Just prior to the plaintiff firing his rifle the second time the police had responded to the scene of the first gun shot report. The sergeant, his partner and two other officers arrived and talked briefly to one of the original tenant's friends. They learned the shot was fired into the porch, found the shell casing, and observed the bullet hole in the corner of the porch floor. According to those at the second address, the police were given the identity of the plaintiff as the person who fired the shot. This fact was not in the police report.

Just moments after their arrival at the second location, the police received a dispatch that a man had just fired a shot downtown. En route to the plaintiff's residence one officer was heard on the radio asking the sergeant whether this incident was connected to the earlier complaints at that same address. That officer attempted to remind the sergeant that he had been at that address earlier in the day, but the sergeant did not acknowledge a recollection of that call.

Two and one half minutes after leaving the house of the first gun shot report, three officers arrived at the location of the apartment. A fourth officer arrived a few moments later. The police pulled up in their patrol cars and stopped across the street from the apartment house. They were informed by a business man there that the person who fired the shot had entered a specific door entering the apartment.

The sergeant removed an AR-15 rifle from his vehicle and ran across the street stationing himself next to the door the man reportedly had entered. A second officer removed a shot gun from his vehicle and followed the sergeant taking up a position behind a vehicle parked near the door. The sergeant opened the screen door with his foot and kicked the door several times yelling, "Open the door-police!" The officers reported hearing some fumbling noises from within the apartment and the door opened. The sergeant jumped back and fired his AR-15 into the doorway. The other officer then fired his shot gun loaded with slugs through the door . The plaintiff was struck in the chest and back and was killed. From the time of the initial call on the first report of a gun shot until the time the coroner was called, ten minutes had elapsed. The coroner was called two and one half minutes after the officers arrived at the second gun shot location.

Subsequent reports and deposition testimony revealed that the plaintiff answered the door to his apartment holding a shot gun in the downward position. The officers testified that he was in the process of raising the gun. They testified they felt they were about to be shot and returned fire. One of the rifle bullets fired by the sergeant entered one of the other apartments nearly hitting a tenant. The second officer involved said he thought the sergeant had been shot when he heard the gunfire. He also said he thought he heard the sergeant yell, "He's got a gun!" Both officers said that they thought the plaintiff was raising his gun, yet the plaintiff was shot in the back and was already turned away from them. It was later learned that the shot gun the plaintiff had held was unloaded and the plaintiff was legally intoxicated.

Issues and Factors Considered

The first issue to resolve was whether the officers had the right to use deadly force. This incident took place a year before the *Tennessee v. Garner* decision. A second issue was whether the officers had other reasonable alternatives open to them before opting for a confrontation with the plaintiff. A question of adherence to agency policy was also raised. A final issue was whether the plaintiff had committed a crime and if so, whether that crime was a serious life threatening felony requiring immediate intervention to save the life of an officer or another citizen.

Commentary

If the officers at the scene actually felt their life was in immediate danger and were sure the gun was pointed in the sergeant's direction, they had the right to shoot to defend themselves. The second officer fired his weapon indicating he thought his partner had been shot or the plaintiff fired a shot. At best, his action was an automatic reaction. Citizens were in the area and on the streets at the time. No attempt was made to clear the area or attempt to identify the plaintiff. It was the author's contention that the sergeant knew who the plaintiff was from the beginning.

In terms of reasonable alternatives there were several more acceptable alternatives open to the officers. The concept of SWAT and other emergency response teams had been operational for over fourten years prior to this incident. The police ideal in such situations has always been that time is on their side. The opinion of the author in this matter was that the response of the officers was premature, unplanned, and an overreaction to the conditions presented to them at the time.

Had the officers followed their own agency policies and followed commonly accepted police practices, they would not have put themselves in a position which resulted in the discharge of their weapons.

A review of agency policies revealed the intent of those policies was not followed. Agency policy recommends immediate communications to headquarters on such indicents and the avoidance of gunfire unless officers or citizens are in immediate danger. Though once in a position to shoot or to be shot at, if the officers version and observations were accurate they had no choice but to shoot. However, if they had followed accepted police standards in place at the time, they would not have placed themselves in the position in the first place. As such, their failure to follow their own policy and accepted police standards resulted in the death of the plaintiff. The author's contention was the officers were a proximate cause of the plaintiff's death.

Accepted procedures for such an event include: (a) establishing an inner perimeter to contain a person in a building, (b) gathering necessary intelligence to determine the identity of the person, (c) obtaining a telephone number to call, (d) getting a layout of the residence interior, and, if time and conditions allow, (e) establishing an outer perimeter to control vehicle and pedestrian traffic. In addition, officers confronting these conditions should establish a nearby command post and carefully evacuate persons in the building who could be endangered. They also could have queried tenants to determine the identity and location of the plaintiff.

The plaintiff could have been contacted by telephone or a bull horn if necessary. All in all, they should have recognized that time was on their side. If, under similar circumstances, the police cannot talk a person out, unless someone is in immediate danger within, it would be best to wait him out. Contemporary police practice recognizes that immediate entry in a building for an armed suspect should only be attempted if there are hostages and a hostage may die if one does not enter immediately. Assaults on buildings are dangerous. Such assaults endanger innocent persons, the individual sought , and the officers.

The officer who fired the fatal shots testified, "Prevention of escalation of circumstances is our prime objective." He also testified "We have to get him out."

Agency policies state that officers must avoid the death of any person and that deadly force by firearms is to be used only after all other reasonable means have been exhausted. Another portion of the policy warns against firing when there is a danger of striking an innocent person. In this matter the sergeant's shot nearly struck an apartment resident in the head.

The plaintiff was voluntarily intoxicated. Any sound reading of all the documents would lead to a reasonable conclusion that he was fearful of retaliation from those evicted. He clearly broke the law in firing the weapon at both locations. While there was no evidence that he intended to fire at any person, he none-the-less fired in an area where others were present. At the very least he was guilty of careless use of firearms and possibly worse.

Had the plaintiff not fired his weapon that day the police would, in all likelihood, not have responded and he would not have been confronted and shot. However, had the police been well trained, followed their polices, and showed some restraint and patience they would not have been in a position to have shot the plaintiff.

The plaintiff lost the case at trial and the officers were exonerated. No fingerprints were found on the gun the plaintiff was allegedly holding. In this case, the court in *Scott v. Henrich* (1992) stated that the gun was unloaded at the time, but unless the officers knew or should have known it, then it was irrelevant. Officers are entitled to assume the weapon is loaded. That court made clear that even a toy gun is sufficient for the federal bank robbery statute. In a second case on this matter in the same federal circuit the court quoted *Graham v. Connor* (1985) on several occasions referring to the fact that officers have to make split-second judgments in such cases. This matter was somewhat problematic for the appellate court when it noted that deadly force cases pose a particular problem because the officer defendant is often the only surviving eyewitness. Thus, the court must be careful to ensure that the officer does not take advantage of the fact that the only witness most likely to contradict his story-the person shot dead-is unable to testify.

The position taken by the author was the officers should have used less intrusive means and should have exhausted other alternatives prior to rushing the building. This position was addressed by the appellate court when it remanded the case for trial. The court said officers need not avail themselves of the least intrusive means of responding to an exigent circumstance; they need only act within that range of conduct we identify as reasonable. As to the departmental guidelines the court said it was not clear whether self-imposed guidelines are relevant as to whether a seizure is reasonable. The position of the author at trial was the conditions confronted by the officers were not exigent as portrayed, but only made so by their actions. A jury returned a verdict of no cause and the defendants prevailed. A critical issue in this case was a question posed to the author. When asked if the plaintiff would be alive today had he not been intoxicated and fired his weapon, the author's response was, "Likely yes." Providing an honest and objective answer during testimony may support a plaintiff's position or a defendant's position.

Case 49: A Ten-Year Commitment, Pending Murder Charge, Leads to a Law Suit

Facts

The plaintiff, an alleged murderer, was confined for ten years in a state mental institution because a psychiatric evaluation determined he was not competent to stand trial. State law allowed the plaintiff to be held in the mental facility until he was declared competent to stand trial. Prior to his official release from his court ordered commitment, the plaintiff was sent to a mental health facility and, while there, walked away. The suit was brought against the arresting agency on his behalf by a close relative. The prosecutor declined to prosecute him and he was subsequently officially released.

Several weeks after the initial investigation and arrest of the plaintiff the focus of the homicide investigation was refocused on a convicted serial killer, who it appeared may have killed the homicide victim. However, certain aspects of the case implicate the plaintiff as having been a possible witness to the murder or he may have been an accessory before or after the fact. The plaintiff's possible involvement has never been established.

On August 1st at 1:30 p.m. the victim left her home to get groceries from a nearby grocery store. Her home and the grocery store are located very near the state line. When her husband returned home after 4:00 p.m. his children told him that his wife had gone to the store earlier. He became concerned because it was unusual for his wife to be gone that long. He called several relatives to see if she was visiting. Then he checked the local hospital on the off chance his wife stopped by to visit his hospitalized mother. At 4:30 p.m., unable to locate his predictable wife, he reported her missing to the local police department. He made it clear to the police that he felt there was foul play. The police normally wait twenty-four hours before putting out missing person reports but based on his checks and insistence, a description of his wife and her vehicle was broadcasted to local police agencies. After he made the police report, the victim's husband notified several relatives. They all began searching the area for the victim.

At 12:35 a.m. on August 2nd a township police officer of a neighboring outstate department checked out the victim's car and noted its license number and location. The vehicle was parked within sight of a Kroger store just over the state line and out of his jurisdiction. It was parked on a dirt road close to a wooded area. The same officer checked the vehicle again at 2:00 a.m. and ran a registration check on the license. The registration came back as registered to the victim's husband. The husband was notified of the vehicle location. While waiting for the husband to arrive the officer met the victim's brother near the store. He said he was searching for his sister. The victim's husband arrived with other relatives who were out searching all night. The husband turned his keys over to the officer. The vehicle was covered with mud and the undercarriage revealed a lot of encrusted mud.

Crime scene #1

The locked vehicle had what appeared to be pieces of wet toilet tissue stuck to the trunk lock and to both door handles. The trunk was opened revealing seven bags of groceries. One bag was split open and a roll of toilet tissue had been opened. The township officer noted in his report that he observed spots on the right front seat of the vehicle that appeared to be blood. Because the vehicle was not in his home state, the officer called the county sheriff department in whose jurisdiction the vehicle was located.

Crime Scene #2

A ranking officer and two detectives from the sheriff department, two police officers from the neighboring township agency, one officer from the victim's city, the husband, and two of his relatives began to search the nearby wooded area for the victim. At 7:30 a.m. the victim's body was located in a wooded area sixty yards from her home state line by her brother-in-law. All nine of the searchers had walked in and around the crime scene for some time.

The victim's body had twenty-one stab wounds. She had six stab wounds to her left breast .75 of an inch to 1.25 inches long, two stabs wounds to the left side of her heart, four stab wounds in her left lung four inches deep, four stab wounds to the right breast, two wounds to her back, two defense wounds on her left arm, and her throat was cut through to her larynx and trachea.

For some reason the county detectives called outstate city police crime lab technicians to the scene to process both scenes for physical evidence. The vehicle was towed to the victim's home city for protection. The vehicle and the body of the victim were both found in the victim's home state. The county's own state crime lab was located within thirty minutes drive of the scene. The second scene was located in a wooded area less than fifty yards from a local fishing site with a bait store and landing on a river. The fishing landing is very close to a mall and the Kroger store. The victim's vehicle and body were both located less than a mile from the Kroger store the victim had frequented.

On August 5th a woman found a bank book belonging to the victim and a pair of sunglasses near the Kroger store. Both were processed by the police for latent prints and a notation made that none were lifted.

On August 9th a township officer from the victim's home state found the plaintiff wandering in an open field near the bait shop and landing. He learned that the plaintiff had been arrested earlier that day by the police from the victim's city for larceny of airplane glue from a local store. The officer described the plaintiff as a homeless illiterate with nothing but the clothes on his back. The officer reported the plaintiff appeared dazed or mentally ill. It was subsequently learned that the plaintiff had been addicted to glue sniffing for several years. According to physicians who had examined him over the years the plaintiff had suffered irreversible brain damage as a result of the habit. He had also been in and out of several mental institutions in other states.

On August 12th the plaintiff agreed to a line up. There was no mention in the reports of the plaintiff's whereabouts from the 9th to the 12th of August. The detectives had earlier interviewed three youths who were riding their bicycles near the Kroger store. Those youths said they saw the victim's car on August 1st near the Kroger store. They said they saw a man doing something to the trunk. He was described as a five foot eleven inch tall white male with long hair, a medium to muscular build, and a pocked-marked face, and was wearing mirrored sun glasses.

At the plaintiff's line up two of the three youths said they "thought" it might be the same man and one said he was positive it was not. There was no description of the composition of the police line up in any of the police reports.

After conducting the line up, the detectives took the plaintiff to a local mission on August 12th. One of the detectives described mission administrator as one of his contacts. Others described him as a police buff. The administrator questioned the plaintiff at length on this murder and urged him to take him to the scene of the crime. Details learned of that unofficial and unethical interrogation reveal that the administrator was aware of several crime scene facts. When questioned on how he learned so much detail he said read it all in the papers. There is little doubt the administrator passed on what he reportedly learned from the plaintiff to the detectives.

Detectives Interview Plaintiff

On August 14th someone brought the plaintiff to the sheriff department for questioning. The plaintiff was read his Miranda rights after telling the interrogators that he could not read or write. He said he understood his rights, signed a waiver, and agreed to talk to the detectives about the homicide. The plaintiff's account, as reported in the detectives' reports, was irrational. He told them when the victim came out of the Kroger store she went to her car with five bags of groceries and put them in the trunk. She then closed the trunk and started to walk to the driver's door when someone yelled at her and she turned around. When she turned she was struck in the face with a rock on the temporal nerves. He said she did not bleed very much, but she was knocked out. She was parked in the second parking spot on the side of the Kroger store.

The plaintiff then said he did not know how she got into the car, but they drove down a side street past some big houses. He remembered a dented mail box on the route. A short distance past the single bent mail box he turned right on to a dirt lane about 40 feet or so. The right front wheel got stuck in a mud puddle and he had to get out to rock the car free. He also said the car got stuck three other times. He claimed when the woman woke up she was mad, yelled at him, and said she would kill him. The plaintiff told the detectives at one point during the ride some boy asked her for oral sex and she just laughed. When the officers asked him why he took her he responded, "So she could be robbed and raped." When asked why she was killed, he said that she was to be his death wife, a member of the living dead and she would be a slave forever.

After hearing his bazaar story the detectives pressed him to explain how the victim was killed. He said she was stabbed eighteen times, once in both eyes, once in the belly, about eight times in the breast, and her throat was cut so she couldn't talk. He also said she was stabbed twice in the back and had several cuts on her hands from the knife. He said she was killed with a red switch blade knife with a three or four inch blade which he threw into the river from the same road on which she was killed. When asked the condition of her body at the scene, he told the officers she was lying on her back, her eyes were open, tears were coming from both eyes, and the blood was still running. He also mentioned that a car came by but the people in the car could not see them.

The plaintiff went on to state he took the body to a place near Dracula's Castle. That location was described as near a weeping willow tree with money trees nearby. That is, a large green leafed tree with leaves that looked like money. The plaintiff reportedly described the victims clothing as a flowered blouse with daisy-type flowers on it. He thought she was wearing blue jeans. He said she had not been raped because when her throat was cut, her brains and heart came out of her throat and wiggled around. He said, "Then no one could rape her."

He went on to describe her brown purse with a silk lining and details of its contents. He said the purse contained a pearl ring, a red squeeze type change purse with a few pennies in it, a driver's license, two pictures of kids, and a bill for a pool table. He then described, in detail, things he found in the glove compartment of her car. Among those things described were, a bottle of pills, a red flashlight without batteries, a pair of prescription glasses, and contact lenses in a K-Mart paper bag.

After these detailed revelations, the plaintiff altered his position and said he had no idea who killed the victim and he definitely did not kill her. However, he said he did see the man that hit her in the face with the rock because he was there. He said he saw all the rest of the stuff he talked about in his head, and not first hand. He also said no one could see us or hear us. He went on to tell the officers the lady was good-looking and very sexy but she was real mad when she woke up and said she would kill him. When asked by a second interrogator why he had said he killed the victim he responded saying, "That was another woman." When asked who the other woman was he said he did not remember, he gets mixed up and isn't sure which one is which, but that did not matter because he did not do it.

In their report the officers note that many times during their conversation with the plaintiff he wandered back into talking about the living dead and that they were the only real people on earth. Moreover, he said that God is a man who lives in Bethlehem and talks to him quite a bit on the phone. He also claimed that God tells him what other men say too, so he knows who is on Satan's side and who is on God's side. He also knew who was above God with the people on Dracula's side. He said he was on Dracula's side, but he likes God too. He hated Satan. The police report indicated that after this interrogation with the plaintiff he was booked in the county jail. At the closing of the interview he claimed he did not kill the lady and was in no way involved.

There were very few details in the police reports that outlined the legal processes the police used. Subsequently, the plaintiff was arraigned on a warrant charging him with murder. The court, after hearing him speak, ordered a psychiatric examination before going forward. The plaintiff was found to be mentally incompetent to stand trial and he was incarcerated in a state mental hospital until he was able to stand trial.

New Suspect Located

On September 9th detectives from the sheriff department learned of the arrest of a killer in the neighboring state in a murder with very similar circumstances. That city was over one hundred miles south. In that killing, a woman leaving a party store type business was hit on the side of the head with a blunt object and dragged some distance. She had her throat slit and also received multiple stab wounds to her breast area.

On September 12th the detectives went to that city and talked to suspect John Doe. They told him why they were there and that he was a suspect in the murder in their state. The suspect nodded and said he would not want anyone to be convicted of a crime they did not commit and, if his lawyer allowed him to talk to the detectives, he would clear it up for them. His lawyer did not allow the officers to interrogate his client.

At the time of his arrest, John Doe had in his possession a four inch blade red Buck hunting knife. His prints were checked against latent lifts from the victim's car, but they did not match. In his property the police located a fishing license issued on the day the victim was killed from the same bait shop and landing near the murder scene.

Follow-up investigation on this new suspect revealed he was well-known at the fishing landing, frequented the deli at the Kroger store, and on the day of the murder he was at the landing and had bandages on his hands. He told persons there he cut them in an accident. He told another friend he cut them in a fight. Two people from the bait shop area knew John Doe and said he always wore his mirrored sun glasses.

On October 5th the three youths who reportedly witnessed a man near the victim's car, on the day of her disappearance, attended a line up on John Doe. He was positively identified by all three as the same man who was standing by her car on August 1st.

There was no information in any of the police reports that this information was relayed to the prosecutor. On November 3rd the psychiatric center advised the plaintiff could not stand trial due to his mental state. On November 14th the plaintiff was admitted to the psychiatric center. Almost ten years later, on March 5, 1991, physicians from the psychiatric center certified that plaintiff was mentally fit for standing trial. The following day the current prosecutor said that he felt the victim's murderer was already in prison for the other killing outstate. The next day the prosecutor terminated prosecution on the plaintiff. Two months after his decision, the prosecutor requested a state police investigation into investigative improprieties on the part of the sheriff detectives.

Though not learned of until the investigation focused on the serial killer in prison, the detectives found the state police in their area had a similar situation eight days after the plaintiff's wife was murdered. In that complaint a woman had left a tavern after work and was struck on the side of the face with a six pack of beer. She was kidnapped and taken to her residence. She was stripped of her clothing, tied spread eagle on her bed, and the suspect brandished a four inch red Buck hunting knife. For reasons unknown, he told the would be victim he changed his mind about killing her, untied her, and left her residence. The description of her attacker and his vehicle were identical to the John Doe held in prison for the outstate murder.

Issues and Factors Considered

The major issue in this case was whether the police conducted a proper and exhaustive homicide investigation. Several factors had to be considered. The lack of an orderly crime scene search and the failure to protect the crime scene from outsiders during the search for the victim was considered. Using outstate crime lab technicians in lieu of one's own state lab is cause for concern, and adds undue complications to an already complicated set of circumstances. The only photos taken were those of the victim's body and those were taken by an out-state technician. Placing a prime suspect in an all-night mission and allowing or encouraging a non-police person to interrogate a suspect is very poor police procedure with little evidentiary value. That practice was also unethical.

Another factor considered was the fact that very little documentation was made of the actions taken at the crime scene or work done by the investigators. The police report was not what one would expect for a major homicide investigation. There was no chronological report of actions taken and no listing of evidence obtained. Though the report indicated there were vacuum sweepings from the victim's car and soil samples taken from the scene, there was no mention made of what was done with the potential trace evidence or of any comparisons made. It was impossible to determine a chain of evidence from reading the police reports.

In short, while the department may have done more than reported they failed to document much of their activity. The plaintiff gave a detailed description of the contents of the victim's purse and the contents of her glove compartment. If any verification was made with her husband as to the accuracy of his testimony, it was not noted in any police report. No mention was made of a search of the area for her purse.

Commentary

Based on the irrational and quasi-confession of the plaintiff the detectives in this case placed the plaintiff in a mission and likely coached the police buff administrator to interrogate him. Two days later, based on the plaintiff's so-called confession and denial he was lodged in jail on a charge of murder. The reports to the prosecutor, outlining justification for a warrant for murder, were never located. The plaintiff claimed the detectives secured a warrant based on false statements. The warrant was obtained on August 14th.

After the plaintiff was released from the mental institution and the current prosecutor refused to prosecute, an inquiry was made as to whether the detectives ever told the original prosecutor of their suspicions. The detectives believed the convicted killer was the prime suspect. The detectives claimed they sent papers indicating their position to the prosecutor. The prosecutor, who by now was a judge, said he never received any such notice. The focal point of the plaintiff's suit was that if they had properly investigated, learned of the identity of the prime suspect, and notified the prosecutor at the time, he would not have been held for ten years.

When the detectives interviewed John Doe in prison they told him that if he cooperated with them the charges pending against him by the state police for kidnapping would be dropped. The state police denied any such arrangement.

The detectives did do a credible job of running down leads, interviewing, and documenting John Doe's activities. They did conclude he was the prime suspect in their murder investigation. The convicted killer had the same method of operation on the kidnapping, this murder, and the murder of the woman outstate for which he was convicted. It was later learned that when he was a juvenile he had killed his neighbor with similar stabbing in the breast and he cut her throat. He was shown to be within fifty feet of the victim's body while fishing. He had a fishing license for the day of her murder, he had worked at that marina and he always carried the red Buck knife on his person. Moreover, he had cuts on his hands on the morning of August 2nd and gave witnesses conflicting stories as to their source. He fit the composite drawings of the suspect and was positively identified in a subsequent line-up. During his interview he made a tacit admission to the killing.

The defendant officers, after interviewing John Doe, should have contacted the prosecutor at that time and recommended the charge be dropped against the plaintiff. Ironically, the victims purse was found less than thirty yards from her vehicle location several years later. That would support the author's contention that no search was ever made for the item. There was no indication that the detectives verified the plaintiff's description of items in the victim's purse with her husband. There was no indication that the detectives attempted to get search warrants for the defendant's clothing and thus attempt to match hairs and fibers. If hair and fiber standards were taken from the victim it was not reported. The search of the victim's car was not documented or reported. There was no documentation that the clothing of the victim was ever checked for trace evidence.

The following chronology explains the plaintiff's situation. First, he was arrested for the victim's murder. Second, he was found incompetent to stand trial. Third, he was legally held for fifteen months pending his regaining his mental capacities. Fourth, he had a proper hearing to determine whether he was a danger to himself or others. Fifth, it was decided he was a danger. Finally, he was held in a state institution for nearly ten years under a civil commitment.

After a trial the jury reached a decision in favor of the defendant detectives. The plaintiff had been released and was last known to be staying at a mission somewhere in the midwest.

One very puzzling issue remains unanswered. Plaintiff's fictitious initials were JFF. When the serial killer was arrested out of state over one hundred miles from the victim's murder scene, the police found a pair of Levi jeans in the trunk of his car. The serial killer was five foot nine inches tall and weighed over 200 lbs. The Levi jeans had a twenty-nine inch waist. The plaintiff is very thin. The initials JFF were sewn inside the jeans. This fact leaves one to speculate whether the plaintiff was with the serial killer before, during or after the homicide. The plaintiff had been institutionalized prior to this incident. A check of those institutions could have been made to see if they sewed initials into their patients' clothing. This was never done and such connections were never attempted. A subsequent check on the plaintiff revealed he had escaped three times from mental institutions and was described as a paranoid-schizophrenic with brain damage and an explosive personality. He was also described by other mental health physicians as having grandiose delusions and as psychotic. He had an arrest record for breaking and entering, assault, and shop-lifting glue for glue sniffing. It appears logical that the convicted serial killer had killed the victim. It also appears the plaintiff may have had something to do with the killing, may have been in the killer's vehicle or witnessed the killing. The poorly conducted homicide investigation prevents reaching any such conclusions.

Case 50: A Questionable Interrogation and Investigation Brings Acquittal

Facts

The defendant in this case was arrested for the murder of his girl-friend's daughter after a four and one half hour interrogation in his own apartment. After the interview the police took him to the police station in a police car and taped a thirty-two minute interrogation in which he reportedly confessed.

At 5:45 a.m. on January 15th the dispatch center received a call from a woman reporting an unknown medical problem with her daughter. She said she did not know whether the child was breathing or not. An ambulance, fire department first responders, and a deputy sheriff responded to her home.

A January 16th police report revealed the four-year-old child was found lying face up on her bed without a pulse or respiration. Her body was cold to the touch and rigor mortis had set in. The ambulance attendants set up a monitor and obtained a straight line indicating death. The deputy sheriff acted as the medical examiner and then requested two detectives. The police report did not indicate any crime scene protection nor was there any evidence in the reports a crime scene investigation was conducted. A few photos were taken of the youngster, but the police reports revealed nothing of any measurements or evidence collection. One detective noted the body was on its back and there was an eight to ten inch blood stain from the nose. He also noted half moon shaped marks on the child's cheek and surmised they were fingernail markings. Forensic experts were not called the scene.

The following day a postmortem examination was conducted. The examining physician noted there was no injury reported in the police report. It was determined that death was due to suffocation. The body had petechial marks on the right side of the nose, contusions on the left shoulder, abrasions to the right ear area, and a scratch on the left side of the nose. Also noted were what appeared to be small half moon type marks believed to be caused by fingernails on her face.

In a police interview with the mother, she said she watched T.V. the previous evening. She had no idea of what time the show started or ended, but it was about a black family. She also could not recall what time her daughter went to bed on the 14th. She said she was sure the daughter got up from a chair and went to bed by herself.

Another officer said he overheard the mother telling someone in the other room that she had gone to bed with her daughter and laid in her bed with her. These two different explanations were never investigated. The mother also advised detectives her separated husband had picked up his daughter from day care on the 14th at 4:30 p.m. and was baby-sitting her at her home until she returned from work about 7:00 p.m. The husband then left for his home. The interview also revealed the defendant, her boyfriend, was also at the house on the night of the 14th and the morning of the 15th of December.

A discussion was held at the police department and it was decided that two detectives would interview the defendant and two others would interview the mother, who by this time, had gone to stay with her mother in a nearby city. The police reports focused on the interview with the boyfriend, but there were no reports to view documenting the interview with the mother.

On December 16th two detectives met the defendant at his second-floor apartment. They asked to speak with him and he welcomed them into his living room. He was advised immediately that he was not under arrest, but was told by the officers they wanted to speak with him regarding the death of his girlfriend's daughter.

He told them he had been seeing her a lot during the past summer. He had filed for divorce and he and the victim's mother had been seeing each other often and are quite close. He said he called her once or twice a day or saw her daily. He mentioned that the mother and her daughter stayed at his apartment on the evening of January 13th. They had placed the girl on the couch to sleep, but he had to spank her to settle her down and for this he was sorry. At 6:30 a.m. the following day he left for work and the mother and her daughter returned home. He called her twice on the 14th and at 4:20 p.m. he left to meet her at the tavern where she worked.

At the tavern, he sat and waited for her and had one beer. She came over and hugged him and they talked of going out for dinner. She then received a phone call from her husband. She told him she made arrangements so they could go out to dinner, but prior to leaving work she changed her mind and said she would rather just go home and spend time with the daughter. She asked for another beer which he obtained for her, but he said he did not want to because she had already had about eight to ten beers. They left the tavern and went their separate ways.

He told the detectives he stayed up watching T.V. at home and fell asleep prior to 11:00 p.m. He set his alarm and arose around 1:30 a.m. and started calling his girlfriend but her line was busy. He then dressed and drove to her home. At her home he entered the back door which was ajar about two inches, but this, he said, was not unusual. He said the house was dark on his arrival and his girlfriend's bedroom door was closed. He found her in bed so he took off his clothes and got in bed with her.

Later in the interview, the detectives report he changed his story saying that he walked in and found the mother sleeping on the couch and the daughter sleeping on the floor. He said he put the mother in her bed and then put the daughter in her bed. Then, he said, he got into the girlfriend's bed, held her hand, and talked to her. On his return from the bathroom he found the mother asleep.

The daughter, he said, started to fuss, and not wanting her crying to wake up the mother, he went in to quiet her down. He sat alongside the daughter on her bed and tried to get her to be quiet. When asked how he quieted her he said in the past he would put his hand over her mouth to keep her quiet. This time he placed his hand over her mouth with his thumb and index finger up against her nostrils. He said he may have held it there five minutes. The police report states the defendant said the child was struggling and thrashing around and then she stopped moving. He said he thought she had gone to sleep so he went back and crawled in bed with the mother. He arose at 5:00 a.m because he had to be at work at 6:00 a.m. Later in the day he received a call from the mother's stepfather reporting the daughter was dead.

A group of former federal investigators, working for the defendant's attorney, report things a bit differently. The defendant confirmed the detectives said he was not under arrest and the questions put to him appeared to be general in nature. During the course of his four-hour interview his wife came to his apartment. He asked if she could come in and the detectives told him no and told him to send her away. These investigators later learned from his wife that the defendant came down to the door and told her, "If you come up they will have to take me somewhere else to question me."

The defendant said the first two detectives were joined by two others and another was stationed outside his door. At this point the questions began to become accusatory. His father called while they were there, but they kept the cordless phone and would not let him talk to him. During the course of the interview he said he asked to talk to his father ten times but was advised against it. One detective said that he should tell them how he caused the girl's death because his father would want him to be honest. Another detective reportedly said, "My God, it was an accident!" Another detective told him he only had a limited amount of time to admit he accidentally caused her death, and if he did so he could avoid a charge of homicide. At one point he got up from the couch to get a drink of water, but the officers blocked his way and ordered him to sit back down. They told him they would get him the water. At the end of four hours the defendant said he was not asked to go to the police station, but was told he had to go. He again asked to talk to his father, but was told they wanted to record his account and then he could call his father. This group of investigators described the defendant as a jealous and unintelligent person with a temper. He is described as having a ninety percent passive personality and he is an enabler.

The police detectives, when examined by the attorney, said it was possible they did not let him get the water. They also admit telling him to tell his wife to go away. The police did not recall blocking the defendants way when he went to get water, but they did not deny it. They also said he was free to go when he was in the police car en route to the police station. One detective said he could have unlocked the door and jumped out.

They also said that he could have used the phone had he wanted to do so. All the detectives were queried on their method of interrogation. Some gave variations of the same theme. Many of their responses support the defendant's version. It appeared the officers were being defensive as to their method of interview. All insisted the defendant was not under arrest. The defendant was not given Miranda warnings until he was questioned at the police station.

At the police station his interrogation was taped. The tape was stopped on three occasions for several minutes. At one time it was reversed so they could record his Miranda warnings. The taped interview lasted thirty-two minutes. The defendant repeatedly said he did not think his hand over her mouth would kill her. It appeared he believed the detectives that he may have caused her death and ended his tape by saying if he did, he didn't mean to. The defendant's taped conversation sounds like he was admitting to accidentally causing her death. He cried through much of the taped recording. He was arrested for murder and lodged in jail.

Issues and Factors Considered

The major issue in this case was whether or not the defendant was in fact under arrest at the time of his interrogation in his own home. If he was, then he should have been Mirandized. Another issue was whether the police, by informing him that he was not under arrest when they entered his apartment, negated the need for a Miranda warning. The manner in which the crime scene was handled was also an issue. The detectives' actions in his apartment provide a reasonable basis to assume that he may have been under arrest. If he was in fact under arrest and was interrogated without being provided the required warnings, evidence obtained could not be used against him in a trial.

Factors overlooked at the scene could have provided a reasonable police officer with grounds to consider the mother of the victim as a potential target for investigation. By not treating the mother's home as a crime scene the detectives lost an opportunity to introduce any potential evidence they may have found there later. If, in fact, the marks on the girl's face were caused by fingernails then it is significant to note that the mother had long fingernails, but the defendant was a nail biter and had little or no fingernails. Fingernail scrapings were taken from what nails the defendant had, but none were requested from the mother. There is no mention in the police reports as to the results of the fingernail examination. Though an early arrest was made in this case there was little or no physical evidence introduced. The entire police case was predicated on a questionable interrogation. The victim's bedroom was not treated as a crime scene and crime scene specialists were not called to the scene.

Commentary

A close examination of the body should have revealed the marks found on the daughter by the physician at the autopsy. That, coupled with the presence of blood, should have alerted the detectives to treat the house as a crime scene and protect it accordingly for scientific examination by professionals. The girl was in rigor mortis and stiffening had started. That observation and her cold skin would have normally been noticed by a mother of a child she could not wake. It is odd that the officers did not think to take fingernail scrapings from the mother as well as the defendant. No connections were made between two different versions provided by the mother of what she did the night before. In short, she was not treated as a potential suspect.

At the conclusion of a district court examination to determine if the defendant should be bound over to circuit court for trial, the case was dismissed against the defendant. When interviewing the defendant he said he put his hand over the child's mouth to quiet her down. The detectives asked him if he held his hand in a v-formation and he said he might have. Based on that conversation they reported he held his index finger and thumb over her nostrils. If defendant was ordered to stay on the couch, it was likely his freedom was restrained in a significant way and he was under arrest. If this were so he should have been Mirandized. What appears to be in the officers' favor is case law. They told him he was not under arrest. Interestingly, en route to the police station in their police car the officers said on the radio, "We are enroute with one." That statement in police parlance indicates they have someone arrested. It is not, however, a legal term.

In *U.S v. Brunson* (1977) the court said an arrest is not in effect if a defendant voluntarily agrees to go to the police station for questioning. In *Dunaway v. NY* (1979) the court said a suspect cannot be taken into custody without probable cause. An arrest is achieved when a person is seized for more than a brief period. *Terry v. Ohio* (1968) states an arrest exist when a person is not free to walk away and that may be twenty minutes. The issue, the *Terry* court said, is the length of the encounter or the use of force, but not the purposes of the officers. The standard is whether a reasonable person would believe his freedom was deprived in a significant way. This requires references to all the circumstances of the interrogation to make a determination of whether custody can be reasonably inferred.

In *People v. Rodney* (1967) the court noted a nervous personality or overly timid person has no bearing on the existence of the custody standard. In *The Government of the Virgin Islands v. Berne* (1969) the court said in most cases, even when the focus is on a suspect as the perpetrator, it does not render custodial an interrogation conducted in a suspect's home unless there is some type of formal arrest or force used which restrains him. *Beckwith v. U.S.* (1976)

notes that cases almost universally hold that interrogation in a person's home is non-custodial. However, in *Rhode Island v. Innis* (1980) that court said interrogation does not have to mean the actual asking of questions by the police, rather, it includes instances that amount to the "functional equivalent" of interrogation meaning words or actions by the police which they know are reasonably likely to elicit an incriminating response. The court went on to state that the term functional equivalent is subjective and difficult to determine.

Had the police in this case treated the scene as a crime scene and had an exhaustive search been done for physical evidence such as hairs and fibers they may have been able to build a case on the defendant or perhaps the mother of the victim. In this author's opinion the defendant was interrogated in his apartment and was not free to walk away. The defendant's case was dismissed and the mother was never charged. A civil suit was not brought against the police.

Case 51: Plaintiff Claims Daughter's Murder Linked to Poor Police Response

Facts

The plaintiff in this case sued the police department after her eighteen-year-old daughter was murdered by her twenty-one-year-old boyfriend while she was out of state attending college. Plaintiff claims her daughter was the focus of long-standing abuse by the boyfriend, and that she reported this to the police. She also claims that her daughter was stalked by telephone by the boyfriend, and the police did nothing to stop it or arrest him.

Over a period of the next twenty-six days from her original call to the police on stalking, the plaintiff reported her daughter being kidnapped once, held for three days by her boyfriend, being threatened, and receiving numerous nuisance telephone calls. She claims some of the calls were threatening to her and her daughter. Subsequently, her daughter reported being kidnapped from her out of state college, brought to her home state, and raped by her boyfriend. Twenty-six days after the series of police reports and incidents the boyfriend shot and killed the daughter in front of at least nineteen witnesses near her college dormitory. He returned to the state and turned himself in to the police.

A review of all the police reports and interviews with the victim's friends revealed she willingly went with the suspect most of the time. She would call him and he would meet her at various places near her home. When her mother saw him she would report him as a stalker or suspicious person. The mother reported to the police that she received upwards of one hundred phone calls on some days. It was later learned that many were collect calls that were accepted.

The first of the plaintiff's complaints was of stalking phone calls. She was advised by the police to contact the phone company and maintain a log of the calls, and the police would get a phone tap installed. Plaintiff was reminded of this process by the police and urged to call the phone company, but she failed to call the phone company for several days.

The first kidnapping report involved the daughter leaving her house with her boyfriend. The plaintiff reported she was taken by force and did not return for three days. The victim called the plaintiff from a phone booth and was picked up on the third day. The plaintiff's daughter told her mother the boyfriend took her to a motel and held her there overnight for one or two days. He then reportedly took her to an abandoned building and locked her in the building. She said she got away and called her mother. In fact, she stayed at the motel one night. The following morning her boyfriend left for a few hours to go to court, but she did not try to leave. He dropped her off at a friend's house where she stayed the remaining two days. The victim's friend reported that the plaintiff knew all along her daughter was at her house.

The day after she made her kidnapping report to the police, the victim and the plaintiff went to the police station to retell their story. When asked why she had lied she said it just sounded better that way. The plaintiff did not want her daughter to go with the boyfriend, but evidence indicates this was not the daughter's desire. The daughter claims she was not intimate with her boyfriend at the motel. His version was that they did in fact become intimate.

Since the plaintiff's first report of the nuisance calls the police had several contacts with her and reminded her to call the phone company. They also made contact with the boyfriend regarding threats he made to the plaintiff and told him to cease and desist.

They checked with the prosecutor who refused to issue warrants for his driving up and down the street or the calling. The prosecutor also concurred that the plaintiff should use the phone company procedure for obtaining a tap on her line.

Six days before she was murdered the plaintiff reported to a nearby metropolitan police agency that her daughter was kidnapped out of state from her college dorm, brought to their city, and raped in an alley. The metropolitan department advised plaintiff to take her daughter to be checked at the hospital and then come in so they could check the scene of the reported rape. Over the next few days the police contacted the plaintiff on at least three occasions asking her to bring her daughter in so they could check the venue of the rape. They also explained the need for this step. Messages were left for the daughter, but she did not return the calls or keep other appointments to meet the police.

The victim's original report to the police was her boyfriend came to her college where they argued. She hit him with a pipe and he forced her into his car, drove her to the city in her home state, put her up against a wall in an alley, and raped her twice. He then reportedly hid her in an abandoned building and she got away and called her mother. The last time the police asked the mother to bring her daughter in she said she could not afford to go get her and bring her back, but perhaps she could come in a few weeks as she was due back in town to attend a function.

Six days later, the victim was seen hugging her boyfriend near her dormitory by several students waiting in a line at the college. Witnesses stated they saw the two begin to fight and they saw him throw her on the ground. She got up and chased him to his car, which he had entered, and she kicked him violently. The boyfriend shot her twice and she ran off. He got out of the car and shot her a third time killing her. He then left and drove home. After arriving home he called the police and turned himself in.

Issues and Factors Considered

The major issue in this case was whether the police failed to properly address the plaintiff's calls for police assistance. A second and more subjective issue was whether the action or inaction of the police in any way was a proximate cause of the shooting death of the victim. A third issue was the inconsistent reporting of the plaintiff and her lack of cooperation with the police. A fourth and final issue was whether the victim was a willing partner with the assailant and whether his advances were unilateral or suggested by the victim.

Commentary

Though the plaintiff made several reports to the police over a twenty-six day period there is ample evidence the police attempted to handle her complaints in a professional manner. They gave her good advise, talked to the boyfriend and warned him, and reported all of her complaints to the prosecutor. The major city police department involved attempted to investigate the report of a rape, but the plaintiff, as well as the victim, did not cooperate by showing them the crime scene. There is every indication that the plaintiff expanded her version of the harassment. Though she viewed herself as the victim of harassment she knew the whereabouts of her daughter during her so-called kidnappings.

A review of statements from the victim's friends revealed that she frequently called her boyfriend and was aware of his temper. According to her friends, it was not uncommon for her to call him and have him pick her up near her home. On the occasions the plaintiff saw him she'd report his presence as a suspicious person or as a stalker. For whatever reasons she had, the plaintiff did not avail herself the services of the police by contacting the phone company or cooperate in the police investigation. Several visits were made to the plaintiff's home by the police and several calls were made. The police responded to all of her complaints and there is little they could have done to prevent the murder of her daughter. After a careful review of all the documents it is the opinion of the author that both of the kidnapping reports were falsified and the rape on the second incident was also a false report.

A day or two before the victim was killed the plaintiff called the chief of the college police department and reported the description of the boyfriend and his car. She informed him that he was abusive and that her daughter had been kidnapped from near her dormitory. The college police called the victim to set up an interview on the reported kidnapping, but she did not show up for an appointment nor did she return other calls. The author supported the actions of the police and did not see any negligence on their part.

Case 52: Attempted "Suicide by Cop" Ends in Death and Award for Plaintiff

Facts

This case is a fatal shooting of a suicidal young man who menaced the police with a knife in the breezeway of his home. After up to seven minutes of attempted mediation the victim lunged at the police with a large knife in his hand and was shot dead.

On a spring evening in an upscale neighborhood of a college town the plaintiff knocked on a neighbor's window and told him his son was trying to commit suicide. He asked him to call 911 and an ambulance. On receipt of the 911 call the city police were dispatched to the plaintiff's home with two officers responding. A short time later a shift supervisor also arrived on the scene. On their arrival they found the plaintiff and his wife in the front yard and the son in an upstairs window wildly ranting and waving a knife. Windows were broken out and blood was smeared on the sashes. The son was bleeding from several wounds. The son threatened to kill his mother and the officers. He said that he had guns and would use them. A short while later the son came downstairs and exited the house through an attached breezeway. He called his mother a bitch and when she and the neighbor, who was standing near her, backed up he yelled, "Run bitch," He threatened to kill his parents and the four officers who were now at the scene.

The son was described by the police as wild and unstable. He ran back into the house through the attached breezeway and into the kitchen. Other officers attempted to remove the plaintiff and his wife from the scene, but were not successful other than keeping them at some distance from the house.

The supervisor and two officers followed the son and entered the breezeway. He remained in the kitchen cutting himself and threatening to kill the officers frequently moving from the inner kitchen to the doorway to the breezeway. He was waving a large butcher knife and had knocked glass out of the kitchen door as well.

During the next seven minutes the officers kept him in sight and attempted to de-escalate the situation by talking to him and asking him to put down the knife. He was reassured he would not be hurt and would receive medical assistance. On at least three occasions he came to the door and lunged at officers. They had their weapons drawn. At one point one officer sprayed the son with FreezeP, but it had no effect on him.

The breezeway was small and the officers backed up each time he came to the doorway. They were less than nine feet from the doorway. Finally, the son lunged at the officers by coming out on the breezeway with the knife raised and he was shot by two officers. He fell backwards into the kitchen and died. During this incident the victim's mother was yelling for the officers not to hurt her son. Plaintiff sued the police for the death of her son. It was subsequently learned that the victim had been drinking most of the day after he broke up with his girlfriend.

The law suit was filed in the circuit court and after depositions and facts were reviewed the court decided the plaintiff did not have a cause of action. That court ruled in favor of the police defendants. The case was appealed to the U.S. District Court and that court decided that there might be a question of fact for a jury to decide and remanded the case for trial. At that juncture, the city made a decision to settle the case and the plaintiff was awarded a very large settlement. Public pressure was brought to bear on the city on behalf of the well-respected family. Ultimately, the chief of police was pressured into retiring.

Issues and Factors Considered

Several issues were raised including whether the police should have entered the breezeway, whether they should have remained at least twenty feet back, as a plaintiff's expert testified, whether they should have left the scene as the mother requested, and whether they had the right to shoot the victim. A primary issue was whether the police were faced with exigent circumstances. The officers' training and agency policy were also raised as an issue. One plaintiff expert testified that the officers should have had specific training in the handling of mentally deranged people.

Commentary

Faced with a suicidal person who was armed, claimed to have firearms, and threatened to shoot several persons, the police were faced with exigent circumstances. The police attempted to contain the victim and maintain visual contact by entering the breezeway to keep him from reaching firearms. They made every effort to mediate and reduce the dangers they faced. They used good judgment in using the non-lethal chemical spray on the victim. The officers faced with this rapidly unfolding volatile situation had a right to draw their weapons for self defense. They were not duty bound to retreat once they made contact. Moreover, had they left the premises under these conditions they would have been negligent to the situation created by the victim. The police officers at the scene were aware of the potential danger to the public had the victim escaped and further armed himself.

The use of force policies of the department were good, and the officers met or exceeded training requirements. An expert for the plaintiff testified that the officers precipitated the confrontation, but this author disagreed with that position. His view that the officers should have kept a safe distance was rejected.

The supervisor gave the victim assurances that he would not be arrested if he would put down his weapon. Furthermore, they offered him medical assistance. The supervisor at the scene called for another police officer, whom the plaintiff knew, to come to the scene to be a possible mediator. It was the author's opinion the officers used all reasonable means available to them to de-escalate the life-threatening situation presented by the victim. They removed potential victims from the immediate vicinity, attempted to mediate, backed up on several occasions when physically threatened, and used non-lethal chemical agents. All of those methods were to no avail. Thus, the use of the firearms by one officer and the supervisor was a proper use of force in that both officers were in immediate danger of a life-threatening injury or death. Moreover, their proximity to the victim with his arms raised while lunging with knives in his hands posed an immediate danger. The victim committed a felonious assault or attempted murder. It appeared the victim wanted the police to shoot him.

Chapter 6

Summary of Conclusions and Suggestions

The Police Environment

The utilization of Section 1983 suits to redress perceived incursions of a citizen's civil rights has probably done more to give substance to police boundaries than any other movement in the past two centuries. Whether a department is small or large, urban or rural, or federal or state, the mandate is clear. The police must be well-selected, well-supervised, well-trained, and well-disciplined. Moreover, the police must stay within the boundaries of the Constitution and the law. If the police fail to do so they will likely be sanctioned. Sanctions may arise from state court law suits or from federal courts. Section 1983 obtains federal jurisdiction and provides a forum for examination of wrongs allegedly committed against the public by the police.

Section 1983 does not apply to federal officers. The means of obtaining federal jurisdiction against a federal police officer is called a Bivens Tort. This type of action obtains its name from a case called *Bivens v. Six Unknown Federal Narcotics Agents* (1971). Briefly, Bivens alleged that federal narcotics agents violated his constitutional rights under the 4th Amendment by conducting an illegal search of his home.

The increase in suits against police departments and their governments has been facilitated primarily due to the erosion of the doctrine of Sovereign Immunity, enactment of civil rights legislation, and court decisions allowing governments to be viewed as persons for purposes of Section 1983 cases. The causal factors of why citizens sue the police are too numerous and varied to discuss in this work. Some of those variables have been made explicit in this book. Others are implied.

The doctrine of Sovereign Immunity evolved from the common law in England where the government was the King. If the King could do no wrong then the direct employees of the King, as agents of the Sovereign, could do no wrong because they were acting on his behalf. The same doctrine was adopted by the American judicial system but has been drastically modified over the years. The doctrine developed from a case called *Russell v. Men of Devon County* (1788).

State legislatures in most states have limited the doctrine and by 1978 only two states fully adhered to the traditional common law practice that the government was fully immune from liability for torts occurring in the exercise of police functions.

Sovereign Immunity and 1983 Suits

In applying immunity to 1983 suits the definition of the word "person" becomes critical. Section 1983 applies to every person. In *Monroe v. Pape* (1971) the plaintiff sued the City of Chicago because he alleged that Chicago police officers broke into his house, beat him, and held him in custody for hours before being charged. The court held the city immune because it said when Congress enacted Section 1983 in 1871 it had not intended for the word "person" to include municipalities. Subsequently, it was held that if cities were immune from such suites then states were as well.

In 1978 the Supreme Court re-examined its own holding of the *Monroe v .Pape* case and in *Monell v. Department of Social Services* (1978) the court concluded that the view held in *Pape* was wrong. That court decided that municipalities were included within the meaning of person. The court however, noted that municipalities were persons only for the purpose of Section 1983, and then only when the municipality inflicted the injury through a municipal policy, ordinance, regulation, or custom. The obvious implications of that decision are that mayors, city managers, and police chiefs had better be sure that they have proper rules, regulations, policies, and procedures in place prior to a suit being brought by a plaintiff.

Unless a police chief or supervisor acts directly in the incident which brought about the law suit, there is little likelihood of them being vulnerable. Most officials are named in the original filings but are often dropped.

Many courts are reluctant to hold supervisors liable under the concept of vicarious liability. First, police administrators and supervisors have very little discretion in hiring decisions. Second, police officials are public officials whose duties are established by government authority that created their jobs rather than by the officials themselves. The police officials are generally viewed as not having as much control over the job of a police officer as their industrial counterparts. However, they are not completely immune from vicarious liability. If the supervisor authorized the focal behavior or was present at the time and did not try to stop it, they may be liable for an officer's tortuous behavior.

What the Police Can Do

Whether officers are pursuing a speeding vehicle, using a degree of force to overcome a suspect's resistance, investigating a possible homicide, or responding to a host of variable police situations, the officers must be keenly aware of their departmental policies. Police officers should not wait for their administrators to hold training sessions. Rather, they should, on their own, review all of the agency policies from time to time and use that opportunity to discuss the concepts included in those policies with fellow officers to insure clear understanding.

Typically, police officers become aware of policy content during their training sessions, if held, or by scanning the documents when they are placed in the agency mandatory reading files. Some officers pour over their policies when preparing for promotional examinations, but that is frequently only every three years and insufficient for liability protection.

Likewise, police supervisors must not only be sure their officers understand the content of their policies, but must also document when such understandings took place. A wise administrator in today's litigious society would be well-advised to devise periodic tests on the more critical policies and document those practices as well. Such testing provides the supervisor an opportunity to conduct retraining when test scores reveal less than adequate understanding. The form of the training is not important. It can be formal in-service training, role call training, or a one-on-one discussion with one's command. The common practice is to post new orders or policies on bulletin boards or in reading files with instructions for the officers to initial the document after they have read the document. Such practices have little value in providing accountability.

Since the emergence of computers and scanable police reports, the now outdated narrative police report has been replaced by one and two sheet reports with check boxes and codes, though supplemental pages are available for the officers' use. The theme today is brevity and efficiency with some concerns for overtime pay. Most reports have a box for the shift supervisor to sign. That signature is designed to indicate the supervisor has reviewed the report and approved it submission. Such a practice is not credible case supervision.

Supervisors should review reports for their content and completeness. Good case supervision gives the supervisor an opportunity to counsel officers, teach them how to properly investigate and report, and cause appropriate follow-up to obtain the necessary detail. It also gives the supervisor the chance to determine if the relevant policy was properly followed.

The movement to the use of in-car computers, while laudable for efficiency, only further complicates this issue. When the clock and concerns for overtime drive the construction of police reports, the chances of success for a plaintiff's attorney are increased exponentially.

The key issue in any law suit is the behavior of the officer involved. Most suits do not come to fruition until years after the incident that prompted the suit. Officers must rely on their recollections supported by a review of their original police report. When reports are incomplete or do not document each step the officer took, supported with explanatory justifications, the plaintiff will more often than not prevail. The old adage "if you didn't write it down, you didn't do it" applies.

For example, in a pursuit case the officer may be asked the width of the roadway, the number of houses along the route, the general description of the area, whether the businesses were open or closed at the time, or how many pedestrians were visible. Such detail is quite easily obtained shortly after a pursuit takes place, but nearly impossible to obtain three years later. During the author's policing years he was once asked by a defense attorney in a criminal case what the weather was at the time of the crime. His response was thirty-two degrees, seventy-five percent humidity, wind out of the southwest at ten miles per hour, overcast and visibility at six miles. When the incredulous attorney asked where he got this information for his report his response was, "I called the weather bureau at the time." Seemingly simple practices like this only enhance an officers ability to testify accurately and are still readily available to contemporary police officers. It is not that the weather may be critical, although it may from an evidentiary point of view, but an attorney attempting to discredit a police officer's testimony is hard pressed when faced with documented facts.

This author does not attempt to demean modern technological advances in policing. To the contrary, they are most helpful, but they do not replace old-fashioned police work and documentation of important details. Automated Fingerprint Systems (AFIS) has been a bonus for policing. Such a system is useless to the police, however, if the first officer at the scene of a potential homicide is not aware of the need to protect the scene or fails to attempt to locate logical locations for the presence of latent prints. The same may be said for DNA and several other modern technological advances.

The question of why there are so many law suits being filed against the police today would require several major sociological research endeavors, and such efforts might only identify some of the variables. An easier question to answer may be why the police lose so many law suits.

An attempt was made in this work to provide some insights by detailing several actual police cases. Some of the answers were implied and some were explicit. To be sure, some cases are disposed of by settlement out of concern for the financial risks of going forward. This is understandable. In those cases where the officers were well-trained, well-informed and well-documented their behaviors the jurisdictions were more inclined to fight the case, and in many cases they prevailed. However, there are some cases in which the officers behaviors were exemplary, but a sympathetic, uninformed, biased, or hostile jury still returned verdicts in the millions of dollars against the accused police departments.

The issue of police law suits cannot be viewed by merely examining officer behaviors. Every action taken by the police department is involved. If the state of community relations in the jurisdiction is poor, one could anticipate negative outcomes from civil suits. If the police exist in a socially or racially polarized community, the same result may be predictable. If the police officers work in departments that are weak in accountability, the same may also apply. It is conceivable that an officer's improper behavior may actually be an artifact of a larger organizational problem. One wishing to embark on identifying long term solutions to police law suits must consider the need to examine the entire agency and its connections with the community it is designed to serve.

Lastly, it has been observed that several police administrators nationwide react to suits against their departments by revising current policies. The more informed departments also initiate necessary training, and when appropriate institute discipline. Some agencies over react and may discontinue a practice such as pursuits. It might be wise to view a law suit as an indicator or symptom of a larger internal problem. The worse approach a police officer can take is to consider the plethora of such suits as the cost of doing police business, and to just continue with an attitude of business as usual.

References

Agnew v. Porter, 247 Northeast 2d 487 (1969).

Alexander v. New York, 371 Northeast 2d 534 (1976).

Alpert, G.P. and R.G. Dunham. 1988. Research on police pursuits: Applications to law enforcement. *American Journal of Police*. 72: 123-131.

____. 1989. Policing hot pursuits: Discovery of aleatory elements. *Journal of Criminal Law and Criminology* 13: (2) 521-539.

____. 1990. *Police pursuit driving: Controlling responses to emergency situations*. New York. Greenwood Press.

Alpert, G.P. and L.A. Fridell. 1992. *Police vehicle and firearms: Instruments of deadly force*. Prospect Heights, IL: Waveland Press.

Alpert, G.P. and W.C. Smith. 1991. Beyond city limits and into the woods: A brief look at the policy impact of City of Canton v. Harris and Wood v. Ostrander. *American Journal of Police* . 10: (1) 19-40.

Amato v. U.S., 549 Fed Supp 863 (1982).

Auten, J.H. 1985. *Law enforcement driving*. Springfield, IL: Charles C. Thomas.

____. 1990. An analysis of police pursuit policy. *Law and Order* (November): 53-54.

____. 1991. *Police pursuit driving operations in Illinois*. Champaign, IL: University of Illinois.

Baily v. Andrews, 811 Fed 2d 1366 (1987).

Baily v. L.W. Edison Charitable Foundation, 284 Northeast 2d 141 (1978).

Basham, D.J. 1978. *Traffic law enforcement*. Springfield, IL: Charles C. Thomas.

Bauer v. Norris, 713 Fed 2d 408 (1983).

Beckman, E. 1983. High speed chases: In pursuit of a balanced policy. *The Police Chief* (January): 34-37.

____. 1985. *Police pursuit: Not safe at any speed: study shows.* Michigan State University, News Bureau Release. 1985.

____. 1986. Pursuit driving: A report to law enforcement on factors in police pursuits. *Michigan Police Chiefs' Newsletter.* (May): 26-34.

Beckwith v. U.S., 425 U.S. 341 (1976).

Bennis, W.G. 1966. Organizational development and the fate of bureaucracy. *Sloan Management Review* 72: 41-55.

Benson, B.L., D.M. Payne, and R.C. Trojanowicz. 1990. *An Evaluation of the University of Iowa Department of Security.* To Vice President of Finance and University Services. Iowa City, IA: (August): A Bound Study.

Bivens v. Six Unknown Federal Narcotics Agents, 403 U.S. 388 (1971).

Britz, M. and D.M. Payne. 1994. Policy implications for law enforcement pursuit driving. *The American Journal of Police* 13: (1) 113-142.

Brooks v. Lundeen, 364 Northeast 2d 423 (1981).

Bureau of National Affairs. 18:(3), 13-14. Officer conducting chase can't be recklessly indifferent to safety. *The Law Officers Bulletin* (August): 1993.

Standards for Law Enforcement Agencies. 1984. Fairfax,VA: Commission for Acceditation for Law Enforcement Agencies. (CALEA) n.p.

California Highway Patrol, 1983. *California Highway Patrol Pursuit Study* . Department of California Highway Patrol, Sacramento, CA: n.p.

Cameron v. City of Pontiac, 813 Fed 2d 782 (1987).

Canton v. Harris, 489 U.S. 378 (1989).

Carter, D.L. 1984. Theoretical dimensions in the abuse of authority by police officers. *Police Studies: The International Review of Police Development* 7: (4) 224-236.

Carter, D.L. and D.K. Dearth. 1984. An assessment of the mission. Texas Police Department. Unpublished Consultants Report.

Carter, D.L. 1986. Techniques for assessment of community for police service. Training Supplement Material. Quantico,VA: FBI National Academy. n.p.

Carter, D.L., D.M. Payne, and P. Embert. 1987. *An Evaluation of the Three Rivers, Michigan Police Department*. For City Manager. (June): A Bound Study.

Carter, D.L.and D.M. Payne, 1989. *An Evaluation of the Blackman Township Department of Public Safety*. For Chairman of Township Board. (January): A Bound Study.

Charles, M., D. Falcone, and E. Wells. 1992. *Police pursuit in pursuit of policy: The pursuit issue, legal and literature review: An empirical study*. Washington, D.C.: AAA Foundation for Traffic Safety. n.p.

Cincinnati Department of Public Safety, Division of Police. (1980). Emergency Operations of Police Vehicles. Section B-1.

City of Akron v. Charley, 440 Northeast 2d 837 (1982) .

City of Kalamazoo v. Priest, 331 Mich. 43 (1951).

City of Miami v. Horne, 198 So. 2d 10 (1967).

Clark, J.M., Jr. 1976. *Emergency and high speed driving techniques*. Houston, TX: Gulf.

Cole, G.F. and C.E. Smith. 1999. *Criminal justice in America*, (2d ed). Belmont, CA: West Wadsworth.

Connecticut Safety Commission. 1978. *A Report to Governor Grasso: Use of Emergency Vehicles in Connecticut*. n.p.

Cornwall v. Larsen, 571 Pacific 2d 925 (1977).

Crawford v. Edmonson, 764 Fed 2d 479 (1985).

Crew, R. 1992. An effective strategy for hot pursuit: Some evidence from Houston. *American Journal of Police* 11: (3) 89-95.

Dearborn Heights Police Department. 1986. General Order 349: *Pursuit Driving Policy*.

del Carmen, R.V. and D.L.Carter. 1985. An overview of civil and criminal liabilities of police officers. *The Police Chief* (August): 46-49.

del Carmen, R.V., 1986. *Civil and criminal liabilities of police officers*. In *Police Deviance* (eds.) T. Barker and D.L. Carter. Cincinnati, OH: Pilgrimage. 300-322.

Donnely, P.J. 1978. Investigation of the use of force. *The Police Chief* (May): 24-26.

Dougherty, E.E. 1961. *Safety in police pursuit driving*. Springfield, IL: Charles C. Thomas.

Dunaway v. New York, 442 U.S. 200 (1979).

Emery, F.E. and E.L. Trist. 1965. The causal texture of organizational environments. *Human Relations* 18: (1) 21-32.

Falcone, D. 1994. Police pursuits and officer attitudes: Myths and realities. *American Journal of Police* 13: (4) 143-155.

Falcone, D., M. Charles, and E. Wells. 1994. A study of pursuits in Illinois. *The Police Chief* (July): 59-64.

Falcone, D., E. Wells, and M. Charles. 1992.Washington, D.C.: AAA Foundation for Traffic Safety n.p.

Fazo, V. 1985. Use of deadly force. *The Police Chief* (August): 54-55.

Fennessy, E.F. Jr., T. Hamilton, K.B. Joscelyn, and T. Merritt. 1970. A Study of the Problem of Hot Pursuit by the Police. Hartford, CT: Center for the Environment and Man, Inc. n.p.

Fennessy, E.F. Jr. and K.B. Joscelyn. 1972. A national study of hot pursuit. *Denver Law Review* 48: (3) 389-403.

Fiser v. City of Ann Arbor, 417 Mich. 461 (1983).

Fyfe, J.J. 1989. Controlling police vehicle pursuits. In *Police practice in the nineties: Key management issues*. J.J. Fyfe (ed.) Washington, D.C.: International City Management Association. 114-123.

Gaines, L.K., M. Kaune, and R.L. Miller. 2001. *Criminal justice in action: The core*. Belmont, CA: Wadsworth.

Galas v. McKee, 801 Fed 2d 200 (1986).

Gallagher, G.P. 1990. Risk management for police administrators. *The Police Chief* (June): 18-29.

Garner, J., T. Schade, J. Hepburn, and J. Buchanan. 1995. Measuring the continuum of force used by and against the police. *Criminal Justice Review* 20: (autumn): 146-168.

Goodwin, M. 1992. In hot pursuit. *Woman's Day* (February): 40-43.

Government of Virgin Islands v. Berne, 412 Fed 2d 1055 (1969).

Graham v. Connor, 490 U.S. 109 (1989).

Halloran, J. 1985. Driving programs teach safer, yet quicker pursuit. *Law and Order* 33: (3) 18-21.

Hamilton v. Town of Palo, 244 Northwest 2d 329 (1976).

Hammon v. Pedigo, 115 Northwest 2d 222 (1962).

Handcock v. Oakland County Sheriff. Statement of U.S. District Judge James Woods at trial.

Hannigan, M. 1992. The viability of police pursuits. *The Police Chief* (February): 46-49.

Herron v. Silbaugh, 260 Atlantic 2d 755 (1970).

Holser v. City of Midland, 48 Northwest 2d 208 (1951).

Hoffman v. Burkhead, 353 Mich. 47 (1958).

International Association of Chiefs of Police. 1965. *Safe Driving Techniques* (Training Key #20) Washington, D.C.: Author.

International Association of Chiefs of Police. 1968. *Pursuit Driving* (Training Key #92). Washington, D.C.: Author

Jackson v. City of Joliet, 715 Fed 2d 1200 (1983).

Jackson v. Rauch, 171 Northwest 2d 551 (1969).

James, C. 1980. The national academy for police driving. *Police Product News* (May): 47-48, 86-88.

Johnson v. Glick, 481 Fed 2d 1028 (1974).

Kappeler, V. E. and R.V. del Carmen. 1990. Legal issues in police negligent operations of emergency vehicles. *Journal of Police Science and Administration* 17: (3) 163-175.

Kennedy, D. R. Homant, and J. Kennedy. 1992. A comparative analysis of police vehicle pursuit policies. *Justice Quarterly* 9: (2) 227-246.

Koonz, J. Jr., and P.M. Regan. 1985. Hot pursuit: proving police negligence. *Trial*(December): 63-69.

Kroeker, M. and C. McCoy. 1988. Establishing and implementing department policies. *The Police Chief* 55: (12) 34-40.

Kuzmics v. Santiago, 389 Atlantic 2d 587 (1978).

Lakoduk v. Cruger, 296 Pacific 2d 690 (1956).

Lansing Police Department. 1984. Pursuit and Emergency Response Procedure. #80-86.

Los Angles Police Department. 1982. Departmental Policy and Procedures Manual.n.p.

Lee v. City of Omaha, 307 Northwest 2d 800 (1981).

Leonard, V.A. and H.W. More. 1974. Police organization and management. (4th ed.) Mineloa, NY: Foundation Press.

Lingo v. Hoekstra, 200 Northeast 2d 325 (1964).

Littell v. Maloney, 593 Pacific 2d 11 (1979).

Lee v. Mitchell Funeral Home Ambulance Service, 606 Pacific 2d 259 (1980).

Marion v. City of Flint, 71 Mich. App. 447 (1976).

Matulia, K.J. 1983. The use of deadly force: A need for written directives and training. *The Police Chief* (May): 30-34.

Mayor and Alderman of Town of Morristown v. Inman, 342 Southwest 2d 71 (1960).

McCoy, C. 1985. Lawsuits against the police.: What impact do they have? In J. Fyfe (ed.) *Police management today: Issues and case studies.* Washington, D.C.: International City Managers Association. 55-64.

Michigan Compiled Laws Annotated: 1979.

Monell v. Department of Social Services, 436 U.S. 658 (1978).

Monroe v. Pape, 365 U.S. 167 (1971).

Moore v. Travelers Indemnity Co., 352 Southern 2d 270 (1977).

Morris, E.R. 1993. Modifying pursuit behavior: The 9 T's approach. *F.B.I. Law Enforcement Bulletin.* (January): 62: (1) 1-6.

Nugent, H., E.F. Connors, J.T. McEwen, and L. Mayo. 1989. *Restrictive policies for high speed pursuits.* Washington, D.C.: National Institute of Justice. n.p.

Oak Park Police Department. 1986. Emergency Vehicle Operations. # 80.

O'Dell v. Civil Service Commission of Flint, 44 Northwest 2d 147 (1950).

Oechsli, S. 1990. Kentucky State Police Pursuit Study *1989-90.* Rockville, MD: National Institute of Justice.

O'Keefe, J. 1989. High speed pursuits in Houston. *The Police Chief.* (July): 32-40.

O'Linn, M. 1992. The Gaps in the use of force policies and training.*The Police Chief* (February): 52-54.

Parker v. Levy, 417 U.S. 783 (1974).

Patikin, H.P. and H. Bingham. 1986. Police motor vehicle pursuits: The Chicago experience.*The Police Chief* 53: (7) 61-62.

Payne, D. M. 1992. *Policy and Training Implications for Law Enforcement Pursuit Driving.* A Report to the Director of the Michigan State Police. Unpublished report.

Payne, D.M. 1993. *Preliminary Findings from the Michigan Emergency Response Study: Phase II.* A Report to the Michigan State Police Training Division. January. Unpublished report.

Payne, D.M. and C. Corley. 1994. Police pursuits: Correlates of the failure to report. *The American Journal of Police* 13:(4) 47-72.

Payne, D.M. 1997. Michigan emergency response study - phase III: Implications of the failure to report pursuits and inaccurate accident reporting. A research note.*Policing: An International Journal of Police Strategy and Management* 20: (2) 256-269.

Payne, D.M. and D.L. Carter. 1997. *An Evaluation of the Sault Ste. Marie Tribe of Chippewa Indians Law Enforcement Conservation Department.* For Prosecuting Attorney. (August): A Bound Study.

People v. Rodney, 286 New York 2d 225 (1967).

Physicians for Automotive Safety. 1968. Rapid pursuit by the police: Causes, hazards, consequences: A national pattern is evident. New York. Physicians for Automotive Safety. n.p.

Placek v. City of Sterling Heights, 275 Northwest 2d 511 (1979).

Powell v. Allstate Insurance Co., 233 Southern 2d 38 (1970).

Pruitt v. City of Montgomery, 771 Fed 2d 1475 (1985).

Rankin v. Sander, 121 Northeast 2d 91 (1953).

Reed v. City of Winter Park, 253 Southern 2d 475 (1971).

Rinaldi v. Livonia, 244 Northwest 2d 609 (1976).

Robinson v. City of Detroit, 462 Mich. 439 (2000).

Rogers v. Detroit, 447 Mich. 125 (1998).

Roll v. Timberman, 229 Atlantic 2d 281 (1958).

Royal v. Ecorse Police and Fire Commissioners, 75 Northwest 2d 841 (1956).

Rowe v. Kansas City Public Service Co., 248 Southwest 2d 454 (1942).

Russel v. Men of Devon County, Court of Kings Bench 100, Eng. Rep. 359 and 16 East (1788).

Rutherford v. State, 605 Pacific 2d 16 (1979).

Scafe, M.E. and J.E. Round. 1979. High speed pursuits. *The Police Chief* (December): 36-37.

Schultz, D.O. 1979. *Police pursuit driving handbook.* Houston, TX: Gulf Publishing Co.

Searles v. Southeastern Pennsylvania Transportation Authority, 990 Fed 2d 789 (1993).

Selkowitz v. State, 389 New York 2d 45 (1976).

Sellars v. Lamb, 303 Mich. 604 (1942).

Sells v. Monroe County, 158 Mich. App. 637 (1987).

Semple v. Hope, 474 Northeast 2d 314 (1984).

Silva v. City of Albuquerque, 610 Pacific 2d 219 (1973).

Simkins v. Barcus, 77 Pacific 2d 717 (1951).

Simkins v. Pulley, 569 Pacific 2d 1385 (1977).

Skolnick, J. H. and J.R. Woodworth. 1967. Bureaucracy, information, and social control: A study of morals. In Bordua, D.J. (ed.) *The police: Six sociological essays*. New York: John Wiley. 99-136.

Smith v. City of West Point, 475 Southern. 2d 818 (1985).

Solicitor General Report., Ontario, Canada. 1985. A Special Report on Police Pursuits. Author n.p.

Sourcebook of Criminal Justice Statistics. 1997. Washington, D.C.: Bureau of Justice   Statistics.

Souryal, S.S., 1976. *Police administration and management.*.West Publishing Co.

Spencer v. Heise, 158 Northeast 2d 570 (1958).

Stark v. City of Los Angeles, 214 Cal. Rprt. 216 (1985).

Tennessee v. Garner, 471 U.S. 1 (1985).

Terriot, L. 1982. Citizen safety: Key elements in pursuit policy. *Trial* (August): 31-34.

Terry v. Ohio, 391 U.S. 1 (1968).

Thorton v. Shore, 666 Pacific 2d 655 (1983).

Traffic Institute. 1981. *Pursuit in Traffic Law Enforcement*. Evanston, IL: Northwestern University. n.p.

United States Code, Title 42 Section 1983.

United States Code, Title 18 Section 242.

United States Code, Title 18 Section 245.

Urbonya, K. 1991. The constitutionality of high speed pursuits under the fourth and fourteenth amendments. *St. Louis University Law Journal* 35: 205-288.

U.S. v. Brunson, 549 Fed 2d 345 (1977).

Wayne County Sheriff Department. 1986. Pursuit Policy Section 8. 6.1.

Whetsel, J. and J.W. Bennett. 1992. Pursuits: A deadly force issue. *The Police Chief.* (February): 30-31.

Winslow, Richard H. Attorney. Personal Communication. May 15, 1989. Battle Creek, MI.

Wisconsin Department of Justice. 1984. Use Pursuit Guidelines. *Training Guide for Law Enforcement Officers* (Sect. 8.2) Madison, WI: Author n.p.